Television Sitcom

Brett Mills

To my Dad.

First published in 2005 by the
BRITISH FILM INSTITUTE
21 Stephen Street, London W1T 1LN

The British Film Institute's purpose is to champion moving image culture in all its
richness and diversity across the UK, for the benefit of as wide an audience as
possible, and to create and encourage debate.

Cover design: Mark Swan
Cover images: *The Office*, BBC; *The Royle Family*, Granada Television; *The Simpsons*,
20th Century Fox Television/Gracie Films; *I Love Lucy*, CBS Television/Desilu Productions
Inc.; *Will and Grace*, KoMut Entertainment/Three Sisters Entertainment/NBC Studios/
NBC Universal Television/Everything Entertainment/New Dominion Pictures Inc.
Stills courtesy of BFI Stills, Posters and Designs

Set by Fakenham Photosetting Limited, Fakenham, Norfolk
Printed in the UK by The Cromwell Press, Trowbridge, Wiltshire

British Library Cataloguing-in-Publication Data
A catalogue record for this book is available from the British Library

ISBN 1–84457–088–6 (pbk)
ISBN 1–84457–087–8 (hbk)

Contents

Acknowledgments

This book is the culmination of about a decade's worth of work, and I thank Mark and Lard for being a reliable constant during that time; how I miss them.

Thanks to those who watched comedy with me in Canterbury as an undergraduate (Lou, Claire, Angus, and Jones) and a postgraduate (Walter, Nathan, Palmer, Zaff, Giles, Steph and Alabaster), and are still great friends. Special gratitude goes to the two people at Canterbury Christ Church (now University) College whose comments on my student work on sitcom helped shape my thinking for over four years; Philip Simpson and Ken Fox. They taught me to ask the most important of all academic questions: 'Yeah, but what does he know?'

Thanks to all my media/culture colleagues at the University of Glamorgan (especially Gill Allard, Vian Bakir, David Barlow, John Beynon, Jon Blackwood, Peter Jachimiak, Tim Robins and Karin Schofield) who've put up with me going on about comedy at every opportunity and have helped make working there a supportive and thoughtful experience. Special thanks go to Philip Mitchell and Richard Hand for discussions which contributed a great deal to this book. All the students from the last three years who've taken my 'Comedy' module and probably hoped it would be a doss, thanks for putting up with my over-enthusiastic rants; the discussions we had inform pretty much everything in this book.

Andrew Lockett and Glen Creeber got this book off the ground, Matt Hills supplied a word somewhere in the middle and Keith Mansfield got it finished.

For the last five years in Cardiff, much appreciation goes to all the people at The House who've given me support and friendship and helped make the place my home; Kris and Greg, Claire and Harvey, Johnny-boy, Lubna, Anna and Quiet John, Karen, Becks, Ruth and Big John, Gretchen, Little John, Fay and Ciara, Ceri, and Jenni and Marijn. See you in the Welsh Club, people.

Elsewhere, Sue Turnbull and Jane Roscoe made me think in much more detail about Australian comedy, and were great companions in Melbourne and Tokyo. Jaime Howell and Sam and Dianne Cox were lifesavers during my time in Warrensburg, Missouri, and gave me heartfelt friendship and cornbread.

Thanks to my family for making me watch so much comedy as I was growing up, supporting my never-ending studies, and letting me have the solitude of the caravan to get some work done.

Special thanks to Sanna, who wrote the funniest email I've ever read. For that, and much more besides: *ausgezeichnet*.

Chapter 1 | Introduction

Basically sitcom is light, family entertainment, which aims to amuse and divert the viewers, not to disturb and upset them.

David Lodge, *Therapy* (London: Secker & Warburg, 1995), p. 56.

In David Lodge's novel *Therapy* (1995), Tubby Passmore is the writer of a successful, mainstream, popular sitcom called 'The People Next Door'. The success and content of the programme is unquestioned by Tubby, who sees little art in what he is doing, and is thankful solely for the money it makes him. However, problems arise for Tubby when one of the programme's stars wishes to leave the series, and return to 'proper' acting in the theatre. As arguments rage about how this can be narratively achieved, questions are raised concerning the expectations and norms for sitcom, with Tubby repeatedly battling with his agent and producer to take the programme off into more complex and socially relevant areas. Tubby's desire to include an episode in which a character has an abortion, for example, is rejected on the grounds that it fails to conform to the audience's expectations for the series, and is a story which cannot successfully (or respectfully) be explored through a comic form such as the sitcom.

The narrative of *Therapy* thus rests on a set of assumptions about the sitcom. In the novel, these assumptions are presented as prevalent within the regimes of sitcom production, in which producers, writers and performers treat the sitcom as a 'known' entity, whose content and form are unquestioned, and whose social position and relevancy are limited and muted. Indeed, in order to get his main character to work through a range of personal issues and explore his role within society generally and within the entertainment industry specifically, Lodge shows Tubby abandoning his interest in sitcom, instead finding reading Kierkegaard a more fruitful way to come to terms with the philosophical enquiry on which he is set. Sitcom and philosophy are thus presented as opposite ends of the intellectual spectrum, with the former a stable entity, incapable of engaging with the complexities of the latter.

In essence, *Therapy*, and the characters within it, assume that the form and content of the sitcom is 'known', and that it is an unimportant form; more importantly, the book assumes that there's no reason why it shouldn't remain that way. In this way, the novel is representative of the approach taken towards the sitcom by academic analysis, and the genre's position within society generally. Considering the popularity and longevity of the genre, it's surprising how little academic work has been carried out on the sitcom; Cook's complaint that a week's research and discussion of sitcom ended after 'we had come across very little written material that helped focus our thinking about sitcoms' (1982, p. 1) would still be appropriate today. Similarly, Bignell almost gives up before he's started, with his lament that 'Theorists of television genre have found it very difficult to establish clearly how television comedy programmes, especially sitcoms, work' (2004, p. 121).

So, while one of Cultural Studies' primary intentions was to investigate popular forms by examining both their production and reception, this has been done without much engagement with the genre of sitcom. This is presumably because the regimes of power central to Cultural Studies' concerns are seen to be so transparently obvious in sitcom that complex analysis isn't required. Similarly, Media Studies has focused on what could be deemed more 'socially relevant' forms, particularly news and documentaries, as the social role of television, and its relationship with the public it serves, have been interrogated. The twin focus of the public sphere and public service broadcasting have repeatedly resulted in Media Studies' lack of engagement with forms whose primary aim is seen as entertainment. The avoidance of the examination of sitcom clearly says something about the priorities which the academy is working from; more tellingly, though, it suggests that the assumptions about the simplicity of the genre, displayed in *Therapy*, are at work here too. After all, why engage with such an immediately understood form, when there are more obviously complex and socially committed genres and texts to be understood?

Of course, this is not to say there hasn't been useful work. However, while the sitcom is dealt with in detail in a number of texts (Wagg, 1998; Neale and Krutnik, 1990), these books use the genre as part of broader debates about broadcast and social comedy, and the relationship between culture and humour. In Britain, the only book focusing purely on the sitcom as a discrete genre is Cook's (1982) excellent edited collection, now well out of date and unfortunately out of print. In the analysis of popular fictional television forms in Britain, the sitcom has always played second fiddle to the soap opera, reflecting that genre's ratings dominance, and the ethnographic and feminist dominance of much study. Indeed, while many genres have discrete entries in Casey *et. al.*'s *Television Studies: The Key Concepts*, sitcom is subsumed under the general term 'comedy' (2002, pp. 29–34); how come news, drama and documentary aren't similarly grouped under 'seriousness'? In America, however, a wider range of works on the sitcom are apparent (for example, Marc, 1989; Hamamoto, 1989; Grote, 1983; Morreale, 2003a), reflecting the continued dominance of the genre in US ratings. Yet again though, such analysis represents a tiny amount compared to that of other television forms.

Perhaps more telling is the noticeable disparity between the amounts of material written on television comedy as opposed to film comedy. General analyses of humour at the cinema can be found in Horton (1991), Karnick and Jenkins (1995), King (2002), Krutnik (2003), Mast (1979) and Rickman (2001), while specific genres of film comedy are explored in Evans and Deleyto (1998), Harries (2000), Matthews (2000), Paul (1994) and Vineberg (2005), and comedians and performance are examined in Dale (2000) and Jenkins (1992). Indeed, there's enough material on film comedy that two readers on the subject have been published (Rickman, 2001; Krutnik, 2003). The analysis of film comedy has thus not only offered a variety of methodological approaches to funny films overall, but also developed towards closer analyses of particular subgenres, finding the term 'film comedy' one that is much too large and which encompasses too broad a range of styles, narratives, ideologies and performances to be dealt with as a complete whole. Furthermore, the relationship between cinema and psychoanalytic theory which has been a primary motivation behind Film Studies is easily demonstrated by film comedy in which 'The realm of comic play might be understood in terms of the Freudian concept of the pre-Oedipal' (King, 2002, p. 78). Sitcom, on the other hand, less easily dovetails with most of the primary concerns of the academic approaches to television, while the approaches used to explore film comedy are not easy to transfer to broadcasting.

What is apparent then, is that 'television comic narratives have received rather less attention than other fictional forms' (Lovell, 1982, p. 19). The causes of this could be many: a belief that the sitcom is simple and already understood; the belief that, as a comedic form, it has little to 'say' about social concerns and the cultures it entertains; the belief that the examination of more 'serious' forms is more pressing; the belief that it's 'only sitcom'. And, as Lodge's novel demonstrates, such assumptions are apparent not only within the academy; they exist within the television industry too and, it can be assumed, are representative of sitcom's social position and the ways in which audiences make sense of them. As Fry and Allen note, despite the millennia-long attempts to examine them, 'humor and laughter are still burdened with a slight hint of questionability' (1998, p. xvii), deeming them unworthy of 'serious' philosophising. If this is the case, if the sitcom has been routinely neglected as an object of study, then why write – or read – a book on them at all? As Butler asks, 'Should we take *The Simpsons* seriously?' (1994, p. ix).

Why Study Sitcom?

So let's take *The Simpsons* (Fox: 1989–) as an example; in what ways has it been, and could it be, examined? We could explore the debate about the programme's effects, especially considering the concerns that were raised over Bart's 'underachiever and proud of it' ethos (Flew, 1994; Glynn, 1996). We could look at the programme's legacy and its important role in the resurgence of prime-time, adult animation in America (Donnelly, 2001; Stabile and Harrison, 2003). We could place the programme within the history of sitcom, demonstrating how Homer comes out of a lineage of male comedy characters (Butsch, 1995). We could examine what the series has to say about contemporary American society, and its critique of consumer capitalism (Cherniavsky, 1999). From this, we could look at the series' oppositional nature and how it is seen to reflect debates about contemporary society, globalisation, capitalism and political unease (Alberti, 2004; Keslowitz, 2004; Turner, 2004). We could investigate its complex and intertextual nature, which has often been linked to postmodernism (Thompson, 1996; Henry, 2003). We could use it as a case study in order to examine debates about philosophy and society, and contemporary moral dilemmas (Irwin, Conrad and Skoble, 2001). And we could look at *The Simpsons* as animation itself, attempting an aesthetic reading of cartoons as a cultural form (Furniss, 1998; Wells, 1998, 2002; Dobson, 2003). Finally and most tellingly, we could examine why it is that this programme has garnered so much critical attention when other long-running, popular series, such as *Friends* (NBC: 1994–2004), hasn't. What does this tell us about academic analysis of sitcom, comedy and popular forms?

One of the main reasons for analysing the sitcom is to attempt to come to terms with the reasons why the genre has maintained its popular cultural position. Since the demise of the Western in the 1950s, 'In only a few television seasons have sitcoms not dominated the network ratings' (Hamamoto, 1989, p. 1) in America. The production of

Analysis of *The Simpsons*
demonstrates the variety of ways
sitcom has been examined
throughout its history

sitcom is an important business, with the financial rewards significant and much industrial power wielded by those who produce popular programmes (Gitlin, 1994, p. 132). The sitcom can, then, be examined to see what it tells us about the machinations of the broadcasting industries and its status as a product whose returns can be considerable.

However, sitcom's ratings dominance in America has not been matched in Britain; while individual programmes, or episodes of particular series, have garnered massive audiences, the sitcom has never maintained the sustained popularity of the soap opera. These differences suggest distinctions which can be made between the UK and the USA, in terms of both the television and entertainment industries, and the ways in which audiences consume and enjoy television. Such distinctions in very similar programming can be explored within broader contexts about national and cultural identities, and the role humour plays within specific nations. It's significant that Mark Thompson, the Director General of the BBC, has stated that the Corporation should invest more time and effort in comedy, because it 'builds genuine public value' and 'plays a critical part in reflecting our national culture and the way we live now' (BBC, 2004, no page); this may not be a statement which could necessarily be made by public service broadcasters of other countries.

Therefore sitcom has a broader social and industrial significance than merely that contained within specific episodes or series. It is also used by television to say something about specific channels and their relationship with their audiences. For example, NBC has marketed its 'Must See' line-up on Thursday evenings for some time now, scheduling two hours' worth of popular, flagship sitcoms in a row (Martin, 2003). NBC's recent line-up – which has included *Friends*, *Will and Grace* (1998–) and *Scrubs* (2001–) – not only consistently beats the programming scheduled by competing channels, but also helps to define the channel as one for younger, urban audiences. This notion of a cluster of sitcoms as a weekly event, aimed at a specific subsection of the mass audience, tries to create an intimate relationship between viewers and channel, in which networks attempt to demonstrate their understanding of their audience's needs. So, when the Fox network began broadcasting in America, it specifically fostered a schedule of 'black' comedy programmes – *In Living Color* (1990–4), *Roc* (1990–4), *South Central* (1994) – 'to distinguish it from the more traditional networks' (Zook, 1999, p. 5) and to attract a specific audience. These series have been used in syndication by channels such as BET, also in an attempt to define their core audience (Tait and Barber, 1996, p. 192). And Lifetime used *The Days and Nights of Molly Dodd* (NBC, Lifetime: 1987–91) as a 'signature piece' (Wilson, 1994, p. 103) when it attempted to redefine itself and its relationship with its intended female audience. So sitcom can be investigated as an industrial tool for cohering specific audience groups, with the implication that such groups find similar things funny, and have similar responses to particular character types.

This relationship between channel and audience is apparent in Britain too, though in a slightly different way. That is, it is only really in the last couple of decades, with the advent of Channel 4, subsequent developments on BBC 2, and the proliferation of cable and satellite channels, that specific sitcoms have aimed to actively engage discrete sections of the audience. Indeed, it is only very recently that the scheduling of a number of sitcoms one after the other, a staple of American television for decades, has become apparent on British television. So, Channel 4 has offered sitcoms on Friday nights for some time now, and it might be telling that many of these series have been American imports, such as *Friends*, *Will and Grace* and *The Simpsons*. In the early 2000s, BBC 2 offered a comedy 'zone' on Monday nights, in which home-grown sitcoms such as *The Office* (2001–3) and *The Royle Family* (BBC 2, BBC 1: 1998–2000) first aired, alongside comedy panel games and sketch shows. Yet the attempt by the most popular channel in Britain – BBC 1 – to schedule clusters of sitcoms has been less successful. In 2003, the series *My Hero* (2000–), *Trevor's World of Sport* (2003–) and *Eyes Down* (2003–) were scheduled consecutively in primetime on Fridays, but within a couple of weeks *Trevor's World of Sport* was moved to a late-night spot on another day and replaced with decades-old repeats of *Only Fools and Horses* (1981–2003). The channel has continued to try out new series in these slots, such as *My Family* (2000–), *The Worst Week of My Life* (2004–), *Wild West* (2003–), *Carrie and Barry* (2004–) and *According to Bex* (2005). While *My Family* has eventually become a kind of success, none of these series has managed to garner massive audiences, though whether this was down to the individual series or the scheduling cluster is debatable. Whatever, this attempt by broadcasters to define certain days of the week as ones dedicated to comedy, as well as the kinds of programmes they schedule on those days, surely suggest something about the role broadcasters assume audiences assign to comedy and sitcom.

Sitcom is used in other ways too. In Britain it is very common for channels to broadcast Christmas specials of popular sitcoms, with these one-off episodes often at the core of the prime-time schedules, and routinely garnering the biggest audiences of the Christmas period. In recent years, specials have been made for series such as *One Foot in the Grave* (BBC 1: 1990–2001), *Only Fools and Horses*, *Men Behaving Badly* (ITV, BBC 1: 1992–8) and *The Office*, with the BBC's advertising of its Christmas schedule in 2001 virtually entirely centred on the return of the immensely popular *Only Fools and Horses* after a few years off-screen. The decision to use sitcoms as the cornerstone of Christmas television clearly indicates an assumption about the relationship between audiences and comedy, the kinds of broadcasting suitable for national holidays, and the ways in which a sitcom can be turned into a 'media event' (McCarthy, 2003, p. 89). Furthermore, the sitcom – particularly one with broad, cross-generational appeal – highlights Christmas's contemporary meaning which is more family-orientated than religious and centred on fun and play. The sitcom, then, is used by broadcasters for purposes beyond purely commercial ones, and so the genre can be explored for what it says about the kinds of audiences broadcasters are attempting to unite, and the kinds of entertainment deemed acceptable for mainstream, family audiences at Christmas. In this way, the sitcom is a useful form for exploring the relationship between industry and audience within broadcasting systems, whether commercial, public service or a mix of both. This is the case the world over, where the use by broadcasters of sitcom imports from Britain and America are carefully selected and scheduled in response to the importers' public service and/or commercial needs.

It is this relationship, in which texts offered as entertainment demonstrate the kinds of audiences that industry imagines their viewers to be, which has led to the primary way in which sitcom has been explored; what it says about representation. Representation is a vital concern of Media Studies generally, for the ways in which individuals and groups are presented to mass audiences are seen to presume something – whether causal or merely correlative – about the ways such individuals and groups are understood outside the media. Furthermore, the existence of those representations is often seen as reinforcing the appropriateness and validity of them. That is, for representations to be successful – and by successful, what is meant is easily understandable – they must conform to and utilise, normalised social conventions. For the sitcom, whose primary intention is the creation of comedy, 'immediacy is imperative, and to find a character immediately funny that character must be a recognisable type, a representative embodiment of a set of ideas or a manifestation of a cliché' (Medhurst and Tuck, 1982, p. 43). Similarly, it's argued that comedy's reliance on deviant aspects of society has meant that it is within sitcom that representations deemed offensive elsewhere have traditionally found their home. Sitcom is seen as offering 'the enjoyment of disruption' (Swanson, 1982, p. 32) and pleasure in 'transgressing boundaries' (Andrews, 1998, p. 51). This assumption has been particularly apparent within the analysis of representations of homosexuality in television, in which gay/camp characters (and, in comedy the two are often conflated) have always had a home within sitcom even if this has not been the case for other forms (Medhurst and Tuck, 1982, p. 49). If work has been carried out on the sitcom then, it is in the area of representation it has been most fruitful; the whole of Chapter 4 is devoted to the issue.

As will be outlined there, the nature of representation in sitcom becomes complex because of the specificities of humour. Debates about the nature of humour consistently highlight its simplicity, its immediacy and its limitations, to the extent that it's assumed that the ways in which comedy works must therefore also be quite simple. The fact that comedy is so vital to sitcom – indeed, is its one true intention – has been one of the barriers to a successful understanding of it, for the examination of humour is still in its infancy. The useful work that has been carried out on joke structure, the relationships between joke tellers, audiences and victims, and the effects of humour, is best collected and summarised by Morreall (1983, 1987). Yet this has repeatedly failed to come to satisfactory conclusions about the fundamental nature and purpose of humour so that, after two millennia of theorising, 'we are still without an adequate general theory of laughter' (Morreall, 1983, p. 1). Part of the reason for this is the number of schools of thought such a theory would need to unite, for humour has been examined via the methods and assumptions of psychology, sociology, philosophy, literature, critical theory and maths, to name but a few. While this is not necessarily a problem – or, more accurately, is merely a problem which afflicts much academic work on any topic – it does seem perverse to explore sitcom without making some sense of the ways in which the comedy within it works. This doesn't prevent analyses such as Badsey's (2001), which criticises *Blackadder Goes Forth*'s (BBC 1: 1989) inaccurate representation of the history of World War I, without an understanding of the role of comedy within the series.

There are then, a number of tensions within debates about how sitcom should be examined. There seems to be an unwillingness to engage with the complexities of humour because of the continued assumption that 'analysing a joke reduces its capacity to make us laugh' (Curtis, 1982, p. 4), resulting in sitcom's pleasures being destroyed by academic theorising. Sitcom is, then, not only a valuable form to study because it can feed into debates about the broadcasting industries, global marketing of programmes and issues of representation, but also because it may offer a new way into much broader debates about comedy and humour as a whole. While a number of theoretical and methodological approaches can be taken towards sitcom then, the genre's primary purpose – to make people laugh – must always somehow be a part of such analysis.

Humour and Society

The burgeoning field of Humour Theory offers numerous ways to explore humour, comedy, jokes and laughter. The main focus of Humour Theory has been an attempt to define precisely what it is that makes people laugh and why. This has resulted in three broad categories of theory – Superiority; Incongruity; Relief – all of which use close readings of particular jokes and comic performances to distinguish the exact components of 'funniness'. In their different ways, all three also acknowledge that humour relies on the relationship between the teller and the audience for its effects, which means that comedy must be examined as a social and cultural phenomenon. Finding out what kinds of things an individual, a group or a society finds funny can tell us more general things about them, such as the distinctions made between serious topics, that which is merely laughable and the interplay between the two. For television, which, is usually organised along national boundaries, the kinds of jokes which exist in sitcom reveal that nation's mass consciousness and the aspects and events of the world which it deems acceptable to laugh at. There is, then, 'a remarkable parallel between the themes of successful situation comedies and the social history of modern society' (Paterson, 1998, p. 66).

This means that sitcom has often been examined for the way it reflects changes within society. So Marc (1989), Hamamoto (1991) and Jones (1992) all trace histories of American sitcom's representation of the family, from stable family units such as *Father Knows Best* (NBC: 1954–60), through the surreal families of the 1960s in *Bewitched* (ABC: 1964–72) and *The Addams Family* (ABC: 1964–6), to secure families of the Reaganite era in programmes such as *Family Ties* (NBC: 1982–9) and *The Cosby Show* (NBC: 1984–92), to surrogate families in workplace sitcoms like *Cheers* (NBC: 1982–93) and *Taxi* (NBC: 1978–83). All of these programmes are seen not as intended critiques of such familial relationships, but instead merely reflect that which broader society finds normal. This is also seen to be the case with the ways in which women have been represented, with series such as *The Mary Tyler Moore Show* (CBS: 1970–7) explored as a reflection of women's changing roles within the workplace (Feuer, Kerr and Vahimagi, 1984; Dow, 1990; Bathrick, 2003).

Sitcom's drawing on social norms becomes more apparent once societies are compared, and it has been demonstrated that the particularities of a culture's sense of humour are extremely specific and often incomprehensible to other societies (Davies, 1990, 2002). This has significant implications for the international trade in comedy, in which programmes produced in one country are understood in slightly different ways in other cultures. So Cunningham and Jacka note how Chinese audiences were offended by the Australian sitcom *Mother and Son* (ABC: 1983–93) because of their differing attitudes towards the elderly (1996, p. 207). The global success of such American programmes as *Friends* and *Seinfeld* (NBC: 1989–98) would suggest that their contents offer some kind of comedic global common ground, yet studies reveal the variety of ways in which, like all media, different audiences read specific texts, as Husband (1988), Gitlin (1994, p. 214) and Feuer (1995, p. 128) demonstrate for *All in the Family* (CBS: 1971–9). Of course, the popularity and comprehensibility of American comedy programming across the globe can be tied into debates about globalisation and cultural imperialism (Strinati, 1992; Cantor, 2003). Yet senses of humour remain stubbornly local, and anyone travelling the globe and seeing forms of entertainment in foreign countries will see the different ways nations decide to amuse themselves. And, as Rixon notes, the attempt by local broadcasting industries to preserve (and define) a nation's cultural identity has meant that while American programmes are broadcast across the globe, they are usually scheduled and understood as 'mere interlopers' (2003, p. 49).

In these ways, sitcom becomes not only representative of a culture's identity and ideology, it also becomes one of the ways in which that culture defines and understands itself. If 'To share humor with someone we need to share a form of life with him [sic]' (Morreall, 1983, p. 61), then group laughter at a joke serves to signal an agreement about the way things are, should be or are understood to be. It is often suggested that vital to the British national identity is the importance of a sense of humour, that the accusation of being humourless has a damning implication in the UK unlike that of other countries (Andrews, 1998, pp. 56–7; Easthope, 2000). Similarly, the ways in which that comedy is presented, and the kinds of topics which are acceptable for humour, feed into the ways in which cultures make sense of themselves. That is, the preponderance of black humour, and the repeated intermingling of serious and comic subjects without clear distinctions between the two can be seen as representative of a particular British way of responding to events. Forms of satirical comedy on British (and much European) television highlight the fondness for examining serious subjects comedically in a manner much less common in America, as series such as *That Was The Week That Was* (BBC 1: 1962–3), *Yes, Minister* (BBC 2: 1980–4) and *Brass Eye* (Channel 4: 1997, 2001) testify. And Richards traces the history of the representation of the English in British cinema, and finds that, particularly in comparison to other countries and especially during World War II, it suggests that 'a sense of humour is the English secret weapon' (1997, p. 87).

Furthermore, comedy also becomes one of the ways in which a culture tries to represent itself to outsiders. Television's national nature requires it to, as much as possible, present a unified national consciousness, scheduling programming comprehensible to all, even though specific channels or programmes may be aimed at particular audiences. Sitcom, then, becomes part of the television process in which broadcasting is used to attempt to define the ways in which a culture presents itself to others. The acceptability of jokes on certain subjects, and the offence caused by jokes on others, are indicative of a (no matter how enforced) understood sense of national identity. Indeed, the arguments over 'political correctness' in the 1980s, many of which were centred around comedy content particularly in terms of jokes about race and gender, are symbolic of cultures wishing to alter how their national identity is perceived. The fact that such comedic political correctness was, if not rejected, certainly derided in many quarters, points not only to the difficulty of containing comedy, but also that television is incapable of finally coalescing its audiences and their ideologies. As 'Joking as a form of human interaction plays disrespectfully on our sense of what is socially respectable or ethically correct' (Littlewood and Pickering, 1998, p. 292), it requires such proprieties not only for its effect but also to necessitate its existence. The British 'Alternative Comedy' movement, with its anti-racist and anti-sexist agenda, did not result purely from comedians' finding this unfunny any more, but instead was seen as a movement away from the 'stylistically and politically conservative' (Double, 1991, p. 111) comedy content which could result in altered attitudes generally (Wilmut and Rosengard, 1989, p. 2). Therefore, jokes about race and gender, and comedians making successful careers from them, still abound; yet the fact that certain inflections of such material are now unacceptable in broadcasting and that media regulatory bodies enforce codes of conduct condemning them, points to an enforced sense of public national identity somewhat at odds with the everyday lives, experiences and attitudes of many individuals. Humour relies, therefore, on an acknowledgment and understanding of the social values it disrupts but it doesn't necessarily require its audience to support such values or the disruption of them.

Indeed, comedy is one of the ways in which identity is constructed at a much more personal level. Since Radcliffe-Brown (1952), anthropological studies of humour show the way in which humour is used for group bonding in many societies. Here, the move-

ment from serious to comedic discourse, particularly among strangers, signals a significant development in social interaction and familiarity. In this way, comedy is a vital social
tool, a significant part of human interaction rather than merely a mode which communication can adopt. Furthermore, the successful invocation of comedy, while bonding
a group together, becomes a useful tool for signalling those who are outside the defined
group. Comedy often involves an understanding of who is 'us' and who is 'them', with
'them' often forming the butt of jokes made by 'us'; racist humour clearly conforms to
such a pattern. In doing this, comedy serves to construct a simplistic version of 'us' in
which a variety of individual differences are glossed over in order for the group bonding to function successfully.

This distinction between social groups is fostered – indeed, is relied upon – for the
success of sitcoms which target specific audiences. Recent developments in animated
sitcom, with such shows as *The Simpsons*, *South Park* (Comedy Central: 1997–), and
Beavis and Butt-head (MTV: 1993–7), demonstrate sitcom being made for specific audiences – young, media literate, urban – which rely for some of their pleasure on the
refusal to be pleasurable to other members of the audience (Donnelly, 2001). That is,
the deliberate offence offered by *South Park* is one which can give pleasure to younger
audiences at least partly because it's offensive to older audiences; in this way, this is 'my'
comedy, not 'yours'. The fact that these series were broadcast on channels aiming for
specific audiences – Fox, Comedy Central and MTV in America, BBC 2 and Channel 4
in Britain – shows how they function to construct an 'in' and an 'out' group. Indeed,
the development of Fox as a realistic competitor to the other networks in America can
be traced to its success in creating programmes for a 'young, hip audience' (Block, 1990,
p. 217). And the development of fan websites and communities devoted to these programmes shows audiences actively creating a group identity in which it is assumed that
the programme is not pleasurable to broader audiences.

It is because of this use of comedy to highlight distinctions between social groups that
it is often criticised for creating or upholding unhealthy divisions within society, particularly through the use of comedy which can be defined as 'racist' or 'sexist'. Yet the
existence of jokes which work from an assumed stereotype about certain people has
been read in a variety of ways. The question remains as to whether comedy is merely
indicative of social inequalities or helps to uphold and normalise them, and much of this
debate rests on the question of comedy's power and the particular circumstances of
specific jokes, audiences, tellers and butts. The most notorious examples of this debate
concern *Till Death Us Do Part* (BBC 1: 1965–75) (Cook, 1982, p. 11; Neale and Krutnik,
1990, p. 261; Cashmore, 1994, p. 105) and its American remake *All in the Family* (Gitlin,
1994, 211–4; Feuer 1995, p. 128; Malik, 2002). Whatever, studies of comedy – whether
broadcast or social – work from the assumption that humour has some relationship with
social structures and power, and that jokes do not exist outside of social and national
discourse. Indeed, rather than merely being a part of discourse, they constitute a specific

discourse of their own, in which the humour intention results in specific inflections of communication.

The concern over the content of jokes assumes that humour either has a relationship with social power, or is in itself powerful. Yet there are disagreements over whether the reiteration of stereotyped assumptions and the use of comedy to present particular ideologies, functions in an aggressive manner or not. That is, the social role of humour may be one in which it serves as a tool of conflict avoidance, in which potential aggression is worked through and dissipated by rendering conflict merely funny. The anthropologist Radcliffe-Brown found that 'a relationship in which insults are exchanged and there is an obligation not to take them seriously, is one which, by means of sham conflicts, avoids real ones' (1952, p. 107). In this manner, potentially threatening and offensive subjects can be broached in a way which allows the teller the pleasure of saying such material, while the butt doesn't have to respond defensively to statements which are contextualised as 'only' jokes.

Yet there are problems with this theory, and these become more manifest once we move from the social arena of comedy to the specifics of television and the sitcom. Radcliffe-Brown notes that such social comedy functions through 'permitted disrespect' (p. 91), in which it is agreed between groups what can be joked about, who can make jokes, and in what manner. Conflict avoidance rests on carefully prescribed and learned 'joking relationships' (p. 90) which signal clearly the manner in which such interaction is intended. For a successful social joking relationship, and for comedy to fulfil its role of voicing aggression without leading to physical violence, it must be signalled, agreed to and adhered to, and there must be the opportunity for the butt of the joke to get revenge by joking back. Joking relationships rest, then, on an equal balance of power, in which part of the reason that insults are unthreatening is because they don't help uphold an unequal power structure.

Clearly, this is difficult to transfer to television. First, those who are joked about on television have little recourse to trading insults back; at least, if they do, they're unlikely to reach the mass audience television can. Second, the institutional nature of broadcasting is one with massive assumptions of power, in which the broadcasting of material serves to legitimise it. If, as noted before, broadcasting coalesces disparate national distinctions and constructs a group identity for the country it serves, the material it presents as funny and the groups or individuals it presents as laughable, become powerful markers for social structures more generally, and, by extension, legitimise those structures. This means that analysis of sitcom, particularly if it attempts to explore the role and effects of humour within sitcom, has to find some way to come to terms with the complex relationship between media texts and audiences, and the implications this has for conventional social analyses of comedy. This difficulty is apparent within the regulations laid down by various broadcasting bodies which, while acknowledging the 'special freedom' (Broadcasting Standards Commission, 1998, p. 24) of comedy, notes that the transference from small-scale communication to the mass nature of broadcasting has significant implications for possible meanings made by audiences, and the potential offence – and other consequences – which may ensue. And the movement away from humour as merely a form of social interaction to a more modern one in which, as a part of consumer societies, comedy becomes a commodity which can be traded and profited from, inevitably affects not only the content of humour, but the function which society, and individuals, see it fulfilling.

Definitions of Terms

One of the major problems in the study of sitcom is that many of the terms associated with it have a range of conflicting definitions. This is partly because many of them have long histories of developing definitions, and partly because, as everyday terms, there's often an assumption that a 'common sense' agreement exists as to their meaning. It's possible, in everyday conversation, to talk of films and books being comedies, or for something that happened to you being funny, without the need to explicate exactly how and why these phenomena are described as such. Indeed, the very everyday, normalness of humour, comedy, laughter and jokes are part of their meaning, and are an essential requirement for their effects to be understood, accepted and pleasurable. This has led to the terms being used in a variety of ways by theorists, depending on the specific points which are being made. Thus Aristotle's insistence on the term 'wit' (1925, Book 4, Chapter 8) as representing a specific form of humour which displays intelligence highlights his insistence on justifying comedy on the basis of it being intelligent or having a social purpose, with jokes that don't have such a purpose rendered mindless and worthless. Freud's notorious insistence on distinguishing between 'jokes', 'wit' and 'humour' only fulfils any purpose if his general theory of comedy is valid (Morreall, 1983, p. 27). Similarly, Neale and Krutnik's desire to examine visual and verbal jokes as separate entities results in them using the term 'gag' to represent only the former, even though they admit that their 'decision to do so is rather an arbitrary one' (1990, p. 51). Olson argues that 'Comedy is precisely a certain freedom from definition' (2001, p. 6) whose power arises from its refusal to conform to any prescriptive understandings of it. The following definitions then, while attempting to find some common ground between these contradictory positions, will inevitably conflict with some writers.

Laughter

Of all these terms 'laughter' is probably the most easily defined, but ironically, also the most often misused. That is, laughter is simply the noise made by the combination of the vocal chords and a release of carbon dioxide resulting in a sound which is usually regarded as being a response to a comic event. Nevertheless, it is important to distance the noise that is made from the common interpretation of it, for much research has shown that the use of the laugh in society is a far more complex and subtle interaction than simply a response to comic stimulus.

Laughter is important to the sitcom not only because it is the genre's intention, but because the use of studio audiences and canned laughter means that it is part of the text. One of the easiest ways to realise you're watching a sitcom is to hear the reaction of the audience on the laugh track. It's unclear whether laugh tracks actually make audiences at home laugh at sitcoms more; certainly there seems to have been a backlash against them in recent British sitcoms, with the majority of new series, such as *The Office, The Smoking Room* (BBC3: 2004–), *Peter Kay's Phoenix Nights* (Channel 4: 2001–), *Green Wing* (Channel 4: 2004–), *Dead Man Weds* (ITV1: 2005–), and *Nathan Barley* (Channel 4: 2005–) not bothering with them at all. There is then a debate about whether laughter is a necessary signifier of the sitcom as a genre, with recent series clearly assuming that it's not.

Laughter is probably instead best understood as fulfilling some kind of social function. Freud (1960) argues that laughter is a result of comedy allowing usually suppressed thoughts to be expressed and is thus a vital 'venting of nervous energy' (Morreall 1983, p. 20). While this reading has been criticised in a number of ways, Provine argues that 'laughter has more to do with relationships than jokes' (2000, p. 3). Provine goes on to outline the contradictory nature of the research into laughter's effects and role but concludes that, even though we don't know precisely how it works, it's clear that its social function is far more important than any benefit it may have to, say, psychological well-being or physical health. The laugh track in sitcom, then, can be seen to function less as a generic signal and more as demonstrating some kind of social unity in the audience that consumes it; it suggests that everyone finds this funny. It may be for this reason that the majority of those British and American series which don't have laugh tracks have been broadcast on minority channels and target themselves at particular, niche audiences rather than general, mainstream ones. Understanding the role of the laugh within sitcom and social interaction is an important part of examining the genre and has implications for its cultural function.

Jokes

The term 'joke' indicates a single construction intended to have a comic effect, and is the smallest possible unit that can do so. Straight away this is a problematic definition: is a joke still a joke if the intention was to have a comic effect, yet none was achieved? The answer is probably yes, for the intention to have a comic effect may be signalled clearly enough for an audience to be aware that a joke has been attempted, even if no comic response occurred. For example, an audience is aware that a stand-up comedian on stage is telling jokes even if they don't find any of them funny. Therefore, the definition of 'joke' relies more on intention than content or effect.

However, this is not to say that content is irrelevant. The 'traditional' format involves a set-up and a punchline, and that structure can itself signal the comic intention even if the joke isn't found to be funny. The phrases 'Have you heard the one about . . .', or

'I went to the doctor's the other day . . .' are so inextricably linked in many societies with the joke format that an audience can be cued to comic intention through their use. Most Humour Theory argues that the punchline must involve surprise, with audiences 'getting' the joke suddenly being vital to a laughter response. This is why explaining a joke to someone who hasn't got it rarely results in them laughing, for they inevitably engage in a slow working through of the joke, rather than an immediate realisation. So, the joke is often regarded as a fleeting, momentary unit, usually at odds with the requirements of film and television narrative. It is perhaps easier to see jokes as individual units when they are performed by a stand-up comedian in which their momentary pleasures are much more foregrounded and offered for pleasure. This is also one of the distinctions between the television sketch show and the sitcom, in which the former uses segmentalised jokes for its pleasure, while the latter attempts to weld these to narrative and maintain character consistency.

Yet surprise becomes severely problematised once we move from one-off performances by stand-ups in which there is an unrepeatable interaction between performer and audience, and television sitcom. While it's clear that part of the pleasure in watching sitcom comes from unexpected punchlines and, in those programmes with strong comedic narratives, surprising reversals of fortune or unexpected farcical developments, the role of surprise becomes severely problematised by repeats. In America, where many channels broadcast syndicated reruns, it's possible to see the same episode of a series a number of times, and in Britain many sitcoms, particularly 'classics' like *Fawlty Towers* (BBC 2: 1975, 1979) and *Dad's Army* (BBC 1: 1968–77), are repeated in prime-time slots to large audiences. Even though it's likely that for many audience members most of the jokes are new, for some viewers the pleasure instead arises from seeing episodes, and jokes within episodes, which are already known. The UKTV channel UKGold, which consists entirely of repeats, even advertises itself as the place where you can see comic moments again and again, their trailers consisting of repeated showings of precisely those moments. And the massive sales on video and DVD of 'classic' series are testament to the fact that viewers are willing to part with money for things they've already seen. In this instance, the pleasure of comedy comes from exactly the opposite of surprise, the joy coming from the reiteration of the known.

For Humour Theory, which has its roots in live performance, this presents a significant problem, for the industrial nature of broadcasting has altered the ways in which audiences can consume comedy. Sitcoms are odd in that they often work for two audiences; the one in the studio laughing 'live' and contributing to the laugh track, and the audience at home watching within the complex variables of the domestic space. While the former can be explored in terms of the surprise of the jokes, this is not necessarily the case for the latter. In this way, television sitcom undermines many of the theories concerning the ways in which jokes work and the social relationships they require to be effective. While this relationship has traditionally been seen as the one between the joke-teller and the audience, for repeats, the one between those viewing the programme may be more significant. For example, *The Day Today* (BBC 2: 1994) was a series I watched with my housemates during my student years, and our pleasure at the time was clearly one of the surprise of the jokes; but when the series was released on DVD last year and we watched it together the pleasure was instead based around us reliving our past, and quoting lines as they were performed. There was, then, very little surprise in the series, but this didn't stop us roaring with laughter throughout. Here the humour was clearly connected to social circumstances, and it these factors which may be the most significant in understanding a joke's meaning.

Thus, while the joke is the smallest unit of comedy, this is not to say that it exists on its own and can be detached from other parts of humour. The joke always exists within discourse and the nature of that discourse can significantly affect its reception. Thus, while it would seem sensible to begin analysis of humour with analysis of the joke, for that is its smallest constituent, this is very difficult to do, as alienating it completely from its context is to detach it from a significant part of its meaning and method of compre-hension. This causes problems concerning a definition of the term, for it is to some extent impossible to pinpoint precisely what is part of the joke and what is just affect-ing it. While this is problematic, it is clear that the term 'joke' is used to denote a segment of text the aim of which is comic and which is the smallest unit capable of being so.

Humour

Humour contains jokes and is the sequential reiteration of a series of jokes. Like jokes, humour exists in discourse, and its meanings are inevitably affected by, and are a result of, that discourse. Whereas jokes are individual units, humour is usually used to denote a process, and is something that is, consciously or unconsciously, grafted onto a text to supply additional meaning; the additional meaning being 'this is funny'. However, whereas jokes are specific instances, and each one has the aim of creating a comic response, humour is more of a general tone, pervading all parts of a text, and existing even when nothing specifically funny is taking place. That is, not all parts of a sitcom are funny, yet the programme as a whole is likely to be defined as humorous. In this instance, we are analysing the overall tone and intention of the programme, rather than every single individual constituent.

Nerhardt finds that 'the term humour is used to denote the funniness of complex stimuli: a single, sudden change in temperature, though experienced as funny, would not be called humorous' (1976, p. 55). This suggests that humour is understood to exist at a level above and beyond that of the joke, and that a joke *is* a joke at least partly because it exists within humour. Zillmann and Cantor remark that 'humour is the result of an appraisal process in which the individual can explain his mirthful behaviour to him-self as fully or partly caused by stimuli which are considered funny in his cultural environment' (1976, p. 111). This is a crucial point. The discourse in which humour exists is always specific – in this case culturally, but also geographically and historically – and this rests on a social understanding of what is humorous. For the sitcom, this suggests that the nature of genre, and the successful cueing of genre expectations, is vital for successful comedic communication.

Morreall remarks that 'Our enjoyment of humor is a kind of aesthetic experience' (1983, p. 93), and it is true that aestheticism exists in discourse, and is always defined by discourse. However, perhaps the most important point made here is that humour usually, though not always, results in enjoyment, and this is its primary aim, at least in the culturally specific discourse which will be explored here. However, it's also important to note that it is the pleasures associated with humour which have been least successfully explored.

Humour is not only placed within discourse but becomes a discourse of its own. That is, the elements which go into creating humour do so partly because they are associated with humour, but also because they exist within humorous discourse. Here, though, we have a paradox: humour exists because of the union of elements required to construct it, but those elements are only humorous if they are placed within a discourse which signals them as such. Thus, humour is both a conglomeration of elements and a tone applied to those elements which is not a part of them. Humour is, then, both the process and the result of this process: we find humour in things which are humorous, and the humorous process results in humour, and we end up going round in circles. This may be why so many analyses of sitcom sidestep the discussion of why such characters, stories and events are funny, and the pleasures that we get from them.

Comedy

The distinction to be made between comedy and humour is based around the production and intention. That is, humour is something which can exist both within and outside of media, whereas comedy suggests material whose primary purpose is one of funniness, usually created by specific people with that aim, and understood as so by audiences. Thus we can talk of comedy programmes, films, books, plays and so on as specific forms whose primary intention is one associated with humour. Therefore a humorous situation is something that can have just happened, without a deliberate intention, in everyday life: a situation comedy, on the other hand, has a deliberate production process and is understood as such by an audience. This is why broadcasters have specific comedy departments, and writers, producers, directors and actors who are known to usually work within comedy.

But for many other media, comedy is a mode through which other forms are presented, or given certain inflections. The idea that comedy in film, for example, is a mode rather than a genre arises because 'any genre might be treated as a subject for comedy' (King, 2002, p. 2), with a range of subgenres such as the romantic comedy, comedy of manners, horror comedy, sci-fi comedy and so on. Here, the characteristics of one genre are inflected through their comic treatment, without losing those characteristics or without being overpowered by comedy. It seems that comedy becomes a specific genre of its own, such as in many of the films of Jim Carrey, only when a film fails to sufficiently deliver the characteristics of another. So, while comedy can be a film genre, it is usually overpowered by other genres with which it is combined, with the comedic intention rendered merely a certain mode through which narrative can be filtered.

The same can be seen in television, most commonly through the hybrid genre of 'comedy drama'. Here again, the term suggests that the primary aim of such a text will conform to the classical assumptions of television drama, with a strong narrative based around cause and effect, and a coherence of character, presented in some kind of 'believable' diegesis. While the construction of that narrative is such that it is easier for the makers to produce and signal comic moments, such intentions only remain understandable – and, presumably, enjoyable – if those comic moments don't undermine to too large an extent the coherence of the drama. In this way, comedy can function as a mode drafted onto something else, and its funniness is limited by the requirements of the dominant genre. This can be seen in series such as *Sex and the City* (HBO: 1998–2004), *Six Feet Under* (HBO: 2001–), *Teachers* (Channel 4: 2001–4) and *Shameless* (Channel 4: 2004–), in which the comedy is forever constrained by the necessities of the drama, and episode endings rarely offer the pleasures of comedy. The difficulty

In *Shameless* the comedy is always constrained by the needs of the drama

in categorising such hybrids was shown by *Six Feet Under*'s production team when they won Best International Comedy at the 2003 British Comedy Awards, who seemed baffled as to why they were included in the nominations at all.

Yet it is difficult to see this happening in sitcom, and other comedy forms. The primary aim of sitcom is one centred on its humour and, on the whole, everything within a sitcom is geared towards that goal. Thus, the ways in which the characters are constructed, the kinds of narratives which are available, the ways in which the whole is shot and performed, and the promotional methods used for the sitcom, all arise from the comedic intent and content of the form. And while some sitcoms are more 'serious' than others – with, say *M*A*S*H* (CBS: 1972–83) being an obvious example – this is merely a matter of degree, rather than an argument that the sitcom ever truly becomes serious. Indeed, one of the ways in which sitcom functions – and a primary argument running throughout this book – is that it is produced and understood as a form which is as distinct as possible from seriousness, upholding the validity of the serious in the process.

Because of this, seeing comedy as a mode – as it conventionally is seen within Film Studies and the analysis of other media – is difficult to argue for some television comedy generally, and the sitcom specifically. If genres differ from modes because they are groups of forms who share similar characteristics and whose intentions and pleasures result from an understanding of the genre and the specific characteristics within them, then the sitcom is clearly a genre, even if it uses the characteristics of the comedy mode as part of its makeup. It is for this reason that the whole of the next chapter will deal with sitcom as a genre.

The Social Position of Comedy and Sitcom

As has been noted, there is a scarcity of academic work on the sitcom and it can be argued that this lack is representative of the position afforded the sitcom within both academia and broader society. One of Cultural Studies' main aims was to attempt to dissect this argument, and to begin to seriously analyse cultural forms which had previously been neglected, particularly when such forms were avoided precisely because they were popular or, more tellingly, were enjoyed by the working class. Yet it is significant that little has been done by Cultural Studies to engage with either broadcast comedy or social humour. This may partly be because the genre is consistently criticised for its conservative nature, in which the pressures of the broadcasting system have muted any radical potential comedy may have. For a subject like Cultural Studies, interested as much in the revolutionary potential of its subject as its meaning, comedy's straightforward pleasures may represent an attack on social structures which are rendered toothless by being laughed away. Indeed, the battle by Cultural Studies to convince other academic subjects and the public at large that their object of study is worthwhile inevitably requires that the subject is dealt with seriously, and this is easier to do if you're dealing with something inherently serious. In a similar manner, Gray notes that 'feminist criticism has generally avoided the discussion of comedy, perhaps in order to be accepted by conservative critics who found feminist theory comic in and of itself' (1994, p. 19).

This has certainly been the case in my experience. For the last ten years, as an undergraduate, postgraduate and lecturer, it's been apparent that there are institutional concerns over the academic value in studying both comedy and television, and so sitcom encompasses a multitude of sins. To tell someone that you're writing an academic book on sitcom is to prepare yourself for questions concerning how this can possibly be done, and to be required to defend yourself from the accusation of being someone wasting taxpayers' money on mere frivolities. Students, perhaps unsurprisingly, assume that a course I teach on comedy will be not only more fun, but also 'easier' than other modules and are sometimes resistant to my perseverance in moving beyond 'common sense' responses to the subject. This isn't intended as a complaint; or, at least, it's not to suggest that these difficulties are more painful than for plenty of other subjects and theories. However, it is to note that it demonstrates certain social understandings not only of what comedy is, but also how it should be thought and written about. There's a weird contradiction – running throughout this book – in which analysts of comedy necessarily adopt an overtly serious discourse in talking about their subject in order to demonstrate that it's not just jokes and laughter, but this inevitably seems to undermine the very pleasure principle which is probably the point of comedy in the first place. Indeed, the fact that so much writing avoids talking about pleasure shows how insistent theorising is on moving away from something seen as so simplistic.

It is probably unsurprising then, that it is Film Studies, with its sense of history and complex theoretical underpinning, which has enough self-confidence in its own worth to risk being tainted by the silliness of studying comedy. While not exhaustive, a broad range of approaches towards film comedy has been adopted by Film Studies, examining the nature of stars, performance style, narrative structure and the visual. Yet here again, the kinds of comedy which are explored indicate the ways in which the study of comedy must be legitimised, with a preponderance of work on writer/performers with a distinctive, near auteur-ist style (Chaplin and Woody Allen being the prime examples), or forms of comedy which have a meaning or social purpose above and beyond mere funniness. In this way, Film Studies works from the assumption that afflicts virtually all study of humour: that comedy is only of interest – and of worth – if it is doing something else at the same time as being funny, for being funny is not in and of itself worthy, and certainly not worthy of understanding.

This can be seen by the ways in which the comic mode is commonly categorised. Forms such as satire, parody and pastiche, in which the humour is coupled with statements about other forms or social events, are routinely examined, while 'simpler' fare, such as romantic (Matthews, 2000) or gross-out comedies (Paul, 1994), are deemed interesting only inasmuch as they somehow entertain the masses. Certainly, in everyday conversation about 'good' sitcom, it's easier to convince someone that *Seinfeld* is an interesting cultural phenomenon by examining either its Jewish heritage (Brook, 2003; Kosalin, 2003) or its vaunted status as a 'show about nothing' (Pierson, 2000) as representative of the modern condition, than it is to say that the gags are good. Of course, I'm not suggesting that those gags arrive without an awareness of their heritage, nor am I saying that audiences just happen to find them funny; instead it's apparent that comedy, in no matter what form, is usually seen as a legitimate mode only if its purpose is complex and, in the end, serious. Thus Thompson calls *The Royle Family* and *The Simpsons* 'art television' (2003, pp. 136–7) not because either is funny, but because the former has an unconventional shooting style and narrative structure, while the latter is highly intertextual and offers different levels of understanding.

Such distinctions are apparent in the ways in which comedy is used within broadcasting. So, while the news is clearly intended to be a serious recounting of recent events, it often incorporates humour. In America, presenters often joke with one another, and here comedy functions to symbolise the personal relationship between a group of workers. Also, such comedy is often focused upon sports or weather reports, and not on news reporters, signalling that the latter are more worthy, or more important, than mere sport. In Britain, *News at Ten* (ITV: 1967–99, 2000–4) ran a slot called 'And Finally . . .' for many years, in which a light-hearted story was told. The fact that this story was always placed at the end of the bulletin, and clearly labelled as separate through its own slot and graphics, reinforces the view that seriousness and comedy must be clearly and appropriately signalled as discrete (Creeber, 2004). In these instances, comedy functions as a kind of 'light relief', a moment whose pleasure is not adulterated by the worries of serious events, just as the fools in Shakespeare's tragedies function not only as a respite from the emotionally draining tragedy, but also serve to highlight how significant the tragedy is. And while the founding principles of Britain's public service broadcasting are 'inform, educate and entertain', it's no accident that entertainment comes last in the list.

Indeed, it is this relationship with the serious which afflicts the production and understanding of comedy completely. Comedy has always been seen as 'contrariety to the serious' (Olsen, 1968, p. 13), and the latter is consistently seen as inherently more worthy than the former. The distinctions made between Shakespeare's tragedies and comedies, with the vast majority of the 'great' roles existing in the former, show that certain methods of representation are prioritised. Moreover, this distinction is one which supports its own existence, for the power and legitimacy of tragedy at least partly rests on it being as distinct from the 'silliness' of comedy as possible. This is why Shakespeare's 'problem plays' are so named, for in their mixing of comedy and tragedy they refuse to conform to the notion that worthwhile stories can only be told through tragedy, and that there are appropriate narrative structures and character types which must be used.

Yet outside media, humour also has a relationship with seriousness which is symbiotic, but in which seriousness is clearly the dominant appropriate mode. Carlson links humour with play, noting both of these are commonly associated with leisure and free time, neither of which occupy as important a social role in modern society as the more important, serious business of work and society (1996, p. 25). Indeed, social structures in Western societies demand that the serious business of work is done before the fun of leisure can take place, as many children barred from their X-Box until they've done their homework will testify.

What is significant in all of this is not merely that a distinction is drawn between the two modes: it is that seriousness is not only prioritised, but normalised. A number of Humour Theories, along with more general theories of social interaction and linguistics, note that the movement from a serious mode to a comic one must use 'metacommunication' (Schechner, 2002, p. 92) to ensure communication is understood as intended. In such analysis, the comic mode is usually the one which is seen as requiring the most obvious cues, and the misunderstanding of intended humour can have potentially offensive consequences. Yet this also notes that seriousness rarely requires cueing, or requires less obvious cueing. It seems that the assumed mode of communication is a serious one, unless cues are given to suggest otherwise. It is this which has led to certain characteristics of the sitcom genre which will be explored in more detail in Chapter 2.

One of the reasons why comedy occupies such a maligned role in society may be because it no longer fulfils the subversive role it may once have done. Analysts of comedy repeatedly cite Bakhtin's (1984) study of the carnivalesque, in which, through analysis of Rabelais' plays, Bakhtin explored the nature of carnival in medieval Europe. He describes a society in which humour is consistently used to mock those in authority and power, to the point where everyone is of equal standing and power becomes meaningless. It is this potential subversiveness which is at the core of responses to comedy, and why, for many, it must be controlled, and expressed only in certain places on certain subjects, as comedians murdered by dictatorial regimes demonstrate (Jenkins, 1994).

For many contemporary thinkers, the industrial, mass nature of contemporary society and the pressures of commercialism have rendered the radical nature of comedy obsolete. Grote argues that 'Everything the traditional comedy stood for, at every level of art, psychology, philosophy, and myth, has been overthrown in this New Comedy of American television' (1983, p. 105). He argues that, while traditional comedy presented change, renewal and development as powerful social forces through the deployment of narratives concerning the overthrow of social structures, the sitcom promotes repetitiveness and stability through its regular setting and characters and trivial storylines. While there are difficulties in comparing the serial nature of sitcom narratives with the self-contained ones of traditional comedy, Grote suggests that the ways in which characters are presented and the kinds of activities which audiences are invited to empathise with are indicative of comedy as a passive form, functioning as nothing other than entertainment. And not only is this a change within the productions of the broadcasting industry, but is instead an extension of developments within society, meaning that 'comedy seems to have given up on the possibility that it could function as a significant critical discourse' (Auslander, 1992, p. 137).

However, none of this takes into account the ways in which the public responds to comedy. Unfortunately, very little work has been done on audiences and sitcom, and that which has commonly uses the genre as a way into more 'serious' debates about significant social issues, such as race (Jhally and Lewis, 1992; Bodroghkozy, 1995; Coleman, 2000). Certainly the pleasures of sitcom have not been explored, nor have the ways in which audiences relate programmes and characters to their own lives. Broadcasters are clearly aware of the public's interest in comedy, as shown by channels devoted to it and, in Britain, a number of recent series in which people were invited to vote on their favourites: *Britain's Best Sitcom* (BBC 2: 2004); *The Nation's Favourite Comedian* (five: 2004); *The Comedian's Comedian* (Channel 4: 2004). However, it was noticeable that in all of these programmes, while the public were allowed to vote, they weren't allowed to express why; it was left to celebrities, other comedians and those within the comedy industry to 'explain' the greatness of particular performers and programmes. And, none of these programmes garnered the same critical and media attention as similar programmes on other subjects, such as *Great Britons* (BBC 2: 2002), *Restoration* (BBC 2: 2003–) and *The Big Read* (BBC 2: 2003). The suggestion is that merely saying something is funnier than something else is incontrovertible, and analysis beyond that is not only unnecessary, but not conducive to the pleasures of comedy.

Comedy, then, occupies a complex social position, in which its function is clearly prescribed as little more than entertainment, and unthreatening entertainment at that. The kinds of comedy produced on television and the repetitive nature of the sitcom are seen as being indicative of, and contributing towards, this role. It is unsurprising then that many academic subjects, with their emphasis on change and questioning social norms, have decided that there are more productive ways of fulfilling their aims. Furthermore, the constant criticisms of television for its failure to present a required public sphere, coupled with its commercial imperatives, means that the medium is often written off as of limited – or, at least, misappropriated – use. The fact that sitcom is, then, a combination of comedy and television means that it's unsurprising that the genre is maligned. It appears that not only does the majority of society see sitcom as a trivial, unintellectual, insignificant form, but that they also like to see it that way. This is not to suggest that I'm attempting to dismantle that understanding here; on the contrary, it is instead to note that the social role apportioned to sitcom and comedy demonstrates significant things about broader social structures.

Examining Sitcom

As has been shown, sitcom can be explored in a variety of ways. Importantly, this is many more than the ways in which sitcom *has* been explored. It's apparent that studies of sitcom audiences are clearly lacking and these would be of particular interest considering the global marketplace for much sitcom production. Most important, though, is the recurring appropriation of sitcom to demonstrate proof for arguments that don't necessarily arise from the genre itself. This book, while clearly drawing on the heritage of sitcom analysis, attempts to think through the ways in which sitcom can be examined rather than the ways it has been examined. It is for this reason that much of the work here is textual, demonstrating that while sitcom can be seen as representative of broader concerns about representation, globalisation and power structures, it is so in ways which are not only specific to the genre, but also inflect the meaning and importance of those concerns in particular ways. That is, analysing what sitcom *says* is pointless unless we have a fuller understanding of what sitcom *does*.

In analysis, this book deliberately takes a general approach to programmes and series. While specific episodes and moments will be examined now and again, on the whole it will attempt to explore series as a whole. This is because one of the problems in textually analysing television is in selecting what to examine. For sitcoms with hundreds of episodes, it's almost always possible to find any moment in one particular episode that's capable of supporting any argument, regardless of whether that moment is indicative of the series as a whole. For example, Rowe (1990) analyses in detail a particular episode of *Roseanne* (ABC: 1988–97) to demonstrate a particular argument about the representation of women in comedy, even though she notes that it's an atypical one. Of course, defining what constitutes a 'typical' episode is virtually impossible, yet it's clear that audiences do this somehow. That is, while people may have a particular episode of a series which is their favourite, it's programmes that they like, rather than episodes. Indeed, repeats and syndication serve to repeatedly undercut any narrative progression or character specificity within episodes, as they help render whole series available simultaneously. This book is about 'television sitcom', not about a particular sitcom, or about particular episodes, and the generalised nature of its analysis is intended to mirror the ways in which audiences make sense of and enjoy programmes. In answer to the question of whether we should take *The Simpsons* seriously, I'd say we should only if the audience does.

Chapter 2 | Sitcom and Genre

'Heartland want you to do a rewrite on the last script.'

'What's wrong with it?'

'There's nothing wrong with it. But you're going to have to write Debbie out of the series.'

'You mean kill off Priscilla?'

'Good God, no. This is a comedy, for Chrissake, not drama.'

David Lodge, *Therapy* (London: Secker & Warburg, 1995), p. 46.

As has been noted, humour is a mode which is a part of virtually all media, whether or not any specific programme would be defined as comic. There is, then, a distinction to be made between comedy as a general mode and those forms whose main aim is humour and whose contents are those most appropriate to that goal. As will be shown, defining exactly what it is that makes the sitcom a discrete genre which is usually understood by both industry and audiences is difficult, particularly as there is much disagreement over exactly which programmes are sitcoms and which aren't. Hybrid forms like 'comedy drama' are notoriously subjective, as shown by series such as *Sex and the City*. Similarly there's sometimes difficulty in distinguishing between sitcoms and sketch shows, particularly those which use recurring characters, such as *The Day Today* and *Knowing Me, Knowing You . . . with Alan Partridge* (BBC 2: 1994). Indeed, there is a long history of producers and production companies insisting their series belong to categories other than sitcom in order to escape its supposed negative connotations, such as MTM's desire to be seen as 'quality television' (Feuer, Kerr and Vahimagi, 1984). Furthermore, a recent trend in sitcom has been the abandonment of some of the genre's most obvious characteristics precisely because they're seen as so simplistically generic; this abandonment, however, has rarely led to confusion over whether they're sitcoms or not. This suggests there's flexibility not only within the industrial structures which produce sitcom, but also within audiences' reading techniques. It also means that the sitcom is a form which, despite the simplistic definitions of it often presented, is instead a complex one, commonly related to many other television (and film) genres. This problem in defining exactly what the sitcom is mirrors broader debates about genre as a whole, and so the sitcom is a useful form for thinking through genre.

Defining Sitcom

The difficulties of genre result from it being used to analyse '(1) the system of production, (2) structural analysis of the text, and (3) the reception process' (Feuer, 1992, p. 144). That is, media industries are commonly structured around departments making certain kinds of programmes; programmes thus contain material which can be read as conforming to generic structures; and audiences make sense of texts by comparison to genre expectations. And these three aspects respond to one another, with audiences selecting certain texts because of their preference for certain genres, and production responding to audiences' understandings of the products it supplies. Certainly sitcom production is focused around specific 'light entertainment' departments, and employs writers, producers, directors and stars because of their previous successes in comedy. Similarly, channels worldwide partly define themselves through the kinds of comedy they broadcast and the audiences they intend to attract. Genre exists, then, as the product of 'the interactions between texts, producers of texts and their readers' lifeworlds' (Meinhof and Smith, 2000, p. 3). In this way, genre becomes an inescapable aspect of media communication, affecting every part of it in a variety of ways. Yet it is this ubiquity which also makes genre analysis a difficult task, for where to begin if it so successfully permeates the industry, the text and the audience?

The sitcom is a form whose structure and content appears to be merely 'known' by both industry and audience, and requires such assumptions in order to be effective. Deciding whether a programme is a sitcom or not is in the end a personal matter, even though there are a number of core characteristics which would be agreed to by most people; indeed, this needs to be the case for genre to have any meaning at all. Analyses of sitcom have often attempted to outline these aspects, noting that such characteristics are not only central to our understanding of the genre, but that their rigidity is representative of the need for comedy to signal its intentions as clearly as possible. Indeed, the characteristics apparent in sitcom are more numerous than those for other genres, incorporating, not only content and narrative structure, but also shooting style, performance style, types of actors, as well as programme length and scheduling. These aspects of sitcom far outnumber those for genres such as the soap opera or documentary; clearly this says something about the nature of sitcom, the social function of humour, and the relationship between comedy, broadcasters and audiences.

Mintz defines the sitcom as:

a half-hour series focused on episodes involving recurrent characters within the same premise. That is, each week we encounter the same people in essentially the same setting. The episodes are finite; what happens in a given episode is generally closed off, explained, reconciled, solved at the end of the half hour ... Sitcoms are generally performed before live audiences, whether broadcast live (in the old days) or filmed or taped, and they usually have an element that might almost be metadrama in the sense that since the laughter is recorded (sometimes even augmented), the audience is aware of watching a play, a performance, a comedy incorporating comic activity.

The most important feature of sitcom structure is the cyclical nature of the normalcy of the premise undergoing stress or threat of change and becoming restored ... This faculty for the 'happy ending' is, of course, one of the staples of comedy, according to most comic theory. (1985, pp. 114–15)

This is a standard definition of the sitcom, concentrating on the recurring set-up and characters, the happy ending and the fact that individual episodes rarely refer to events in previous ones. However, what such a definition does is to look at the structure of the form, while ignoring the content. That is, the cyclical, closed-off nature of the sitcom is not complete enough as a definition of sitcom because it is applicable to many other genres within television. Indeed, such a narrative structure, with recurring characters and a central situation, is the central premise of most drama series, such as *Casualty* (BBC 1: 1986–) and *er* (NBC: 1994–).

Furthermore, many sitcoms ignore the rule of the closed-off storylines. *Soap* (ABC: 1977–81), for example, deliberately ignored this structure, and constantly incorporated narratives which lasted over many weeks, using the cliffhanger form which is so central to the soap opera. And, in its final years, *Only Fools and Horses* expanded to encompass developing storylines, with tales of Rodney and Del Boy's continuing romances. Furthermore, *Only Fools and Horses* has also gone beyond the half-hour structure, expanding to fifty-minute episodes, even though episode length is a recurring characteristic of sitcom definitions (Marshall and Werndly, 2002, p. 45). And *Friends*, with its continuing development of Ross and Rachel's relationship, uses episodic narratives which are self–contained but which often gain extra meaning (and funniness) through knowledge of the soap-like complex backstory.

Mintz notes that sitcoms are capable of going beyond his boundaries; his example is *M*A*S*H*, which 'departed significantly from several sitcom traditions and formulas, beginning with its use of film, the elimination of audience involvement, and the elaboration of setting and movement. The show does not look like a sitcom' (1985, pp. 112–13). Indeed, *M*A*S*H* is a problematic programme, particularly as incarnations with and without laugh tracks were broadcast. Mintz argues that *M*A*S*H* is indeed a sitcom, albeit one that 'developed beyond the limitations of a strict adherence to the formula' (p. 113), with a clear implication, fostered by the programme-makers and other critics, that it was 'more' than mere entertainment. Gitlin (1994, p. 236) outlines the debates within *M*A*S*H*'s production team as they grappled to reconcile that

As *M*A*S*H* played with the genre's boundaries, is it a sitcom, a 'dramedy', or a 'hospital drama'?

series' sitcom origins with its wartime setting, resulting in a shooting style which signals its distinction from conventional sitcom, at least partly in order to ensure that it is not seen as offensively making flippant jokes about war and death. While Morreale calls the programme a 'dramedy' (2003b, p. 152), Jacobs instead places *M*A*S*H* within the category of 'hospital drama' (2001, p. 25) demonstrating the personal nature of genre definitions and the ways in which different pleasures can be taken from programmes.

The problem here is defining the point at which a programme stops belonging to a genre. For sitcom, this is a valid point. Donnelly's (2001, pp. 73–5) analysis of the 1990's growth of prime-time adult animation does so without a single reference to sitcom, even though programmes such as *The Simpsons* and *South Park* clearly use its narrative structure. Here, the 'cartoonalness' (Wells, 2002, p. 94) of the series, in which the animated, visual aspects of the programmes are so distinct from the live-action, theatrical nature of most sitcom, is seen as enough to render it something else. Indeed, the fact that Creeber's *The Television Genre Book* (2001) includes a separate section for adult animation within its comedy section demonstrates the assumption that visual form is enough to mark cartoons as a coherent subgenre distinct from sitcom proper. Similarly, the decision not to include a laugh track on a sitcom has usually been justified by the argument that the programme is something other than a sitcom; or, more patronisingly, as more than 'just' a sitcom. While such difficulties highlight the pointlessness in attempting to come to a precise definition of what does and doesn't make a sitcom (or any other genre), this renders problematic the seamless way in which audiences seem to have little difficulty in making such distinctions and responding to generic programmes accordingly. Of course, differences clearly exist within individuals' responses to programmes, and these are often inexplicable: for example, what contradiction with sitcom conventions do I feel are occurring when I argue, as I do, that *The Flintstones* (ABC: 1960–6) is not a sitcom, when I'm quite happy accepting that *The Simpsons* is? While Neale remarks that 'generic specificity is extremely difficult to pin down in general statements that are anything other than rudimentary and banal' (1990, p. 48), I would also add, therefore, 'or personal'.

This is perhaps a result of genre conventions not being set, but simply accepted; 'Genre is what we collectively believe it to be' (Tudor, 1970, p. 38). Furthermore, for many genres the very 'naturalness' of genre conventions is vital to the efficient understanding of them. If comedy cannot function successfully in confused communication, the sitcom must be a form which signals itself as quickly and unambiguously as possible. Yet, in the same way that semiotics argues that language exists only through a set of cultural conventions, so too does genre, which then affects interpretation of the texts it contains; in addition, it also means that genre definitions are varied and can be individualised. This is why it is easy to find many definitions of the genre of sitcom which, while broadly similar, have enough differences for a text to be read differently depending on which definition is used. Some of these definitions are so at odds that they are capable of excluding programmes which, on the whole, are generally accepted as sitcoms. So Clarke (1987, p. 106) rejects *The Young Ones* (BBC 2: 1982–4) as a sitcom, while Abercrombie argues that the series instead 'pushed the conventions of the situation comedy to their limits' (1996, p. 43). Similarly, Cantor defines *Married . . . with Children* (Fox: 1987–97) and *The Simpsons* as 'satires' (1990, p. 284) rather than sitcoms and sees a significant difference between the two. This is not to argue that these definitions are 'wrong', merely to remark that definitions are varied and contested, that this is a primary factor of genre, and it seems particularly pertinent to sitcom.

Part of the reason for this is that 'Genres are inherently temporal' (Neale, 1990, p. 56). So, as genres develop over time, characteristics of them are lost to the past. While this highlights the problems in concretely defining genres, it also shows that genres are a process that exist in the developing relationship between the text, its producers and its receivers. This results in a continual development of genres, and it is not uncommon to see television reviews stating that programmes have 'reinvented the genre'. In fact, this reinvention is likely to just be a more obvious, foregrounded playing with the genre conventions, without the sense of overt novelty that the phrase implies. After all, if the difference outweighed the repetition too severely, it is doubtful that the text would be comprehensible and it certainly wouldn't be associated with such a genre. This means that 'Genres do not only change because society changes, they also evolve as distinct entities' (Lacey, 2000, p. 142). They also change, however, in response to trends within television more generally. Certainly, the recent move towards 'comedy vérité' (Mills, 2004a) can be partially attributed to audiences' acceptance of certain shooting styles thanks to the boom in documentary and reality television in the 1990s (Dovey 2001, p. 134). While some of these series – *The Office*, *The Larry Sanders Show* (HBO: 1992–8), *People Like Us* (BBC 2: 1999–2001) – use documentary and docusoap techniques to comedically examine the consequences of such productions, others – *The Royle Family*, *Curb Your Enthusiasm* (HBO: 2000–) – merely adopt them. Here genre development has responded to broader changes in television aesthetics; the bigger question remains, however, why it is the sitcom which has so actively and successfully commandeered such aesthetics when other popular fictional forms – particularly American drama series and British soap operas – haven't.

The term 'genre' is now often a pejorative one, representative of popular culture devoid of any originality or creativity, mass-produced by an industry whose only concern is the successful selling of its product (Willemen, 1992, p. 2). Neale notes how this is a complete inversion of previous understandings of culture 'which saw "high art" as rule-bound and ordered (as evident in genres like the sonnet and tragedy) and "low art" as unconstrained by the rules of decorum' (2001, p. 2). Current social conventions certainly prioritise series which foreground their lack of generic specificity or, more commonly, which question, interrogate or overhaul accepted genre conventions. Thus British sit-coms like *The Royle Family* are lauded for their non-sitcom-like shooting style and experimentation with comedic narrative (by not really having one) just as *The Larry Sanders Show* used the form to interrogate the nature of television production, experimenting with the boundaries of language within comedy on the way. It is notable that both of these programmes are commonly talked about as the individual vision of one person, with *The Royle Family* associated with Caroline Aherne, and *The Larry Sanders Show* seen as developing from Garry Shandling's career as a stand-up and the formal experimentation with sitcom he carried out in *It's Garry Shandling's Show* (Showtime: 1986–90). Such understandings clearly resonate with filmic understandings of the 'auteur', in which, like most novels and theatre, the product of single creative voice is seen as higher 'art' than that of the collaborative, commercial sector commonly associated with most genre products. Programmes which don't display a desire to experiment with or interrogate the genre of which they're a part thus occupy a low cultural position on two counts – as being the product of many people; as being repetitive and formulaic – with these two aspects symbiotic responses to one another. It is these two aspects of sitcom which help support the genre's low cultural position as 'only entertainment' (Dyer, 1992).

In attempting to define the sitcom, Jones instead looks at narrative. He finds that the sitcom has, always the same basic structure: Domestic harmony is threatened when a character develops a desire that runs counter to the group's welfare, or misunderstands a situation because of poor communication, or contacts a disruptive outside element. The voice of the group – usually the voice of the father or equivalent chief executive – tries to restore harmony but fails. The dissenter grabs at an easy, often unilateral solution. The solution fails, and the dissenter must surrender to the group for rescue. The problem turns out to be not very serious after all, once everyone remembers to communicate and surrender his or her selfish goals. The wisdom of the group and its executive is proved. Everyone, including the dissenter, is happier than at the outset. (1992, pp. 3–4)

While such a definition is indeed true for much sitcom, the same problems exist here as for Mintz's definition; that it covers programmes other than sitcoms and it does not apply to all sitcoms. Much drama, particularly the soap opera, relies on narratives in which a character has to fall back on the group to be rescued from a difficult situation, and yet soap opera is not sitcom. And series such as *The Young Ones* and *The Strange World of Gurney Slade* (ITV: 1960), while very clearly sitcoms, do not use this narrative structure. So, yes, *most* sitcoms do conform to such definitions, but the question remains concerning how audiences are capable of reading programmes as sitcoms which do not conform to such criteria.

Neale and Krutnik note that the model they construct in an attempt to define film comedy 'is so schematic and so general that it can be applied to genres like the Western, the thriller, and the detective film, as well as to the genre of comedy' (1990, p. 29). There are structures apparent in many drama forms, whether primarily serious or comic, and these are norms which are associated with narrative as a whole. Instead the differences between genres are signalled purely by the ways in which such narratives are motivated. So Neale and Krutnik note that the limits of a genre 'are determined largely by considerations of tone' (p. 18). For them, the sitcom is not defined by a certain narrative structure, but by that narrative structure being motivated towards humour and having the tone of humour. It is usually the treatment of narratives which makes them sitcoms, and not the narratives themselves. This treatment is one which not only means that the script is written in a certain way, but also that it is performed, shot and recorded in a certain way, so that there is a 'look' which is indicative of the sitcom just as there is a visual style associated with many genres. Indeed, Mintz would not be able to argue that *M*A*S*H* did not 'look like a sitcom' (1985, p. 112) if this was not the case.

This notion of the sitcom 'look' is an important one, for it is one of the most obvious ways in which sitcom signals its generic adherence and comic aim. Conventionally, sitcoms are shot as if the performance was taking place in a proscenium theatre, with the audience positioned as the fourth wall. Indeed, the sitcom is commonly not just shot to look theatrical, it often is actually shot in a theatrical manner, with a real, live audience watching the recording. The performers are thus able to respond to the audience's reactions, leaving pauses for big laughs. Sitcom aesthetics usually require programmes to be recorded under very bright lights, with sets clear and full, again reminiscent of the theatrical experience. And camera moves in sitcom are often limited, with the directorial style often more about capturing the events in a manner conducive to the comic event than in creating any kind of diegetic atmosphere or complex televisual world.

It is significant when sitcoms abandon this look, for it signals an attempt to use the visual possibilities of comedy television for means other than those traditionally seen as available to the sitcom. As noted, *M*A*S*H* used a visual style which meant it did not 'look like a sitcom', and it is no accident that this occurred in a programme which was a metaphor for the Vietnam War, exploring the complex moral decisions faced by surgeons in the field, and the use of humour to combat everyday horrors. This tinkering with the sitcom look has become more common in recent years in both the UK and America, and many such programmes attempt to use comedy and the nature of media to be more than 'just funny'. *The Larry Sanders Show*, for example, uses both video and film to distinguish between the public and private personae of its eponymous character. *The Royle Family* and *The Office* use handheld cameras in an attempt to latch onto the visual style of the recent docusoap trend and to make a connection between those series and the British social realism trend which dominates British broadcasting. In both of these programmes, narrative is downplayed and replaced by the slow accumulation of comic moments and idiosyncratic detail, both aspects often pinpointed by the documentary form but perhaps too subtle for the conventional sitcom look. Both *The League of Gentlemen* (BBC 2: 1999–) and *Spaced* (Channel 4: 1999–2001) have a more visually complex aesthetic drawn from cinema. *The League of Gentlemen* repeatedly uses the shooting style and lighting techniques of British horror film, which underlines its horrific representation of the town of Royston Vasey. *Spaced* uses camera movements and performance styles from a range of sources, most commonly action films, horror and anime, to demonstrate the characters' inability to make sense of their own lives other than through the media they consume which offer a rare element of stability in their lives.

What's significant in all of these series are the ways in which non-sitcom aesthetics are incorporated into the sitcom format and how they signal the distinctions between comic and non-comic moments. For example, *The League of Gentlemen* uses horror aesthetics most often at those points where its primary intention is not to be funny, whereas the more obviously comedic scenes, such as those in the local shop, are shot in a very traditional sitcom manner. It is also significant that the programme's third series, which incorporated interlocking plots and a less obviously sitcom visual style, was seen as far less successful than the earlier ones which more clearly signalled their sitcom conventions. Similarly, while *Spaced* uses many very quick pans to signal the end of scenes, within scenes the programme clearly looks like a sitcom. And those moments which

The League of Gentlemen signals in its shooting style the distinctions between its moments of comedy and horror

draw on cinema aesthetics, such as Daisy's *Matrix*-style fight with customs officers 'exaggerates' (Harries, 2000, p. 83) that film's visual style so that it parodies its source rather than copying it.

The notion of excess is vital to comedy, and is a central principle of sitcom. As will be shown in Chapter 3 this is certainly the case with performance, but it can also be seen in the way in which sitcom is shot, and what it does when it draws on the conventions of other forms. By rendering the conventions of both horror and action cinema as merely aesthetics that can be drawn on and played with, the 'seriousness' associated with them is undermined. That is, while many of the themes of *The League of Gentlemen* are clearly horrific – murder, cannibalism, wife abduction – because they are placed within the conventions of sitcom their dreadfulness is undercut and, most importantly, rendered merely laughable. Similarly, anything *M*A*S*H* has to say about war is rendered more palatable because of the comic tone which permeates it. So, while sitcom often does attempt to make serious statements about the world, politics and society, it repeatedly downplays the significance of its statements because they are presented through the mode of humour.

This is because sitcom has an aesthetic which is quite different to the codes and conventions of 'realist' television which dominate Western broadcasting. Corner notes that the aesthetic criteria by which entertainment television is judged are different to those for other, more serious forms of television and this is due to their implied relationship to 'the real' (1995, p. 175). So, the characteristics which make *M*A*S*H* different from other sitcoms (Mintz, 1985) are those which attempt to push it nearer to the conventions of realism on television. Thus the laugh track is removed, the audience is not positioned as the fourth wall and film is used instead of video. And by attempting to create links between sitcom content and serious forms, such series belie the assumption that the sitcom form is in itself severely limited, and that comedy should be used for some purpose other than mere funniness. How successful this is, though, is extremely debatable.

The difference between sitcom and non-comic television forms can also be seen in the ways in which they use narrative. Cook finds that sitcom narrative is read in a much more structural way than is the case for the rest of television (1982, p. 16). That is, every single bit of sitcom narrative is assessed by the audience in terms of its funniness; a sitcom is only as good as its last joke. In this sense, the narrative becomes less a story and more a sequence of comic events, with the audience offered a series of small, short-lived pleasures rather than the narrative ones which would be offered by a drama programme. Neale and Krutnik state that comedy 'not only permits but encourages the abandonment of causal motivation and narrative integration for the sake of comic effect, providing a generically appropriate space for the exploration of and use of non-causal forms of motivation and digressive narrative structures' (1990, p. 31). Similarly, Mellencamp argues that rather than story being vital to the genre, sitcom instead 'uses narrative, offhandedly' (1992, p. 334). Sitcom's relationship to narrative is purely functional, as if story is there only because that's a convention of communication in Western cultures. Mellencamp suggests that the primary pleasures of sitcom are ones based around moments and narrative is little more than a useful organisational tool to string such moments together. King, in calling film comedy 'a cinema of attractions' (2002, p. 25) makes the same argument for movies, and relates the whole back to music hall pleasures of performances and moments. This argument suggests that comedy is in and of itself antithetical to the conventional pleasures of narrative, such as a good story well told, and the anxieties of suspense and development.

Yet, this insistence on seeing comic narrative as little more than a structuring principle for comic moments ignores the many pleasures offered by stories within comedy. In those more farcical extremes of sitcom, in series such as *Fawlty Towers*, one of the main pleasures is indeed the development of the narrative towards a coherent and logical (comic) conclusion. The acclaim for *Fawlty Towers* rests partly on the ways in which it manages to logically interweave a number of plotlines per episode, which collide as a pleasurable comedic conclusion. Once an audience has an understanding of *Seinfeld*, pleasure can be taken in the ways in which each episode manages to find some connection between seemingly unconnected events. And while it's clear that such narrative pleasure functions in a manner different to that for other genres, to dismiss sitcom as a form in which narrative is of little importance misses not only one of its pleasures, but also one of its most obvious defining characteristics.

One Foot in the Grave has many episodes whose point is that nothing at all happens

Yet while sitcoms do often offer pleasure in a complex narrative, it is true that parts of their narratives (and these are likely to be the comic parts) will be non-causal. Particular jokes often rely less on narrative and more on the ways in which characters respond to it. This lack of narrative is seen most obviously in series such as *Hancock's Half-Hour* (BBC 1: 1956–60) and *One Foot in the Grave*, which contain many episodes whose point is that virtually nothing happens. The *One Foot in the Grave* episodes 'Timeless Time', 'The Trial' and 'The Beast in the Cage' occur in (almost) real time, with their protagonists in a bedroom unable to sleep, a house waiting for a phone call and a traffic jam, respectively. None of the episodes offer any narrative development or resolution, but instead consist of a series of comic moments whose meaning and funniness rely on character reaction and the quality of each individual joke. This is true for virtually all sitcom, yet assumptions about narrative which dominate broadcasting require the genre to at least pretend that story matters. Yet jokes' reliance on suddenness (Hobbes, 1914; Kant, 1952; Schopenhauer, 1958; Palmer, 1987) inherently disrupts narrative. This can be seen most obviously in *Friends*, where the most conventionally narrative segments – the relationships of Ross and Rachel, Rachel and Joey, and Monica and Chandler, and the pregnancies of Phoebe and Rachel – are predominantly serious matters. Indeed, the serious, emotional aspects of Joey's character only became apparent very late in the series once he became narrativised by the non-comic plotline of his love for Rachel. Sitcom, then, must forever unite narrative conventions and comedic requirements, displaying the complexity of the former while actually relying on the latter for its effectivity.

What this suggests is that for the sitcom, the audience is offered a 'dual reading focus' (Cook, 1982, p. 18). That is, viewers are offered pleasures common to most narrative television (a story well told; likeable, recurring characters; enigmas and solutions), but, undercutting these, are the pleasures common to comedy itself, which do not coincide with those of narrative drama. Goddard argues that for comedy to work it has to disrupt expectations and norms; but to do so, particularly in a narrative form such as the sitcom, it has to also present those norms, so that there is something to disrupt (1991, p. 80). So an audience's reading of a sitcom depends on their ability to believe in the norms presented by the programme, but also to believe that which deliberately disrupts such norms. And, because that which often disrupts – such as absurd narrative, deliberately comic performance, and so on – is usually constructed in a manner which also contradicts the realism which such a programme has built up, the audience is simultaneously presented with the realism of the programme and also distanced from it. So the naturalism presented by sitcom is based on an audience 'suspending disbelief in return for pleasure' (ibid.). There is, then, a tension within sitcom, and it is one that has to be understood by the audience to be able to make any sense of the genre.

This is what problematises analysis of the sitcom, particularly in terms of representations, because there is often a conflict between the ways in which people, groups, events or organisations are represented by the narrative as a whole, and how they are represented within individual comic events. In *The Simpsons*, for example, there is often a disparity between the way in which Marge and Homer's relationship is portrayed within specific comic moments and the narrative as a whole. Jokes in *The Simpsons* often centre on Homer's selfish uncaringness for Marge, in which he treats her as a drudge and fails to understand the work she carries out as a housewife. Yet a number of episodes have dealt with the difficulties within their relationship, all of which conclude with a re-establishment of their love for one another and the stability of the family as a whole. It is noticeable that most of the instances of Homer's display of his love for his wife are presented not as comic moments but instead as serious conclusions to narrative, with incidental music that clearly cues scenes to be read as non-comic. In this way, definitively deciding whether Homer is a sexist pig whose downtrodden wife should leave him, or merely a thoughtless fool who is capable of demonstrating his love when required, rests to a large extent on whether jokes or narrative are taken as evidence. The difficult thing about *The Simpsons*, as shown by Cherniavsky's (1999) multifaceted approach to the series, is that, while the sitcom is conventionally seen merely as a comic form, specific series often refuse to prioritise one reading over another. The pleasures of the series are both comic *and* emotional, and each of these pleasures often requires its opposite for its effectiveness. This suggests that while Cook argues that audiences require a 'dual reading focus' to make sense of the sitcom, the precise ways in which this functions for individual viewers and individual episodes is difficult to gauge.

As has been shown, defining the sitcom is difficult. Not only is it hard to define the genre textually, it is also difficult to state the ways in which audiences make sense of and get pleasure out of it. Sitcom has traditionally been defined by its narrative structure, with an acknowledgment that this must be filtered through the comic mode essential to humour. This reliance on narrative has supported analysis that examines such things as sitcom's radical potential and representative strategies. What's rarely explored in generic analysis of sitcom, however, are the ways in which this stuff is rendered funny, how humour actually works, and what consequences this has for sitcom's effects and relationship with its audience. What's even more significant is the repeated use of sitcom to demonstrate the effects and limitations of genre, which surely suggests assumptions about the form as a whole. There's clearly a view that sitcom is more limited by its generic status than many other forms, and evidence of sitcom experimentalism is often leapt on in order to demonstrate the radical possibilities which many assume are the point of comedy. Yet sitcom can instead be used as a way into thinking about genre, and the difficulties in coherently defining it are representative of the problems within genre analysis overall.

The Origins of Sitcom

The story of the sitcom mirrors that of broadcasting as a whole, and television in particular. Yet this history is problematised because the sitcom hasn't evolved through definitive leaps and bounds, or through the desire of any creative team to create new forms, but through the conjunction of comedy forms that existed before broadcasting, and the natures of radio and television. So, when Taylor (1994) attempts to construct a history of the sitcom, he inevitably runs into problems in deciding where the comedy show ends and the sitcom starts.

Sitcom has its origins in the desire of the broadcasting institutions to exploit the already famous comedians who performed in music hall and vaudeville prior to the invention of television and radio. Such comedians' acts were commonly a string of gags, and there was little or no narrative structure in their patter in the manner which we now associate with sitcom (Fisher, 1976). When transferred to broadcasting, the serial nature of the medium encouraged the performers and writers to construct jokes around narratives, thus conforming to the 'institutional imperatives of commercial broadcast radio' (Neale and Krutnik, 1990, p. 214). And while comedians in music hall had to spend many years touring the country to build up a following, the industry realised that such audience awareness could be achieved in a matter of weeks in broadcasting. Furthermore, by creating extra characters to bounce off the main star, and by developing situations and gags which ran over many weeks, audiences were rewarded for their continued commitment to a particular programme. Broadcast comedy, then, seized the advantages offered by the nature of the medium which were unavailable in theatre. The sitcom form is found only in broadcasting precisely because that is the only place in which it can work, and it is the logical result of the synthesis of the broadcasting medium and comedic content.

It is significant to note that the sitcom has not fully escaped its music hall origins, and virtually all forms of television comedy remain 'video approximations of theater' (Marc, 1996, p. 11). This can be seen not only in the performance style and the method of shooting which, as in theatre, usually relies on the audience being positioned as the fourth wall. Whereas other televisual forms have evolved so as to distance themselves from their theatrical origins – indeed, one of the codes by which much modern drama is signalled as 'realist' is its abandonment of the fourth wall (Jacobs 2000) – and have embraced the shooting possibilities the medium has to offer, the sitcom resolutely resists this. And this theatrical construction is still apparent when sitcoms are recorded; sitting in the audience for a sitcom recording is like being at the theatre.

Medhurst and Tuck (1982) argue that this continuing recreation of the music hall experience (but in the home) is an attempt to recreate the kind of relationship between audience and text which music hall relied upon. To this end the industry uses the laugh track, which is the convention which has traditionally most simply and effectively defined the genre. Medhurst and Tuck see this as 'the electronic substitute for collective experience' (p. 45), used by the industry to convince the viewer that they are part of a much larger audience. It is significant that sitcom does this, that it actively attempts to construct a mass audience and to make that mass audience know that others exist; other forms and genres in broadcasting do not so actively foreground their audience. Clearly this says something about the communal nature of humour, in which we are more likely to laugh if others are doing so. So, while the sitcom is resolutely a broadcasting form, it has not fully escaped its music hall origins, and still attempts to recreate that kind of experience.

The movement from theatrical comedy to television comedy was facilitated by the success of comedy on radio, particularly during the 1930s and 1940s, 'the classic years of American radio' (Neale and Krutnik, 1990, p. 211). The most important series in developing sitcom's most obvious characteristics is *The Jack Benny Program* (CBS, NBC: 1950–65), which increasingly incorporated recurring characters, linear plots, and, most importantly, a unified sense of character for Benny himself, meaning he wasn't just a performer spouting gags, but instead a character whose actions were predictable for an audience. This character was then placed within comedic situations recognisable to the audience, taking advantage of the domestic nature of media consumption. The conflicts which continue to define sitcom when compared to other genres – particularly the difficult relationship between the overtly comedic performance of many of its stars and the near-naturalist situations which render such performances extreme – are, then, not only found in *The Jack Benny Program*, but are a result of the evolutionary process which produced it.

Yet defining the point at which sitcom emerged as a discrete and recognisable form is problematic because of this evolution and the range of possible definitions of the genre. So, while Taylor suggests that the earliest British radio sitcom was *That Child* (BBC: 1926) (1994, p. 250), Neale and Krutnik (1990) see *Mr Muddlecombe JP* (BBC: 1937), over a decade later, as the genre's first example. Morreale argues that *Mary Kay and Johnny* (Dumont, NBC: 1947–50) was the first television sitcom (2003a, p. 1). Taylor's analysis (1994) of the significance of the radio series *Band Waggon* (BBC Home Service: 1938–47), starring Arthur Askey and Richard Murdoch (1994, p. 250 and pp. 28–9), shows how developments in British broadcast comedy were often an 'attempt to emulate American-style comedy formats' (Neale and Krutnik, 1990, p. 221). *Band Waggon* evolved over time from a string of gags to a 'situation'; two comedians living in a flat at the top of the BBC's Broadcasting House, replete with recurring characters and catchphrases. Other radio comedies following a similar evolution were *It's That Man Again* (BBC Light Programme: 1939–48) and *Take It from Here* (BBC Home Service: 1948–60). Radio comedy was a phenomenally successful form in Britain both during and after World War II, with *It's That Man Again* garnering audiences of sixteen million in 1942 (Taylor, 1994, p. 123). *Take It from Here* was significant in its creation of The Glums, 'considered by many to be a watershed in comedy' (p. 246). Throughout these programmes there existed a tension between the non-narrative music hall tradition and the requirements of the serial form of broadcasting. It is as a compromise between these two concerns that the sitcom can be placed and which are vital to an understanding of it.

The 'Three-Headed Monster'

While the transfer of *The Jack Benny Program* to television was successful, the visual aspect of the medium created new problems for sitcom. It is *I Love Lucy* (CBS: 1951–7) which most effectively dealt with these difficulties. It was Lucille Ball, along with Desi Arnaz and cinematographer Karl Freund who constructed the 'three-headed monster' (Mellencamp, 1992, p. 322), the 'three-camera set-up with studio audience format that freed television situation comedy from its stiff stage restraints' (Putterman, 1995, p. 15). The three-camera set-up meant that in any filmed exchange between two characters, one camera would shoot both characters together, while the other two covered close-ups of each of the characters. This format was implemented 'to capture the spontaneity of Lucille Ball's comic performances, particularly her rapport with audiences' (Anderson, 1994, p. 68). This kind of camera set-up is still very much in evidence in sitcom today and enables performers to get two laughs out of a joke; one from the funny thing that is said and another from someone else's reactions to it. The reaction shot is far more central to the sitcom than many other genres, and shooting comedy in this way highlights the cause-and-effect nature of the comic sequence. Indeed, much of the quickfire dialogue in *Will and Grace*, for example, is shot using this format, with the detached framing and rapid editing serving as visual cues to the comedy's rhythm. In this way, an exchange can be understood by an audience to be comic, even if they don't find particular jokes within it funny, purely because of the way it's shot.

However, Putterman overstates the case. As has been noted, the sitcom still clearly acknowledges its music hall origins, more than forty years after *I Love Lucy*'s supposedly revolutionary move. Instead, what was created then, and is still apparent now, is a form which is a hybrid, recreating the collective experience of the theatre with that available from the social nature of television. It is significant that these genre characteristics are those which most effectively aid sitcom's social functions, combining the social nature of comedy's pleasures with the narrative strands and domestic setting common to much broadcasting consumed within the home. It also means that the ways in which sitcom is shot remain one of its most important genre characteristics.

The Britcom

Up to the 1950s, the sitcom on British television was dominated by American series, with home-grown efforts never able to compete successfully with imports. Furthermore, British sitcoms were very similar in shooting style, form and content to those from America. This situation altered significantly in Britain with *Hancock's Half-Hour* (BBC Light Programme: 1954–9; BBC 1: 1956–60). It is at this point that the differences between American and British sitcom were forged. Even though the rationale behind the creation of a programme for Hancock mirrored that for virtually every sitcom on television, per-

Hancock's Half-Hour was responsible for making the sitcom the dominant form of comedy on British television

haps suggesting a straightforward continuance of the sitcom lineage, the entire tone and style of the programme was unlike anything seen in the genre before, in Britain or America.

For example, Goddard finds that, among other things, *Hancock's Half-Hour* was responsible for making the sitcom the dominant form of comedy on British television. Furthermore, it distanced itself significantly from the methods of comic performance which were associated with music hall, foregrounding situation and characterisation over the gag (1991, p. 86). Much of this, Goddard argues, was a comic extension of the social realist movement pervading much popular culture at that time, with Osborne's play *Look Back in Anger* (1956), films such as *A Taste of Honey* (Tony Richardson, 1961), and *Saturday Night and Sunday Morning* (Karel Reisz, 1960). Such 'kitchen sink' drama also influenced other television programmes, such as early episodes of *Coronation Street* (ITV 1: 1960–), and remains one of the most influential movements in recent British cultural history. Goddard argues that *Hancock's Half-Hour*, in following this tradition, attempted to portray 'life' as it would have been understood by its audience, offering a critique of many social concerns (p. 87). This was obviously a far cry from the knockabout, gag-obsessed American sitcoms, and 'enabled home-produced shows to compete for the first time on an almost equal footing with American imports' (ibid.).

However, in terms of its influence, it is probably the character of Tony Hancock himself which is of most importance. Self-obsessed, pretentious, stubborn, a loser, the character of Hancock was unlike the witty, intelligent heroes of American sitcom (Casey *et. al.*, 2002, p. 30). This difference can still be seen; it's no surprise that the most popular comedies of recent years have, in Britain, been *One Foot in the Grave*, *Only Fools and Horses* and *The Royle Family*, whereas America offers up *Friends* and *Seinfeld*. The differences between British and American sitcom are, then, ones which are based around character, and they may be representative of broader social and cultural norms within those countries. British sitcom repeatedly focuses on characters who are incapable of communicating and for whom relationships and family are problematic and stifling; it's no surprise that the 'classic' British sitcoms are painful series such as *Dad's Army*, *Steptoe and Son* (BBC 1: 1962–74), *Fawlty Towers*, *Only Fools and Horses* and, more recently, *The Office*. All these programmes deal with groups who the audience is intended to find funny because of their inability to understand one another. *Peep Show* (Channel 4: 2003–) may be the logical conclusion of this trend in British comedy, as the programme allows viewers to hear its characters' inner thoughts, finding comedy in the disparity between them and what the characters actually say.

While American sitcom also deals with characters for whom life's problems are the comedy's source, these are presented differently to British series in two main ways. First, American series demonstrate that while friends, family and colleagues may be a source of life's problems, they also constitute a significant support network; it's unlikely that

British series would have theme tunes promising that there's somewhere 'everybody knows your name' and friends will be 'there for you', as *Cheers'* and *Friends'* do. Second, American sitcom characters commonly have a degree of self-awareness about their own predicaments and are able to comically reflect on their own drawbacks. This is seen as a result of the Jewish heritage of the majority of American comedy (Epstein, 2002; Brook, 2003), which means that even WASP characters like Chandler in *Friends* are funny because of their weary joking about the human condition. British characters are rarely so self-aware. The comic force of characters such as David Brent, Alan Partridge, Tony Hancock, Del Boy, Basil Fawlty, Captain Mainwaring and Harold Steptoe lies in the gap between how they wish to be seen by others, and how they actually appear. It is their lack of self-awareness that's funny. This means that while American sitcom often invites us to laugh *with* its characters, Britcom instead offers pleasure in us laughing *at* them. This may say more about British and American assumptions about people and society than any amount of complex social and cultural analysis. Whatever, there are clear tendencies within Britcom which mark it as different from its American counterpart, and these can be traced back, within broadcasting, to *Hancock's Half-Hour*.

Sitcom and Social Change

It can be argued that little has changed in the sitcom over the last fifty years or so; this rigidity is fundamental to Grote's (1983) criticism of the genre. Indeed, the structure of the sitcom is pretty much the same as it was when it first evolved, and many of its influences go back much further than that. While this is a factor often used to deride and criticise the sitcom, such an argument fails to take into account two important points. First, the repetitiveness of sitcom is to be understood in term of its position within genre which, as Neale points out, deals with 'repetition and difference' (1992, p. 48). Second, it ignores the fact that while the form of sitcom has remained unchanged, the content has developed significantly, particularly as the sitcom has, as in the days of *Hancock's Half-Hour*, attempted to explore contemporary social concerns. Furthermore, sitcom is inevitably affected by wider comedic trends, as the relationship between stand-up comedy and the sitcom demonstrates. Thus, to examine the evolution of sitcom it is necessary to explore comedy as a whole, whether on television, in theatre or within society, and to see the sitcom as coming out of a broad set of social concerns, influences and debates.

Nathan finds the three major influences on contemporary British comedy (though he is writing in 1971) to be *Take It from Here*, *The Goon Show* (BBC Light Programme: 1952–60) and *Beyond the Fringe* (BBC2: 1960) (1971, pp. 14–17). While none of these is a sitcom, their choice of comic subject was responsible for developments within the

Father Ted is a recent example of the absurdist childishness that can be traced back to *The Goon Show*

sitcom. Thus *Take it from Here*, in its establishment of The Glums, was a major influence on *Hancock's Half-Hour* and in establishing the sitcom form; *The Goon Show*'s influence can be seen in the work of Vic Reeves and Bob Mortimer and, in the sitcom, in the absurdist childishness of *Father Ted* (Channel 4: 1995–8) and *The League of Gentlemen*; and *Beyond the Fringe*, which ushered in a wave of comedians from Oxbridge, resulted in political satire and biting humour which can be seen as a precursor to the whole of the Alternative Comedy movement which not only resulted in *The Young Ones* but also affected most broadcast comedy produced since. Just as early sitcom was a collaboration between comedy existing prior to television and the nature of the medium, so this process still occurs. Stand-up comedians still write and perform sitcoms as they always did and what is happening in comedy outside sitcom today is often what is happening in sitcom tomorrow.

Indeed, sitcom's development is a result of the constant attempt by writers and producers to create situations and comedy which, like *Hancock's Half-Hour*, tap into the ways in which their audiences live their lives. So Hough, when grouping American sitcoms, finds that there are distinct historical phases in which representations of the family are seen to develop, from traditional families, through nuclear families, followed by eccentric, bizarre families, to families which represented the complex ethnic makeup of contemporary society (1981, pp. 204–5). Since then, the American (and British) sitcom has repeatedly centred on surrogate families, symbolising the fragmentary nature of the family in contemporary society. Examples of this in America are *Cheers*, *Seinfeld* and, most obviously, *Friends*; in Britain the surrogate family can be seen in *The Thin Blue Line* (BBC 1: 1995–6), *Oh, Doctor Beeching!* (BBC 1: 1995–7), *Father Ted*, *Red Dwarf* (BBC 2: 1988–97), *Dead Man Weds*, *Men Behaving Badly* and *Spaced*. And programmes which portray actual biological families, such as *The King of Queens* (CBS: 1998–), *My Wife and Kids* (ABC: 2001–), *Family Guy* (Fox: 1999–), *Two and a Half Men* (CBS: 2003–), *Frasier* (NBC: 1993–2004), *Everybody Loves Raymond* (CBS: 1996–), *The Bernie Mac Show* (Fox: 2001–), *One Foot in the Grave*, *Two Pints of Lager and a Packet of Crisps* (BBC 2, BBC 3: 2001–) and *My Family* show the family to be a less reliable, more complex unit than was previously the norm, often demonstrating that the power relationships between parent and child are significantly blurred.

Not only have the situations in sitcom developed in an attempt to portray social changes, but so has the humour contained within it. And, when such changes do occur, it is common for such programmes to be vilified and complained about. Thus Johnny Speight's attempt to satirise bigoted views in *Till Death Us Do Part*, which necessarily incorporated humour of a ferocity and language that had not been used on television before, caused an outcry when first broadcast, even though Speight argued he was attempting to portray a 'realistic' view of inner-city attitudes that had come to prominence due to social changes (Taylor, 1994, p. 254; Malik 2002, p. 93). The same occurred with the American remake of the series, Norman Lear's *All in the Family* (Miller, 2000; Mills, 2004b).

Similarly, the development of humour which took on board the feminist movement and attempted to portray women's contradictory roles within society, has often caused consternation. Prominent in this movement in Britain is Carla Lane, whose many series have dealt with the various roles women can occupy in modern society and whose *Butterflies* (BBC 2: 1978–83) was criticised for its central premise of a woman on the verge of an extra-marital affair (Andrews, 1998, p. 45). To confound this, the programme also touched on subjects, such as sex and teenage pregnancy which, at that time, were also uncommon in mainstream sitcom. Lane has repeatedly explored the role of women in society, in 'housewives comedies' (p. 60) such as *The Liver Birds* (BBC 1: 1969–78, 1996), *Solo* (BBC 1: 1981–2), *The Mistress* (BBC 2: 1985–7), *Screaming* (BBC 1: 1992) and *Luv* (BBC 1: 1993–4). It's significant, though, that while Lane experiments with sitcom content, the form of her programmes remains predominantly traditional. Mellencamp (1992) finds a strain of feminist thought running though the history of American sitcom, in series such as *I Love Lucy* and *Roseanne*, in which the effects of women unwilling to conform to patriarchal versions of femininity are presented in a funny, and thus positive, manner. A more extreme version of this argument is proposed by Rabinovitz, who suggests that sitcom 'has been the television genre most consistently associated with feminist heroines and with advocating a progressive politics of liberal feminism' (1999, p. 145). Certainly a writer/producer such as Susan Harris can be explored in terms of the novel ways she strove to represent women and traditionally feminine genres, in series such as *Soap* and *The Golden Girls* (NBC: 1985–92). Of course, the precise ways in which such representations exist narratively and performatively affect the progressiveness of such portrayals, and audiences' responses to them. Yet it's clear that, while soaps have commonly been examined as feminist texts, the disruptive nature of comedy has allowed certain series and performers to present (some) female characters so far unseen in other genres. These issues of representation are discussed in more detail in Chapter 4.

There is, then, ample evidence that the sitcom is a genre which has repeatedly responded to changes within the societies which produce it. However, sitcom's domestic focus means that, on the whole, it has responded to the politics of the family and, with a few exceptions, rarely explicitly explores either macro social structures or the relationship between the individual and society as a whole. Again, this focus on the domestic and the individual has been one of the reasons for the criticism of sitcom's failure to comically interrogate and undermine dominant ideologies. Sitcom has been a reflection of social changes, rather than an intervention into them. This means that it 'has remarked upon almost every major development of postwar American history' (Hamamoto, 1991, p. 2), and the same might be true of British series.

Alternative Comedy

It is impossible to look at the current form and content of British sitcom without acknowledging the influence of the Alternative Comedy movement of the 1980s (Macdonald, 2002). Alternative Comedy, like many popular culture terms, is notoriously difficult to define, not least because most of the comedians associated with it often refuse to acknowledge its existence. While there may not be specific characteristics which define Alternative Comedy, there is no doubting that, as Putterman suggests, 'the constant factor in their [the comedians'] varied styles was a revolt against the unctuous and comforting qualities of the television sitcoms and variety shows they had grown up watching' (1995, p. 162). Furthermore, he finds that Alternative Comedy, by deliberately making itself unpleasant and distancing, is reminiscent of the 'regional comedy that dominated early century burlesque' (p. 169). To Putterman, Alternative Comedy was not just an attempt to construct a 'counterculture' (p. 178), it was also a way for individuals who felt disenfranchised by comedy to discover that there were other people out there who felt the same way. Thus Peter Rosengard, whose opening of the stand-up venue The Comedy Store in London in 1979 is seen as the starting point of Alternative Comedy, denies the usefulness of the term while remarking that he set the place up as a deliberate attempt to escape from 'the northern club comics and their mother-in-law jokes on TV' (Wilmut and Rosengard, 1989, p. 2). Certainly, the fact that the movement had its roots in stand-up and theatre is seen as significant, for 'At the popular end of the performing arts, humour is possibly the most widely influential medium through which people are introduced to "other" perspectives in everyday experience' (Tompsett, 1996, p. 261).

However, Alternative Comedy didn't just liberate. While it proved that there are other possibilities for comedy besides those traditionally explored, it also denounced the use of 'sexist' and 'racist' material which was hitherto a staple of comedy. So Double finds that Alternative Comedy was a 'return to the basic subversive roots of comedy' (1991, p. 203), as opposed to the 'stylistically and politically conservative' (p. 111) nature of music hall and working-men's clubs' comedy. There is, then, a tension within Alternative Comedy that is rare within comedy's history, in which performers deliberately used comedy to subvert social norms and make jokes about previously unacceptable subjects while simultaneously instituting taboos of their own, centred on race and gender. This resulted in the eventual removal from British television of Speight's Alf Garnett, and the vilification of old comedy favourites like Bernard Manning and It Ain't Half Hot, Mum (BBC 1: 1974–81). So, while it is important to be aware of the liberating force which was Alternative Comedy, it is also important to note that such freedoms imposed restrictions of their own.

Yet there's a problem in such non-sexist, non-racist ideology being presented on television by white men with a university education. Furthermore, the ideology of Alternative Comedy may be inconsistent, condemning some forms of representation as stereotypes while merely creating new ones. So, while Mike, Vyvyan, Rik and Neil in The Young Ones were novel forms of representation, their lack of complexity is on a level with those stereotypes which Alternative Comedy banished as offensive. The debate concerning Alternative Comedy's lasting influence, and whether it matched the criteria it purported to endorse, is a common one, as Housham notes:

> in the wake of Benny Hill and Frankie Howerd's adjacent deaths in 1992, the media's commissars of popular culture seem to have been in a constant dither about comedy. They've been struggling to place it in a new, meaningful context, worrying whether alternative comedy should now be disparagingly viewed as too po-faced and puritanical, and whether the sexism, homophobia and racism evinced in British comedy in the old days should now be weighed as inconsequential traits against the more admirable and considerable grasp of stagecraft, timing and delivery displayed by Hill, Howerd, Tommy Cooper and others of their generation. (1994, p. 10)

Such an argument symbolises the difficulties inherent in analysing broadcast comedy, in which there is often a clash between performance and what is being performed. The desire to admire traditional comedy because of its performers' skills is representative of the wish to see comedy as politically neutral and incapable of negative social effects. In this way, there is a longing to return comedy to the social position in which its content remained uninterrogated, and there was an assumption that what was joked about was normal, neutral, agreed to by all and representative of a general social consensus. If Alternative Comedy did anything, then, it was to highlight the ideological content in comedy which, in Britain, rested on forcing audiences to accept a white, male standpoint for the jokes to be in any way pleasurable. In doing so, it showed that comedy doesn't just exist within a society without developing from dominant ideological positions, and nor is its use of such positions irrelevant to their continuation.

This may explain the difficult and contradictory position British sitcom seems to occupy. So, while Alternative Comedy has experienced a backlash as witnessed in the blossoming popularity of such 'New Lad' comedy (Barber 1996, p. 15) as *Men Behaving Badly*, it is clear to see that those themes Alternative Comedy deemed out of bounds – racism and sexism – are, on the whole, still so, at least in their most obvious forms. Cook charts the movement of Alternative Comedy from its position as counterculture to the mainstream force, even though post-Alternative Comedians are keen to distance themselves from it (1994, p. 11). The difficulty is that, in its truer form in the 1980s, Alternative Comedy *was* an alternative, if only because it reached such small audiences. While Channel 4 was the 'TV station that invented the eighties' (p. 1), it still did so to a minority audience of a certain age and socio-economic grouping (McQueen, 2001, pp. 55–6). Indeed the legacies of the Alternative Comedy movement may be less ones of comic content and more to do with the relationship between broadcasters and their audiences. That is, if we look at the current trends in sitcom, in both Britain and America, we can see that Alternative Comedy's resistance to mainstream humour may have had consequences which weren't intended.

Contemporary Sitcom

In America, the sitcom continues its five-decade-long dominance, though there have been concerns raised as to how long this will last. Long-running series, such as *Friends* and *Frasier*, as well as genre-defining series such as *Sex and the City*, have not been replaced by newer series with either the same ratings or cultural clout. Morreale argues that the terrorist attacks of 2001 have meant that people have turned away from comedy (2003b, pp. 249–50). The rise of reality television has meant that the number of sitcoms in the Nielsen ratings has reduced and broadcasters are keen to develop more reality formats as they are significantly cheaper than scripted comedy. Newer sitcoms, such as the *Friends* spin-off *Joey* (NBC: 2004–), haven't been the hits that were hoped and it is instead drama spin-offs, such as the various *CSI* (CBS: 2000–) franchises, which have been more successful. Of course, sitcom has been in this situation before and the death of the genre is announced every few years.

Similarly, debates continue concerning the genre's reactionary or progressive nature. The considerable amount of analysis that has gone into *Will and Grace* (Battles and Hilton-Morrow, 2002; Dow, 2001; Feuer, 2001; McCarthy, 2001, 2003) shows that a leading gay male character in a popular, mainstream sitcom is still a matter of historical interest, even if there's little agreement on exactly how Will should be read. Furthermore, *Will and Grace* has so far failed to have the kind of impact on British audiences that, say, *Friends* did, even though it's scheduled in the same slot on the same channel. The lack of interest in *Will and Grace* is possibly a result of Britain having a longer tradition of gay/camp characters, against which the performative histrionics of the character of Jack look decidedly old hat (McCarthy, 2003, p. 101). However, it could also be due to British sitcom (and some American ones) recently moving away from the theatrical visual style associated with sitcom and towards a more documentary-style one in which acting is relatively downplayed; this will be explored in the section on *The Office* at the end of this chapter.

Because sitcom is the dominant genre on American television, spotting trends within its content is not only a recurring occupation of academics and journalists but also a vital part of the industry's creative process. While previous decades have seen feminist sitcoms and fantasy sitcoms (Marc, 1989; Jones, 1992), both Brook (2003) and Zurawik (2003) see the 1990s as the decade of the Jewish sitcom, a trend seen in, among others, *The Nanny* (CBS: 1993–9), *Mad about You* (NBC: 1992–9), *Friends* and *Dharma and Greg* (ABC: 1997–2002), all in response to the success of *Seinfeld*. Of course, lumping together such disparate series is always problematic, but it does demonstrate the ways in which the form's concerns and representations develop; whether this says something about the society which produces and consumes such fare is another matter, however.

What's noticeable is that the popularity of British sitcom appears to be in decline too;

or, at least, there hasn't been a massive, mainstream hit on B
of *Only Fools and Horses*. *My Family* and *The Vicar of Di*
attracting decent ratings, certainly aren't age-defining in the
understood. Both Channel 4 and BBC 3 have experimented
series such as *Green Wing*, *Peep Show*, *Nathan Barley*, *Outl*
(BBC 3: 2005–), but none of these have managed to become massive
the majority of the series examined by critics and academics are not those made by the
main networks in either country, or which reach massive audiences. Thus lauded British
series such as *The Office*, *Marion and Geoff* (BBC 2: 2001–) and *The League of Gentlemen* – which Thompson (2004) argues contribute towards the 1990s being a 'golden
age' in British comedy – were not on either of the main channels, just as America's HBO
produced *Curb Your Enthusiasm*, *The Larry Sanders Show* and *Sex and the City*. The
same has occurred in Australia, with SBS producing comedy series like *Pizza* (2000–). By
presenting itself as a genre which can offer the pleasure of experimentation, sitcom has
begun to abandon some of its theatrical origins; at least, it has begun to stop displaying them so obviously. And in doing so, it has become a form actively used by 'minority'
channels to target specific audiences, resulting in the proliferation of multiple kinds of
comedy, many of which are only intended to reach minority audiences. Certainly the
growth of 'adult animation' (Donnelly, 2001) or 'anicom' (Dobson, 2003, p. 85) as a
subgenre of sitcom can be attributed predominantly to the desire of new and niche networks to produce series for specific, minority audiences, with *Beavis and Butt-head* on
MTV, *Ren and Stimpy* (1991–4) on Nickelodeon, *South Park* on Comedy Central, *Mon-
key Dust* (2003–) on BBC 3 and, most notably, both Fox in America and Sky in the UK
initially defining themselves virtually entirely around *The Simpsons*. Of these, only *The
Simpsons* has achieved a truly mass audience, and only then in America; instead these
series serve to define and identify the rationale and characteristics of broadcasters, which
is a vital function to aid audiences confused by the proliferation of channels. Adult animation also represents the logical synthesis of 'two similarly degraded genres – the
situation comedy or sitcom and the cartoon' (Stabile and Harrison, 2003, p. 2). This plu-
ralism of sitcom shows that the industry is becoming more attuned to what specific
audiences want, but at the expense of mainstream sitcom, meaning that contemporary
series fail, on the whole, to unite audiences in the way that postwar radio comedies did.
While this implies changes not only within sitcom but also within the social role of
humour, it also suggests that, in a broadcasting industry in which the number of channels continues to increase, the sitcom's once universal appeal may continue to splinter
into ever more individualised examples.

The Laugh Track

One of the ways that sitcom highlights its concern with the momentary pleasures of
jokes and signals its content as intentionally humorous, is through the use of a laugh

noted above, Medhurst and Tuck see this as 'the electronic substitute for col-
experience' (1982, p. 45), an attempt to recreate the social experience vital to
hour and most obviously a leftover from the theatre. The laugh track is so central to
the sitcom that, when channel-hopping, it is the most obvious signal to the kind of programme you've just found. Yet noise created by a live audience at the recording exists
in other genres too; most obviously in quiz shows and variety shows, but also at sport-
ing and other public events, such as election announcements and state and government
proceedings. There's a distinction to be made, though, between those programmes
where the audience would exist if television cameras weren't there – such as sport and
public events – and those where the audience exists only because a programme is being
made, such as the sitcom. In public events the audience functions as a signal of 'reality',
suggesting that television is merely recording things that would have occurred anyway.
In the sitcom, however, the laugh track signals precisely the opposite; it underlines the
artificial, theatrical nature of the genre, and the fact that sitcom requires an audience
for its existence to be at all meaningful.

The sitcom is an obvious demonstration that television is a medium sold on its 'liveness' (Bourdon, 2000), and is able to respond to real world events quicker than film and
newspapers. Yet much television fiction doesn't attempt to recreate the live experience,
instead taking advantage of the possibilities of recording to create complex narratives
and visual trickery. So how come sitcom does? It's because comedy needs to signal its
relationship with the audience to be fully effective, and therefore must appear as a live
experience. It is this relationship to liveness which most clearly distinguishes sitcom, and
which it relies on to signal its comic intent.

Yet the idea of 'liveness' is complex, and can be understood only in terms of its
relationship to mediation. As Auslander points out, 'Prior to the advent of those tech-
nologies (e.g., sound recording and motion pictures), there was no such thing as "live"
performance, for that category has meaning only in relation to an opposing possibility'
(1999, p. 51). The liveness of sitcom, then, is one which requires the conventions of
recorded media for its effectivity, and marks itself as different from most television by
foregrounding its liveness. Auslander notes that, in a media-saturated world, live performance is not the dominant mode it once was, and instead has connotations of
authenticity, for it suggests that the events recorded existed before the media decided
to record them. Yet the power of the live act is that it can only ever be experienced once,
and the pleasures associated with it are about 'being there'. The sitcom is an odd hybrid
of the live and the recorded, and it may be this inherent contradiction that means the
sitcom has never achieved the cultural status that Auslander says is usually associated
with live events. Indeed, it is only through abandoning its theatrical origins and instead
using the television aesthetics of the live – the documentary form – that sitcom as a form
has achieved some kind of cultural status. It is no coincidence that *The Office*, which is

the most obvious example of this trend, was the first non-American programme ever to win the Golden Globe for best comedy series.

Importantly, the laugh track is also a signal for the ways in which sitcom is intended to be understood. By placing laughter at jokes, a comic moment is signalled as such even if an audience member watching the programme at home doesn't find it funny. In doing so, the sitcom signals a distinction between that which is and isn't funny, whether the non-comic moments just happen to be not funny for some purpose such as narrative development or, as is often in the case of *Friends*, is purposefully intended as serious and emotional drama. In this way, the sitcom attempts to close down alternative readings of its content, by suggesting that if you're not laughing at one of its jokes, then you're the only one.

Because of this, the recent abandonment of the laugh track by much sitcom (particularly in Britain) is meaningful. The combination of a visual style unlike the traditional theatrical aesthetic and the removal of the laugh track results in texts which must signal their comic intent in a different way, or lay themselves open to the possibility not only of audiences failing to spot all the jokes, but of failing to realise they're watching a sitcom at all. Certainly, the sophisticated use of the documentary look in series such as *The Office* and *Marion and Geoff* make it perfectly possible for audiences to think, for a short time at least, that they're watching an actual documentary. This development could be a result of a number of factors. First, it could be because the traditional sitcom look appears artificial and staged to younger audiences for whom the theatrical experience has little meaning. Second, it could be that the attacks by recent documentary hybrid forms upon traditional documentary's claims to truth have rendered its aesthetic nothing more than a bunch of visual formulae (Bruzzi, 2000; Winston, 2000). Third, it could result from the development of niche channels, for most of the series which have abandoned the laugh track have not been broadcast on the main channels in either Britain or America. Coupled with this, it could be programme-makers' desires for their series to be understood as something 'more' than sitcom, for the channels on which these series have been broadcast – HBO, Channel 4, BBC 2, MTV – are ones associated with innovative broadcasting. Whatever the reason, the abandonment of the laugh track represents the most significant development in the sitcom form since the introduction of the 'three-headed monster', and it remains to be seen what long-term consequences it will have for the genre.

Yet sitcom continues to ransack live material. American sitcom has commonly been based around stand-up comedians, whose television performance clearly draws on skills learned in live performance. And when actors appear in sitcoms instead of stand-ups, such as Jack and Karen in *Will and Grace*, they are ones who've often made their names in live performance such as theatre. While this is less obvious in British sitcom, there are many series based around stand-ups, and this was particularly the case during the

Alternative Comedy boom in the 1980s. Indeed, the success of series such as *The Young Ones* led to a revival in attendance at stand-up gigs. This complex relationship between the live and the mediated, coupled with recent developments in the sitcom, suggest there are significant changes occurring within the television industry, which the genre is both responding to and indicative of.

The Sitcom Industry

Analysis of sitcom has usually explored it textually, examining its representations and what these suggest about the society that produces them. Yet sitcom is also a product which results from complex and highly structured broadcasting industries. The money-making possibilities for the genre can be seen in the financial successes of global phenomena such as *Friends*, *The Simpsons* and *Seinfeld*. Because of this, sitcom production occupies a significant and powerful position within the broadcasting industries as a whole; analysis of it as an industrial product thus offers valuable insights into the relationship between media, entertainment and commerce.

The industrialised nature of sitcom production is shown by the structure of the industries which produce and broadcast them, in which specific writers, producers and directors generally work within the genre, rarely venturing outside it. The existence of light entertainment or comedy departments within the majority of broadcasters shows that it is felt that a certain group of people, whose talents are best applied towards

Porridge draws on Ronnie Barker's comic connotations from other popular sitcoms, such as *Open All Hours*

entertainment (as opposed to drama, documentaries, news and so on) should work together and, on the whole, not go outside these areas. This is applicable not only to writers and producers, but also to stars, who carry with them significant comic connotations. Actors such as Ronnie Barker can move from series to series – *Open All Hours* (BBC 1: 1973–85), *Porridge* (BBC 1: 1973–7), *Clarence* (BBC 2: 1988) – carrying with them not only the connotation of comedy, but also a certain kind of comedy. In Barker's case this is a much more mainstream, family connotation than an actor such as Rik Mayall – *The Young Ones*, *The New Statesman* (ITV: 1987–94), *Bottom* (BBC 2: 1991–5), *Believe Nothing* (ITV: 2002) – carries. So, while performance is vital to sitcom, who performs affects the ways in which programmes are understood and the expectations audiences bring to them.

This is significant because, as noted, sitcom is one of the ways in which channels attempt to define themselves. In America, the fledgling Fox network used *The Simpsons* in much of its promotional material and continues to do so. This is not only because, as animated yellow characters, they are highly distinctive. It's also because the humour contained within the programme is that which is attractive to younger, media-literate audiences, as opposed to the demographics which other networks were reaching. Similarly, MTV's move away from non-stop music videos towards a broader range of programming styles was kick-started by the success of *Beavis and Butt-head*, a series about MTV's viewers. The casual violence and celebration of a lack of education in the series was attractive only to certain audience groups, and in broadcasting such a programme, MTV attempted to connect to them. And in recent years, Comedy Central's continual use of *South Park* to promote itself could sometimes make it appear as if it doesn't broadcast anything else.

In Britain, regulations imposed upon channels mean that sitcom is not just a way of defining a channel, but also a requirement for experimental broadcasting. Channel 4's remit requires it to be innovative and to cater to minorities, which resulted in the only successful, long-running 'black' sitcom in British television history: *Desmond's* (1989–94). It has also resulted in sitcom/drama hybrids such as *The Book Group* (2002–), whose complex narratives and graphic depiction of sex would be unlikely on more mainstream channels. And, like the Comedy Network, Channel 4 has used the *South Park* characters in its own promotional idents, merging the characters with the channel's usual visual logos. Similarly, BBC 2's requirement to be innovative (as part of the BBC's overall remit) is what has led to the development of 'comedy vérité' (Mills, 2004a), with series such as *The Office*, *Marion and Geoff* and *People Like Us*. One of the ways in which the BBC promoted its new digital channels was through sitcom, making clear the kinds of audiences the networks were aiming for through the kinds of comedy they broadcast. Thus BBC 3's *Two Pints of Lager and a Packet of Crisps* (transferred, oddly, from BBC 2) is about the problems associated with a working-class, youth lifestyle, in keeping with the channel's target audience. BBC 4's purchase of the American series *Curb Your Enthu-*

siasm (the only new comedy programme on the network) draws on the high culture, improvisatory style of the series, as well as the programme's relationship to *Seinfeld*, as signifiers of quality.

This use of sitcom is unsurprising considering 'Comedy is, after drama, the second most popular genre in British television' (Tunstall, 1993, p. 125) and the most popular genre in America. By successfully producing popular sitcom, a series can run for many years and make considerable profits around the world, either sold directly or as a format to be remade for domestic audiences (Moran, 1998). In the last decade, with the advent of adult animation, spin-off merchandise has also become an important part of the financial possibilities of sitcom, as has the release of box sets of sitcoms on video and special editions on DVD, often with extra scenes and production commentaries. Sitcom, when successful, not only helps to define channels and audiences, but can also be a highly profitable business. Yet the risks in the production of them are high, for 'Comedy is also the second most expensive programming to produce' (ibid.), with its requirement for actors, writers and sets. The standard production process in America of producing pilot episodes, which can be tested with audiences and used as a tool to explore the long-term possibilities of series, is becoming more apparent in Britain. The risks involved in sitcom production are then quite high, and it is this problem which, as Butsch remarks, is likely to contribute to a lack of risk-taking and repetitiveness in the form, particularly on the mainstream channels (1995, p. 406). Certainly, the continued use of the same writers, producers, actors and production companies, in both Britain and America, demonstrates the networks' reliance on trusted bankers. The 'family tree' of British sitcom production has been shown in the BBC 1 series *Comedy Connections* (2003–), which traces the lineage of the writers, producers, directors and actors associated with a particular programme, and shows how the same people have dominated mainstream British sitcom for decades. Because of this, it is possible to list producers (Dennis Main Wilson, Mike Stephens, David Croft) and writers (Galton and Simpson, Clement and Le Frenais, Perry and Croft) who've produced sitcoms for decades, and in many cases show no signs of stopping. A similar list can be made for producer/writers in America (James L. Brooks, Norman Lear, Susan Harris), many of whose series have produced spin-offs continuing their comedic lineage. While it's apparent that many television genres repeatedly employ some producers (Steven Bochco, for example), for most genres it is nowhere near as enclosed as in the sitcom world. While this may be indicative of the unwillingness of broadcasters to take risk with unknowns, it may also point to the limited number of people actually capable of making sitcom work for a mass audience.

British and American Sitcom Production

This power of writers and producers highlights one of the many ways in which sitcom differs in Britain and America. So, while in both countries a great deal of creative power rests in the hands of writer and producers, there is a distinction in the precise ways in which this is structured. In Britain, the writer usually creates a programme, seeks a producer, retains much of the control over the programme's development and the series usually ends once the writer no longer wishes to write it. In America, producers usually create and control programmes and employ writers to write them, retaining the artistic control which, in Britain, is much more firmly in the hands of the writer. The growth of the independent television production sector in Britain has begun to blur this distinction, as writers have set up companies such as Hat Trick and TalkBack to produce their own programmes. The British industry's desire to produce longer-running series has led to the BBC recruiting the US producer Fred Barron to create *My Family*, which is written and produced using the American system and is currently Britain's most popular sitcom. Yet this is the exception which proves the rule and the distinctions between the two countries' production systems remain overwhelmingly intact.

These different working practices lead to noticeable differences in the content of resulting series. Because any American sitcom uses many writers, some or all of whom may leave the programme to be replaced by new ones, it is virtually impossible for any of them to place their individual stamp upon it. A writer for an American sitcom often functions solely as a gag writer, with perhaps only one joke in any individual script, the rest of which would have been constructed by the rest of the team. He/she is likely to have no control over the original set-up of the programme, the idea for any individual story, or the development of the characters. The American sitcom writer is a much smaller part of a much larger process, whose overall control is in the hands of the producers.

Because the writer in Britain is responsible for many more creative decisions, he or she is a more central part of that process. Of course, this means that any writer for British sitcom has to think up every situation and every joke for any episode of a series, placing a much larger creative burden upon them. It is probably this reason above any other that results in American sitcoms being deemed by critics funnier than British ones; after all, if there is a large group of writers, each of whom only has to think up a limited number of jokes and isn't required to spend creative energy on other parts of the process, then it's likely that the script which is produced will contain a larger number of 'better' jokes than one written solely by a single person. However, this is not to suggest that better jokes necessarily result in better sitcom, as the joke is only one element.

The use of multiple writers also removes the chance for a writer to express an individual voice: this is allowed to flourish, and is actively encouraged, in the British industry. So, whereas it's clear to see that the ideology, type of humour and overall voice of British sitcoms differ to a great degree – for example, *Keeping up Appearances* (BBC 1: 1990–5) is very different from *Father Ted* which is very different from *One Foot in the Grave* – such differences are arguably less apparent in American sitcoms. Without wishing to overstate the case, the role of the author in British sitcom does lend itself to the fostering of individuality in a manner perhaps more difficult to achieve within the American system.

Further, there are other factors which are responsible for the difficulty in individual voices making themselves heard in American sitcom. While in Britain sitcoms are performed by actors who are used because they fit in with the writer and producer's vision, in America sitcom is performed to a much greater degree by, and very often based around the routines of, stand-up comedians. Examples of this are *Roseanne*, *The Cosby Show* and *Home Improvement* (ABC: 1991–9). Indeed, it was the movement by *Hancock's Half-Hour* away from using comedians and comic actors which, as noted above, began the split between British and American sitcom (Goddard, 1991, p. 86). This use of stand-up comedians results in a different comic performance style in America and means that resulting programmes are inevitably geared towards humour to a more obvious extent than is the case for programmes performed by actors. After all, the performance is intended as a showcase for the comedian's talents and the American networks, after spending much money to secure the services of a famous stand-up, will want them foregrounded within the programme as much as possible. Such differences can be seen in Bill Cosby's most recent sitcom, the American remake of *One Foot in the Grave*, where his importance is signalled in the programme's new title, *Cosby* (CBS: 1996–2000).

The fact that stand-up comedians are used in American sitcom reduces possible individuality in other ways too. On the whole, the stand-ups used in American sitcom are those who are most successful and popular and for whom a large audience already exists; that is, they conform to the kind of comedy which already exists on American television. More innovative, obscure comedians are unlikely to build up a big enough following to attract the attentions of the television industry executives. In this way, the dominant comic ideology is forever reiterated, as stand-ups become successful if they reproduce this and, once they are given their own programmes, become a part of the reproduction of it. American comedy exists within an institutional loop which promotes the reiteration of that which is already known to a greater extent than its British counterpart.

Due to the highly efficient, industrialised nature of the American sitcom industry, programmes are usually constructed to be broadcast very soon after their recording. A week's episode of a sitcom is usually written, rewritten, rehearsed and recorded in the week that it is broadcast. This means that American sitcom is able to refer to topical events quite easily; during the O. J. Simpson trial, *Roseanne* made many jokes about events within it. This is very unlike British sitcom where it is common for there to be a considerable gap between recording and broadcast. For example, Christmas specials of sitcoms are commonly recorded months in advance, as part of the long-term planning often involved in schedules at such times. This means that a script has to be commissioned and written even earlier than that, resulting in there often being a gap of over a year between such an episode being initially conceived and eventually broadcast. When a British sitcom is made using the American process this uniqueness is often its selling point, as in *Drop the Dead Donkey* (Channel 4: 1990–6), promoting its topicality and ability to refer to that week's news.

This ability to refer to the world outside the programme means that it is possible for an American sitcom to reflect contemporary social feelings and attitudes. Because there is such a long gap between an episode of a British sitcom being written and being broadcast, the writer has to make sure that all references within it will still be relevant in that later time. In this sense, British sitcom exists in a 'timeless now' (Eaton, 1981, p. 34), with little or no explicit regard or reference to the world outside the series. American sitcom, however, is able to reflect social and topical concerns more immediately, and analysis of it in America has repeatedly focused on the genre as a social barometer (Marc, 1989; Hamamoto, 1991; Jones, 1992; Feuer, 1995), in a way much less common for the Britcom. Of course, this is a comparison of degree for, as Hamamoto notes, the sitcom inevitably articulates the social concerns of the society for which it is made (1991, p. 147). It is not that this does not occur in British sitcom, but that it is not the place which most actively acknowledges this function.

American sitcom positions itself even further within social concerns by being the dominant genre on American television. In Britain, the sitcom exists as part of a mixed schedule and it is rare to find two sitcoms following one another on the main terrestrial channels. Moreover, if there is a sitcom on one channel, it's unlikely that there'll also be one on another channel. However, in America, the sitcom dominates prime-time television. They are often scheduled as a sequence, for up to two hours, from 8pm to 10pm, on many nights. As this can happen on many networks simultaneously, an audience may not have a choice between different kinds of programmes, but between different sitcoms. And once any sitcom reaches a significant number of episodes (usually 65), it can be syndicated. That is, it is shown on one of the many local or cable channels stripped across the week and is also likely to appear on the main network in reruns too. The sitcom is ubiquitous on American television, far outstripping its prevalence on British television.

In this sense, it can be seen that form and content comparisons of British and American sitcoms very often miss the important point that the function of the genre in the two countries is markedly different. Complaints concerning the depiction of social concerns in British sitcom suggest that audiences do not associate such concerns with the genre, that the British audience looks to other forms, like the soap opera, for this. This is not to say that the sitcom can't say serious things, nor that audiences can't enjoy them for reasons other than comedy; however, it is to say that on British television there are other genres more clearly associated with reflecting social concerns and which audiences are more likely to turn to for those kinds of pleasures. However, in America, the major place where social concerns are played out in a popular form is in the sitcom, and this factor becomes a significant part of the audience's expectations for the genre in a manner quite different to that for British audiences. The question which arises out of this is, of course, why it should be that Britain commonly articulates social concerns in a serious cultural form, whereas America does the same through a comic one. While this may be seen as undermining the cliché of the importance of humour to the British, it could instead highlight the distinct difference between seriousness and humour. After all, the British are 'known' for their sense of humour as much as they are for their stiff upper lip (Richards, 1997, pp. 4–5).

Readings of an American sitcom by a British audience are, then, liable to be affected by the differences each culture associates with the genre, and these come about from the different social roles of humour. Strinati notes that British audiences read American programmes in certain ways precisely because they are American, altering their expectations accordingly (1992, p. 73). Furthermore, he finds that while American television is critically celebrated in Britain, such assessments are often out of step with what the majority of the audience is actually thinking (p. 75). This can be seen if the audience ratings are studied; while *Friends* is by far the most written about sitcom for years, its audiences, while large for Channel 4, show that it is really a minority programme, especially in comparison to many other series which are less likely to be categorised as 'popular'. The vast majority of American sitcoms shown in Britain are seen on BBC 2 and Channel 4 and, while these channels have smaller audiences than BBC 1 and ITV, they are associated with 'quality' which inevitably informs the ways in which audiences make sense of them. This may be why most British critics argue that 'compared to the best of the US offerings ... the domestic UK programmes generally pale into insignificance' (Mullan, 1997, pp. 47–8).

Transatlantic Sitcom Remakes

The similarities and differences between British and American sitcom can be shown by those programmes which have been exported across the Atlantic. This process works differently each way: while Britain broadcasts American series, American television usually buys the format of British programmes and remakes them with an American production team and cast. Recent examples of this are *Men Behaving Badly* (NBC: 1996–7), *One Foot in the Grave* (retitled *Cosby* in America), *The Kumars at No 42* (BBC 2: 2001–) (renamed *The Ortegas* [Fox: 2004–] in America) and *Coupling* (BBC 2: 2000–), which only survived for three episodes in America (NBC: 2003). After a very long gestation period, the American remake of *The Office* was finally broadcast in March 2005. While Britain does sometimes remake American sitcoms – such as *The Upper Hand* (ITV: 1990–6) (adapted from *Who's the Boss?* [ABC: 1984–92]), *Loved by You* (ITV: 1997) (from *Mad about You* [NBC: 1992–9]), *Brighton Belles* (ITV: 1993–4) (from *The Golden Girls)* and *Married for Life* (ITV: 1996) (a remake of *Married ... with Children*) – it is a much rarer phenomenon; also, from this evidence, it is not particularly successful.

In itself this suggests something about a dislike in America for showing foreign programmes to a prime-time mass audience. Of more significance are the differences in the series when they are remade by the American industry. For example, the American version of *Birds of a Feather* (BBC 1: 1989–97), which was renamed *Stand By Your Man* (Fox: 1992), altered the reason for the characters' husbands' absence from their incarceration in prison to them being long-distance lorry drivers. Bishop finds that in the American *Men Behaving Badly* 'scenes are being linked by a voice-over ... distancing the audience and apologising to them' (1996, p. 23). Furthermore, the characters are less 'laddy', the audience are invited to laugh *at* rather than *with* them, and the viewpoint of the female characters is made more prominent. This means the series becomes a critique of men's bad behaviour rather than, as in the British original, a celebration.

Similarly, in the American version of *Fawlty Towers*, the American producers instructed the writers 'to change Basil and Sybil's relationship to one of love not hate' (Baker, 1996, p. 25). Perhaps the most infamous recent attempted transfer is *Absolutely Fabulous* (BBC 2, BBC 1: 1992–), whose American rights were bought by Roseanne. However, the series has never made it to the air. This is because the producers in America were so afraid of offending the audience with the characters' 'politically incorrect' behaviour that,

> so much of the rawness of *Ab Fab* – the drug abuse, the gratuitous sex, the drunken swearing – has been watered down or removed from the format, [so] that the US version now seems sanitised and unremarkable, lacking the rawness and cutting edge which made the show such a notable hit in the UK. (Baker, p. 24)

Clearly there are differences here in available subject matter, which suggests that British audiences are more willing to accept a range of sitcom content.

It seems that we have a tension here, then. While the American sitcom is by far the dominant popular television form on television in the States, and is critically celebrated in the UK for its funniness and social awareness, British sitcom content offers a considerable threat to American audiences. This could be purely down to social differences within the two countries generally, rather than anything specifically to do with the sitcom. However, it could also be because in Britain the sitcom is less commonly read in terms of its reference to 'reality', whereas subject matter in American sitcom is limited because the genre is the place audiences look to for popular social analysis. And the reverse is true for the soap opera, which foregrounds its melodramatic excesses in America but which, in Britain, retains links to its social realist heritage and thus is forever aware of its responsibilities towards its audiences. Genres which actively foreground their desire to engage with and explore the social world around them are inevitably restricted in the ways in which they deal with their subject matter; perhaps sitcom can get away with more in Britain because the genre is not seen as a socially responsible one in the first place.

Consequently, analysis of British and American sitcom must go beyond matters of content if their differences are to be understood. A straightforward comparison of the two countries' popular media fails to acknowledge that there is 'a quite radical difference in the place occupied by television in the two cultures and a consequent difference in the way it is written about by cultural critics' (Corner, 1995, pp. 159–60). While this implies that the differences within sitcom are as a result of social factors, it also suggests that the sitcom is not a rigid, defined form. If it can mean such different things to two different countries, what are its other possibilities? Variations in form, content and social position of the sitcom in Britain and America indicate that none of these are necessary or unmotivated. The construction and content of the sitcom arises out of the concerns of the society which produces it. Putting this in a global context, the question arises as to why the genre remains a curiously Anglo-American form. That is, while many countries produce domestic sitcoms – see Mills (2004c) on Australia's *Kath and Kim* (ABC: 2002–), Horrocks (2001) on the repeated failure of all comedy forms in New Zealand, Pettitt (2000, pp. 197–201) on Northern Ireland's *Give My Head Peace* (BBCNI: 1998–), Rivero (2002) on Puerto Rica's *Mi Familia* (Telemundo: 1994), Roome (1999) on South African sitcom and Buonanno (1999, 2000) on a whole range of European series – these rarely compete successfully with imports, and the genre as a whole does not have the social or industrial position it occupies in the UK and America. The sitcom remains an Anglo-American product; what does that say about us?

The Office	Case Study

As has been shown, one of the recurring ways in which sitcom has been understood – certainly by audiences but particularly by the academy – is through its stability. Its theatricality is seen as a reminder of television's origins which other genres have long-since abandoned, which may underscore its conservative nature. It's been argued that theatricality is also necessary for sitcom to signal the differences between it and serious forms, ensuring the genre's comic intentions are unproblematically understood. Similarly, the acknowledgment of the audience through the use of the laugh track, as well as a performance style which dismantles any notion of realism, forever destroys any possibility that the genre might be either radical or progressive. In Western culture, where naturalist and realist forms are prioritised and employed whenever socially relevant statements are to be made, the theatrical nature of the sitcom consistently positions the genre as one whose main concern is entertainment.

Yet there have been small but significant developments within the sitcom in the last decade or so, which challenge these assumptions. The most critically lauded sitcom in Britain in recent years has been *The Office*, which was shown to great acclaim on BBC America in the States, and eventually remade in 2005. The series, like most traditional sitcoms, has a regular setting and characters; in this instance, the workers at a stationery distribution office in Slough. The main character is the office's boss, David Brent, played by Ricky Gervais who, along with Stephen Marchant, also wrote and directed the series. Much of the acclaim for the series has been centred on Brent, and Gervais

Because of its shooting style, *The Office* challenges the idea that sitcom can't be radical or progressive

won BAFTAs for 'Comedy Performance' in 2002 and 2003 and the 2004 Golden Globe for 'Actor in a Leading Role: Musical or Comedy Series'. The character of Brent is egotistical and vain, with a complete lack of self-knowledge; while he's convinced he's a hilarious comedian beloved by his employees, he is instead a sexist and racist who gets away with humiliating his workforce only because of his position of power. The main employees are Gareth, Brent's second-in-command who is the only character who adores him; Tim, who most clearly symbolises the hell of working in the office by his desire to leave and return to university; and Dawn, the office secretary who, like Tim, dreams of escape. The hellish manager lording it over workmates cowed by the need for employment is a staple in sitcom and can be seen in Basil Fawlty in *Fawlty Towers*, Louie De Palma in *Taxi* and Lou Grant in *The Mary Tyler Moore Show*. So far then, *The Office* adheres to the narrative and genre structures of the conventional sitcom.

However, the programme differs notably from most sitcom in its performance and shooting style. Instead of looking explicitly theatrical, *The Office* is shot and acted to look and feel like a documentary. The camera is hand-held and follows the characters around as they work in the office, which means that shots are often jerky and small pieces of action are missed as the camera attempts to keep up with what's going on. Because of this, the series is incapable of using the 'three-headed monster' which conventionally defines sitcom and which ensures all aspects of an actor's performance are captured. Instead, to catch character reactions the camera has to pan very quickly across the office, often recording the end of reactions rather than the whole of them. The use of cameras to rove the office as characters work within it creates a more fully realised narrative space than that of traditional sitcom. Similarly, the camera's constantly changing position continually alters the distance between the audience and the performers, and viewers aren't kept

Kath and Kim exemplifies the recent Australian trend in shooting sitcom using a documentary style

at a distance from the action in the manner traditionally seen as vital to the comic reaction. Therefore, the series consistently refuses to use sitcom's visual characteristics, and so fails to signal its comic intent in the traditional manner. Fundamentally, it also has no laugh track.

The Office is not the only series to be shot and acted in such a way. Indeed, it is merely the most famous example of a trend in such shooting styles in recent British comedy, with series such as *The Royle Family*, *Marion and Geoff*, *Human Remains* (BBC 2, 2001) and *People Like Us* all abandoning the laugh track and three-headed monster. Similarly, American series such as *The Larry Sanders Show* and *Curb Your Enthusiasm* are shot using a documentary style. Interestingly, this trend is also apparent in Australian comedy, even though that country has a less prevalent sitcom tradition; it can be seen in *Frontline* (ABC: 1994–7), *The Games* (ABC: 1998–2000), and *Kath and Kim*. It's not too difficult to see a relationship between the role of public service broadcasting in Australia and Britain and this experimentation, as opposed to the commercial imperatives of the American networks which have, on the whole, upheld sitcom conventions. So, *The Office* was not the first sitcom to adopt this shooting style, and nor was it the most popular or long-running. However, the critical acclaim heaped on it, coupled with its success in a number of countries, may mean that it most vividly signals an irrevocable sea change for sitcom and highlights the point at which the traditional sitcom form died in Britain and Australia.

The use of a documentary shooting style positions the audience in relation to the events portrayed very differently than traditional sitcom. The three-headed monster gives the audience an omniscient position, in which the events being played out are readily understandable. Often, sitcom relies on the disparity between characters' knowledge and audiences' knowledge for its comic effect, and audiences can laugh securely in their superior position. It is rare in sitcom for the audience to not be aware of all that has happened, even if comic surprise sometimes rests on them not knowing what will happen next or how a character will react. In this way, the laugh track functions as a signal of the audience's omniscience and ubiquity; even when characters in a series' diegesis are on their own, the inescapable audience can be heard by viewers, even though the characters remain oblivious to their observers. Because of this, it's possible to relate the audience position in conventional sitcom with the Superiority Theory of humour, in which comedy functions to allow an audience to reassert their intellectual mastery over misinformed, unaware and unintelligent characters (Hobbes, 1914). It is this audience position which supports the argument that sitcom, and comedy generally, offer hegemonic social ideologies and repetitive, simplistic characters.

By removing the laugh track, however, this position is altered, as it means sitcom is failing to reassure its audience that what it's finding humorous is also being laughed at by society at large. Laughing alone, at home, at a sitcom which doesn't recreate the 'music hall experience' (Medhurst and Tuck, 1982, p. 45) means that the only laugh that's heard is your own, and this not only means the text doesn't clearly signal what is and isn't intended as funny, it also fails to reassure viewers that what they find funny is the same as everyone else. The removal of this collective experience – and collective justification – allows for the possibility that audiences might laugh at different things, which seriously undermines the hegemonic criticisms of most sitcom.

The documentary style of shooting also positions audiences relative to the narrative and characters in particular ways. In traditional sitcom, audiences commonly have access to knowledge which the programme's characters don't and they witness the absurd behaviour of those characters who don't know they're being watched. The pleasure of sitcom, then, lies in offering some kind of comic voyeurism. The documentary format, however, means that characters do know they're being filmed, and that an audience at home is observing their actions. In *The Office*, Brent repeatedly makes sure that the camera is on him when he's about to do something that he thinks will make great television and sees the making of the series as his opportunity to impress a television producer and maybe get his own 'real' television series. *Marion and Geoff* takes this to an extreme, as it consists of little more than the series's only character, Keith, sitting in his car talking to a camera on his dashboard, recounting various stories from his life. Keith directly acknowledges the audience at home, saying 'hello' when he turns the camera on and sometimes moves the camera to make sure his audience knows what's going on. Traditional sitcom, then, gives the audience access to the private lives of its characters, whereas in this new form all we see is the behaviour the characters feel is appropriate in front of a camera. David Brent is clearly performing, and he's doing so for the explicit amusement of the audience at home, for it's noticeable that he behaves differently in those moments in the series when he doesn't realise he's being filmed.

This means the audience's relationship to *The Office*'s characters differs from those to traditional sitcom. Even though comedy often rests on embarrassment, it's noticeable that critics have often stated that it's difficult to watch *The Office* and it's a programme that makes you squirm as much as laugh. Its humour rests less on laugh-out-loud gags and pleasurable moments of excessive performance (though there are some of these) and more on smaller incidents and character moments, few of which invoke the belly laughs of traditional sitcom. Yet sitcom has repeatedly relied on absurd, unthinking, monstrous characters for its humour and this has rarely led to the creeping feeling of awfulness and cringing which is the comic material of *The Office*; how come Brent makes us squirm when so many other similar characters don't? It's because traditional sitcom's three-headed monster shooting style, theatrical performances and characters who don't know they're being watched distances the audience from the characters they're invited to laugh at. In *The Office*, however, Brent's flaws are not only on display, but he flaunts them in front of the camera, convinced that the audience at home will adore him as much as he believes his colleagues do. *The Office* is uncomfortable for the audience at home because it presents us with laughable characters without distancing us from their actions. We don't have the omniscient position of most comedy and we're therefore consistently called to account by the series as it puts us in the difficult position of laughing at someone whose only wish is to entertain us and be liked. The series forces the audience to take responsibility for the spitefulness of its laughter. While sitcom conventionally allows us to laugh at idiots behind their backs, *The Office* still says we can laugh at these people, but we'd better be prepared to do it to their faces. Worse than this, it says that laughing at them will only encourage them, as Brent's awful dancing, singing and mugging to the camera demonstrate.

Therefore, this new sitcom form has significant implications for the genre's relationship with its audience. It begins to seriously question the long-standing Humour Theory assumption that com-

Brass Eye uses the conventions of television current affairs programmes for its comic material

edy requires unambiguous cues to signal its intention and the distinction between comic and non-comic moments. That those cues have been sitcom's shooting and performance style are easy to see; what happens, then, when *The Office* not only abandons those cues, but replaces them with the cues of another genre, particularly one like the documentary which normally connotes seriousness? Much of *The Office*'s material is similar to that in programmes from the docusoap boom which characterised British television in the 1990s, and which led to the global rise in reality programming at the beginning of the twenty-first century (Bruzzi, 2001; Kilborn, 2003). Whether any of these series conforms to the characteristics of documentary is irrelevant; what's significant is that audiences have become more accustomed to being entertained by programmes which mix the characteristics of factual and fictional genres. While sitcom and comedy have often used the conventions of television forms for their comic material – see Chris Morris's series *Brass Eye* and *The Day Today*, and *The Larry Sanders Show* – what's significant about *The Office* is that even though it uses the conventions of the docusoap for comedy purposes, it is not in and of itself a parody of that genre. That is, while it clearly shows how documentary participants alter their behaviour because of the presence of a camera, the main pleasures of the series lie in the same kinds of interpersonal conflicts and absurd characters which have always characterised sitcom. The fact that it is precisely these characteristics which, along with those of soap opera, are the pleasures of docusoap, demonstrate that it is the supposedly serious, documentary forms which currently have a crisis of faith in their own worth (Corner, 2004, p. 294). If a sitcom can recreate the look and feel of a documentary and combine those with its own pleasures, without the resulting series being about the nature of documentary itself, what other possibilities are there? Furthermore, that audiences weren't 'fooled' into thinking this was a 'real' documentary, points not only to audiences' sophisticated understanding of generic hybridity, but also suggests that traditional distinctions between the comic and the serious may have far less meaning for them. Most importantly, it means that those criticisms about generic and ideological stability which have forever been used to deride sitcom fail to take into account recent specific examples and work from an assumption that because the genre had developed little since its inception, it was therefore incapable of doing so.

However, it's clear that not all the series mentioned above use the documentary style in the same way. *The Royle Family*, for example, may look like a documentary, but doesn't pretend to be one as the characters don't know they're being filmed. While the series uses the hand-held format to place itself in the British realist, working-class tradition which is appropriate to its setting and content, it still places the audience in a superior position where the characters are to be laughed at, like traditional sitcom. The same is true for *Curb Your Enthusiasm*. More confusing and complex are the interplay of styles in *Kath and Kim* and *The Larry Sanders Show*. *Kath and Kim* uses hand-held cameras and, importantly, incorporates character voice-overs which suggest the characters know they're in a programme. However, at no point during the series do characters visually acknowledge the fact they're being recorded and they're therefore performing accordingly. This results in an unresolvable contradiction, in which the voice-overs suggest the characters know they're part of a programme, yet the narrative and performance never allow for this reading. *The Larry Sanders Show*, on the other hand, relies for its comedy on the contradiction between that which is performed for the purpose of being consumed by an audience (Sanders' chat show) and that which isn't (all the backstage stuff). The programme takes great pleasure in presenting Sanders as a professional, charming host who likes his guests on the show, and a vain, insensitive man who has problematic relationships with them off it. While the backstage material is shot in a hand-held manner, like *The Royle Family* the characters don't acknowledge they're part of a series. Instead, the joke is about the disparity between public and private behaviour, with the public arena defined as that which explicitly takes place in front of a camera.

What implications does all this have for the sitcom, as both an industrial product and the focus of academic analysis? It's important not to overstate the significance of this new form of sitcom, especially as it has yet to produce a truly popular, mainstream example which unites audiences in the ways sitcoms from earlier decades did. Similarly, it may be too tempting to argue that this new form undermines all those arguments about the stable, conservative nature of the genre. However, it is significant that comedy has begun to alter its relationship with its audience, particularly as the traditional position was one of the clearest characteristics of the genre. It also raises the question of how many of these conventions can be altered without sitcom becoming unrecognisable. The long-term effects that this documentary-informed sitcom trend will have on the genre are too difficult to assess at the moment, and it may turn out to be nothing more than a brief interlude in the same way as socially relevant sitcom was in America in the 1970s, and Alternative Comedy was in Britain in the 1980s. However, these developments do have consequences for the ways in which sitcom can be interpreted and criticised. Fundamentally, it points to those conventions which have usually been seen as most central to sitcom as being merely window-dressing: that is, sitcom cannot be defined by the way in which it is shot or its hegemonic representations and we need to find newer and more complex ways of thinking of sitcom as a genre. If we're going to find what it is that helps define sitcom as something distinct from other television forms, maybe we have to look at some of its other aspects; and performance may very well be one of those.

Chapter 3 | Sitcom and Performance

'The cameramen yawn and look at their watches to see how long it is to the next coffee-break. The actors stretch and pace about the set. Phoebe Osborn practises ballet steps in front of a mirror. Making television programmes consists very largely of waiting around.'

David Lodge, *Therapy* (London: Secker & Warburg, 1995), p. 75.

A man is standing at a bar with a friend, chatting generally about business troubles and trying to impress the upmarket clientele around him with his references to money. He realises that he's caught the attention of two attractive women and tells his companion that he thinks they might have a chance with him. He goes to lean on the bar but doesn't realise that the barman has raised its trapdoor. He falls through the bar, spilling his drink and his friend looks confused as his companion appears to have disappeared. Embarrassed, the man gets up, and demands the two leave.

This scene from the 'Yuppy Love' episode of *Only Fools and Horses* is often cited as the funniest moment in the history of British television comedy. It is endlessly repeated in programmes about the show, trailers for repeats, and profiles on the actor who plays the character Del Boy, David Jason. It certainly contributed to that series winning the public vote in *Britain's Best Sitcom*. Recorded in front of a live studio audience, the soundtrack shows that it elicits a massive reaction, with long drawn-out laughter, and a round of applause. And when it was first broadcast, I remember it being the moment that friends and family talked about the day after, as it quickly attained its status as a 'classic comedy moment'. Yet it's one of the oldest jokes in the world: it's merely someone falling over. How come this particular fall was successful as comedy and is regarded with so much admiration?

It seems unlikely that we can find the answer to this question through genre analysis. *Only Fools and Horses* conforms almost entirely to the conventions of sitcom, so that wouldn't make this moment funnier than any other in the programme or, for that matter, in any other series. While the joke makes sense within the narrative – Del's fall is made more embarrassing because it occurs at the moment he's trying to impress – this is also not markedly different from most of the jokes in the programme, which is often centred on the disparity between Del's desired appearance and the reality of his existence. And the moment certainly contains surprise, which is common in much comedy but again, much of the programme's comedy does so. Instead, it makes sense to see this gag as a moment of spectacular performance, in which the skills and techniques of David Jason – along with the way in which the scene is directed and shot – somehow make the joke funnier. The fall is not natural, as Jason's body remains completely straight as he falls and he doesn't put his hand out to stop himself as would be most likely. Yet this still doesn't entirely explain why this should make this moment so memorable or even funny at all. Acting clearly plays a significant part in the ways in which comedy is made to make sense, so it's necessary to examine these aspects in order to understand the genre better.

Like much else when discussing sitcom, the analysis of performance is one informed by the lack of critical thought and vocabulary available. For example, both Horowitz (1997) and Mellencamp (1992) laud Lucille Ball's performance in *I Love Lucy* for its feminist possibilities. Yet they do so through description of the acting, without placing it within either a historical or genre context, or acknowledging the variety of ways in which such acting can be understood and enjoyed. This is unsurprising considering the lack of work in this area and Naremore, in the only full-length single-authored book on media acting (though, in this case, film), notes that writing on it often results in 'unwieldy tables of statistics or fuzzy, adjectival language' (1988, p. 2). It's all too easy to end up simply describing a performance and it's difficult to know whether that actually tells us anything. Acting is phenomenally complex, both as a part of the industrial production of media, and within completed texts. Similarly, acting has to be understood within the nature of television as a whole, where it is only one part of what an audience sees and hears. Therefore there's a complex range of possible analytical approaches to acting and simple description often tells us very little.

To understand the sitcom it is vital to explore the performances within it. First, this is because it conventionally employs styles of acting not used within other genres; indeed, one of the most obvious markers of sitcom is these kinds of performance and the roles they play within the text. Sitcom foregrounds performance more obviously than other forms. As will be shown, this is a result of historical factors relevant to comic acting which derived from theatre and film but which the majority of television has evolved away from. Second, it is within performance that the possible radical potential of sitcom is most obvious. It may be no surprise that a number of feminist critics have chosen performance as the aspect through which to demonstrate how certain series offer pleasures which are resistant to patriarchy, particularly as that performance commonly revolves around the body. For Mellencamp, 'If Lucy's plots for ambition and fame narratively failed ... *performatively* they succeeded' (1992, p. 329), demonstrating that acting and story can offer quite different meanings within the same programme. The specifics of sitcom acting also point towards the social role of sitcom as a whole, for distinctions between comic and serious acting must result from cultural meanings which are associated with both of those modes. Third, we can explore performance for the pleasures it offers, particularly as these are often made so obvious in sitcom. Not taking account of acting in sitcoms means failing to get to grips with important aspects of it as a genre, a political text and a piece of entertainment.

Defining Acting and Performance

The lack of critical work on acting has meant that the vocabulary appropriate to it is often conflicting, having to unite academic understandings of it with everyday, common-sense ones. For example, how can we make a distinction – or, even, is a distinction required – between 'acting', 'comic acting', 'clowning' and 'performance'? This is particularly troubling considering these terms are used in various ways by a number of disciplines, such as Sociology, Theatre Studies and Psychology, as well as Media and Cultural Studies. Since Goffman (1959, 1974), 'performance' has become a word with a much wider sociological meaning than its everyday use about what professional, paid actors do. 'Performance Studies' has forced Theatre Studies to examine exactly what it is that distinguishes theatrical from everyday performance, if such a distinction exists at all. Schechner defines performance as 'actions', and notes that it is 'so broad-ranging and open to new possibilities, no one can grasp its totality' (2002, p. 1). Analysing performance engages with questions about everyday life, reality and its representation and recreation, and whether the distinctions between these concepts should be dissolved. This may seem an unnecessarily complex debate when thinking about sitcom but, as will be shown, not only does sitcom incorporate performance, it often finds humour in the ways in which its characters perform in particular social circumstances.

It is important to distinguish between acting and performance. For Naremore, 'acting is nothing more than the transposition of everyday behaviour into a theatrical realm' (1988, p. 21). Here, the quality of acting is assessed through reference to the world outside of the media text and good acting is that which we easily describe as like 'real life'. Of course, this ignores a whole range of narrative and visual techniques used by media to construct such naturalism and realism. These techniques dominate Western film and television and won the century-long battle between them and more abstract methods of representation (Meyer-Dinkgräfe, 2001, p. 27). Such acting attempts as much as possible to downplay its role within a text and instead tries to appear as though it hasn't been through any kind of production process (Durham, 2002). This style of acting is usually seen in 'serious' drama, but is also apparent in the speeches of politicians, which are rehearsed performances which pretend not to be. By this definition, it is difficult to equate sitcom with acting for it is a genre which rarely makes claims towards television's forms of realism and instead has generic structures which signal its production and intentions.

'Performance' is different to acting as it has connotations of 'mastery, skill or inventiveness' (Naremore, 1988, p. 26). In this sense, a performance is more (or less?) than the attempt to recreate the real world; instead it relies on forms of excessive display that are centred on the star performer of the text. It is significant that Naremore consistently uses comedy to examine performance, as he repeatedly examines Chaplin. Comic performance's pleasures often rest on a display of such skill; the quick verbal banter, coupled with excessive gestures and well-timed movement within the frame supply many of the laughs in *Will and Grace* and the 'three-headed monster' shooting style developed precisely out of the need to capture as successfully as possible the comic skills of Lucille Ball. For Double, 'learning to be a comedian is like learning any other set of performance skills' (2000, p. 18). Auslander notes that the stand-up Andy Kauffman, who went on to play Latka Gravas in *Taxi*, was such a controversial live performer because he refused to display skill in anything and instead 'many of the things he did were seemingly things anyone could do' (1992, p. 141). For comic performance to offer pleasure it must demonstrate the abilities of the person performing it far more obviously than non-comic forms do. So Humphrey's tortuous, long-winded monologues in *Yes, Minister* are pleasurable less because they are inherently funny and more because of the skill displayed by Nigel Hawthorne in successfully completing them. Peter Kay's multiple roles in *Peter Kay's Phoenix Nights* allow him to demonstrate his acting range, just as Paul Whitehouse's do in *Help* (BBC 2: 2005–). It is noticeable that it is comedy that has a tradition of allowing actors to play more than one part, such as Peter Sellers in *Dr Strangelove, or: How I Learned to Stop Worrying and Love the Bomb* (Stanley Kubrick, 1964), Alec Guinness in *Kind Hearts and Coronets* (Robert Hamer, 1949) and Alan Ayckbourn's *Intimate Strangers* (1985). On television, certain comic actors have been given series made up of one-off episodes, so they can show off their ability to play a variety of characters. The most famous of these is Ronnie Barker's *Seven of One* (BBC 2: 1973) because it eventually led to full series of *Porridge* and *Open All Hours*, but the same is also true for Maureen Lipman in *About Face* (ITV: 1989, 1991) and Steve Coogan in *Coogan's Run* (BBC 2: 1995). What binds these series together is the performance skills of the central star, and the audience is invited to be impressed by their range above all else.

Naremore notes that acting is commonly about characters who 'have become agents in a narrative' (p. 23), so that the actor's job is not only to create a character which make sense within the story, but whose characteristics act as a motivator for the narrative's continuance. Performance, however, has no such limitations and narrative can be abandoned in sequences where performers display their skills. Naremore notes that many of the most famous scenes in Chaplin's films are narratively redundant; indeed, they may be best remembered precisely because knowledge of the plot is unnecessary for the comic pleasure offered by them. These pleasures instead rest on 'our feeling that an actor is doing something remarkable' (p. 26) and, within comedy, we're willing to trade off narrative for the pleasures offered by such performance. Sitcom is a genre which often requires its cast to be able to fulfil both acting and performance, depending on particular moments in the script. In *Friends*, for example, David Schwimmer plays Ross

In *Friends*, David Schwimmer plays Ross differently in his serious scenes with Jennifer Aniston's Rachel compared to his more farcical moments

quite differently in the serious, romantic scenes he has with Jennifer Aniston's Rachel to the way he does in the farcical ones when he's, say, pretending to have a British accent in order to impress some students, or dealing with the problems of wearing leather trousers; the former's acting and the latter's performance. While most genres will sometimes flit between acting and performance, most don't do so this explicitly, and this is a requirement of the comic mode. It means making sense of what actors do in sitcom is very complicated, for their actions will depend upon particular series, narratives and comic moments.

Acting and Performance: Actors and Performers

The examination of acting in media has fallen predominantly to Film Studies, and has often been related to the analysis of stars. Lovell and Krämer outline a history of this approach, placing it as a response to the 'semiological/psychoanalytic position' (1999, p. 3) central to the study of cinema. In this way, acting has been rendered as little more than a series of visual elements, particularly as Film Studies has often positioned actors, especially female ones, as something to be looked at by a voyeuristic audience (Mulvey, 2001). While such an approach has allowed useful work to take place on the limited and repetitive ways in which representation functions, it has failed to examine acting as more than something to be merely looked at and the variety of possible ways audiences can make sense of, and get pleasure from, performance. By rendering actors and acting as just another element of the film text, the ways in which certain actors work, and distinctions between certain types of acting, most notably between the comic and the serious, are downplayed. Carlson argues that this is partly because of the literary-based origins of much media analysis, which not only places the text as the core of study, but which sees acting and performance as a 'troubling distraction' (1996, p. 82) to its coherence.

Yet it is precisely this troubling aspect of acting which can be seen as its most potent force, particularly when related to comedy. That is, while most texts within the dominant naturalist mode of Western contemporary media try to hide the process behind their selection and use as much as possible, acting, and the meanings associated with actors, often rests on a non-naturalist display of their position within the text (Dyer, 1998). The expectation that particular actors will give certain kinds of performances and so offer certain kinds of pleasures is what the star system rests on, and these pleasures often rely on whether an actor is a comic or serious one. Performance is one of the ways in which the naturalist diegesis of texts can be disrupted and not in a manner undesired by audiences. The existence of sitcom spin-offs attests to this; by taking a character such as *Cheers*'s Frasier and giving him his own series, the implication is that, while the setting, narrative structure and supporting characters will change, the performance of Kelsey Grammar in the title role will be the same as that in the original series and will therefore offer similar pleasures. Spin-offs are based around character/actor, not setting, director, music or any other aspect of genre and this is because acting is a central aspect of genre coherence and audience pleasure.

Award-winning performances are often not the most 'realistic' or appropriate; instead they are the ones which most pleasurably balance the naturalistic requirements of the text with the expectations and pleasures associated with the star performing them and the 'skill' which this process involves. The pleasures of, say, Jerry Seinfeld's performance in *Seinfeld* are ones which makes sense of his acting as part of the narrative and diegesis of any particular episode, coupled with the clear acknowledgment that such performance is informed by his success and skill as a stand-up comedian. Indeed, early series included scenes of Jerry (simultaneously stand-up comedian and sitcom character) performing in a comedy club explicitly offered the audience the pleasures of Seinfeld's stand-up skills, as if his ability to perform within a 'realist' sitcom diegesis may not be pleasurable enough. This notion of skill is apparent in comedy acting done by non-stand-ups too; the massive audience reaction to David Jason's portrayal of Del Boy in *Only Fools and Horses* is one that finds pleasure in the character's position within the series and individual episodes' narratives, coupled with the comedic skill and displayed performance expectations garnered by Jason's audience through seeing him in previous series such as *Open All Hours* and *A Sharp Intake of Breath* (ITV: 1977–81).

This sense of skill is important, and is one of the pleasures offered by much performance. The academy's insistence on seeing acting as nothing more than a process which results in objectified (particularly female) performers presented in a powerless manner for audiences to voyeuristically gawp at means that 'the considerable skills of abilities of a wide range of actresses ... go ignored' (Lovell and Krämer, 1999, p. 3). It is necessary to move away from an assumption that performances are nothing more than texts to be read, and instead move towards examining the rehearsal and production process which creates them and which rely for their effectivity on the abilities of individual actors and audiences' abilities to recognise and take pleasure in them. Lovell and Krämer note that by concentrating on the visuals of acting, analysis has ignored vocals, which is odd considering how some actors become famous for their voices. Indeed, the skills offered by actors in animated series such as *The Simpsons* and *South Park* are based solely around their vocal talents; the fact that such actors are nowhere near as famous or recognisable as would be expected from such long-running global series demonstrates how the social position of actors is one which assumes the superiority of the face over the voice.

Acting is significant as it represents the 'human agency' (Carlson, 1996, p. 3) in media production. The pleasures related to acting are centred on the specific abilities and talents of a particular individual and their willingness to use and display those for the enjoyment of others. And while this display of skill is apparent in all media – such as literature and art – in the performing arts, there is a conflation between the 'artist' and the material they use to display their work. So, we can look at a painter's paintings, as they were intended, without the agency of the painter: performance and acting, however, require the agency of the actor as their body and voice are themselves the medium through which skill is expressed. The artist and the art are one, which is often what makes distinguishing between performer and performance difficult.

This is most noticeable in stand-up comedy, which is usually performed in venues as bare as possible with no technology other than a microphone and a spotlight. In stand-up, all that is on offer is the performer, who delivers a routine by drawing on personal experiences which are turned into jokes through their writing and delivery skills. Significantly, stand-ups usually perform using their real name. While it's obvious comedy characters and the actors who perform them are not the same, they do often rely on a conflation of the two for their potency and pleasure. This is what American sitcoms based around stand-up comedians' routines capitalise on and explore. The (pseudo-)-autobiographical nature of series such as *Curb Your Enthusiasm* and *It's Garry Shandling's Show* are unheard of in serious fictional series, because the comedy star system allows this conflation between actor and character – indeed, relies on it – whereas serious acting is often judged on actors' abilities to immerse themselves in something they resolutely are not. In addition, comedy's 'metalinguistic function' (Fiske and Hartley, 2003, p. 63) means it can critique television itself, allowing such autobiographical series to unite star and character. Displays of skill in serious acting revolve around becoming 'something else'; the fact that comedy performers often play what are assumed to be extensions of themselves is the cause of much of the critical antipathy towards it.

Much analysis of performance looks at the physical presence of actors. Stand-up comedy is 'bound up with the here and now' (Double, 2000, p. 22) and its pleasures often rely on the production and consumption occurring simultaneously. It's possible for television to demonstrate its relationship to the 'here and now' also, as shown by live news broadcasts and some parts of reality television. Yet sitcom is recorded, which means there's a massive temporal and geographical disparity between performance and its consumption. This is unsurprising, for most fictional forms rarely suggest that audiences are seeing events as they occur, which is necessary in view of the long and considered production process they've been through. We can make a rough distinction then between factual and fictional forms, based on the ways they associate themselves with the live. These distinctions, and the common prioritisation of the factual over fiction, have led to what Barish calls 'the antitheatrical prejudice' (1981).

As sitcom is a fictional form it shouldn't, then, attempt to make claims for simultaneity. Yet it commonly does, using a range of theatrical signifiers and an audible laugh track to, if not convince the domestic audience that the performance is happening as they watch it, at least signal that what is being watched was once a performance which relied on the 'live' relationship between an audience and the performers. Bourdon argues that all of 'television remains deeply influenced by the possibility of live broadcasting' (2000, p. 531), yet it's apparent that this functions in a much more obvious way for comic forms than serious drama. Why this should be is unclear and is more than just a residue of the theatrical origins of these forms; after all, drama itself mutated from theatre. Hayman (1969, pp. 102–14) argues that film and television acting downplays the role of the performer, and instead the editor and director have more control over meaning-making yet this is clearly not the case for comedy. This might be because, as noted before, comedy is commonly seen as requiring surprise and spontaneity, as well as a reciprocal relationship between audience and text for its comic effectivity (Hobbes, 1914; Kant, 1952; Schopenhauer, 1958; Palmer, 1987). In these ways, the physical presence of actors and the ways in which they perform to, and respond to, the audience which signals its comic pleasure, become vital to understanding the development of sitcoms and the ways in which audiences enjoy them. There are, then, specifics of comic acting, which are carried out in particular ways in a television form such as the sitcom.

Seriousness and Comedy

Television sitcom acting is best understood by highlighting its differences from acting in other media and other modes. Rather than suggesting that there are more 'natural' forms of acting which just happen to appear in certain kinds of texts, it's better to see acting as one of the conventions which define genres, media and historical periods. Sitcom acting is a device used to signal specific comic moments within an episode, and not just the comic mode of the text as a whole; we could distinguish, say, between expositional acting in sitcom and that required for punchlines. Acting is thus a technique which not only helps define a text as a whole, but also defines the 'intentionality' (Elam, 2002, p. 67) of specific moments; indeed, it may well be the performance itself that is funny. The moments in sitcom which are probably the most famous in the UK and America – Del Boy falling through the bar in *Only Fools and Horses* and Lucy's tango with a dress stuffed full of eggs in *I Love Lucy* – may rest on their position within the respective episodes for their narrative justification, but are funny predominantly because of how they're performed. Both of these moments are physical jokes, demonstrating that while sitcom has often been analysed through its dialogue, there are many comic incidents in sitcom which rely very little on dialogue for their funniness.

Sitcom acting and performance must also be understood in relation to the conventions for other forms and genres. The fact that such acting is taking place on television not only affects logistical possibilities, but also contributes to the meanings made by actors. It is noticeable that the majority of analysis of screen acting examines film and this is perhaps logical considering that medium's more consistent use of stars. Television's domestic nature, its relationship to naturalism and its theatrical heritage all contribute to the expectations audiences bring to bear on sitcom which are different to those for other media. Some of this distinction relies on seeing film as a more 'worthy' medium than television, an assumption which helps support the development of Film Studies as a separate discipline to Media Studies. That this distinction is seen by comic actors, writers, directors and producers is apparent in many of their careers, in which television is used as a stepping-stone towards the more legitimate – and lucrative – world of cinema. This distinction assumes that film acting is in some way 'better' than that for television, which rests on the belief that the conventions of cinema are more authentic and natural. This hierarchy can be seen in the ways tragedy and comedy are judged, for 'serious' acting and actors are seen as 'good art' (Quinn, 1990, p. 155), as shown every year in film and television awards ceremonies where drama inevitably wins over comedy. And while television's 'impulse is almost constantly towards a spectacle of realism' (Durham, 2002, p. 82), the sitcom's artificiality marks it off as different to the majority of the medium's fiction.

Indeed, distinguishing between realism/naturalism and other forms of acting are vital to an examination of sitcom performance. Broadly speaking, the 'usefulness' of any form of culture is measured by its ability to respond to, examine and demonstrate 'truths' about the real world. Those countries which have public service broadcasting repeatedly require television to demonstrate that it is fulfilling such roles in order to justify receiving public funds. The Reithian mantra of the BBC – inform, educate, entertain – makes it clear what the corporation's motivation should be, and it is rarely criticised for not being entertaining enough in the way it is for not being informative or educative enough. It is this repeated insistence on culture's relationship with reality which has led to sitcoms being lauded more often for their humorous reflection of social structures than for their comic ingenuity or performance skill. It has also often meant that sitcoms justify their existence through such a comparison, no matter how successful. This is apparent in the ten documentaries broadcast by the BBC as part of their *Britain's Best Sitcom* series. In attempting to entice viewers to vote for a particular programme, each series' proponents often spent far more time remarking on their candidate's social importance and reflection of contemporary concerns than they did talking about how funny it was or how well it was acted.

More so in the UK than in America, television acting is evaluated with reference to some 'common-sense' notion of how people would really behave in such a situation. The pressures of naturalism and realism have promoted performance which is 'invisible' (Naremore, 1988, p. 17) but which might more accurately be deemed 'transparent'. That is, serious television acting has become a process in which actors, through understanding of character motivation and extensive research, attempt to *become* the person they're portraying. The performance itself, then, is merely a 'transparent' medium through which to transmit a learned psychological and sociological reality. Because of this, it's quite common to hear actors talk about acting as a rehearsal process centred on psychology and truth, with little reference to a whole range of simple, acting techniques which have particular effects (Barr, 1997; Milter, 1992; Milling and Ley, 2001; Tucker, 2003). Therefore, 'the credibility of performance is created out of coherence and harmony' (Klevan, 2005, p. 5) with the narrative and diegesis of any particular text.

Comedy acting, on the other hand, rarely makes claims of verisimilitude. That is, while sitcom may strive to reflect cultural reality, the acting and shooting style through which such meaning is presented instead highlight its artificiality, resulting in 'self-conscious performance' (Bignell, 2004, p. 122). Because comedy occupies a social role which sees it as less valuable than seriousness, it must repeatedly mark its comedic purpose through various signals, of which acting is one. Considering the fact that the 'frame' of the television screen already marks anything on it as 'not real', comedy's requirement to signal its artificiality must be a result of the nature of comedy itself. Of course, considering sitcom's recent foray into the signifying strategies of other forms, particularly documentary, it might be expected that concerns would be raised about comedic texts undermining the veracity of documentary; that this hasn't happened is a result of the batterings documentary aesthetics took in the last decade, as seen in forms such as the docusoap and reality TV (Bruzzi, 2001; Winston, 2000).

The self-consciousness of comic acting is so widespread that it might be easier to note those programmes that don't use it. Suffice to say, the list of great sitcom characters – Del in *Only Fools and Horses*, Hancock in *Hancock's Half-Hour*, Ralph Kramden in *The Honeymooners* (CBS: 1955–6), Fletch in *Porridge*, Bill Cosby in *The Cosby Show* and so on – is a list of differing kinds of successful excessive performance full of the 'facial gri-

South Park's 'limited animation' signals its comic intentions

maces' (Shepherd and Wallis, 2004, p. 22) which have always categorised comic acting. It is not insignificant that animation is a form popularly associated with comedy, for it is in and of itself artificial; how come there aren't any animated drama series, soap operas, news programmes or documentaries regularly running on mainstream television? Series such as *The Simpsons*, *South Park* and *Beavis and Butt-head* deliberately employ 'limited animation' (Furniss, 1998, p. 135) in which the 'bad' drawings display their 'cartoonal-ness' (Wells, 2002, p. 94), distancing these series from serious forms as obviously as possible.

Examining acting requires techniques which make sense not only of performance's narrative function but also its importance within specific moments. Semiotics allows the examination of movements, gestures and voice, while placing these within the context in which they are presented and consumed. Particularly since Eco (1977), semiotics has been used to explore the nature of communication in theatre, primarily because theatre has rarely made claims to verisimilitude in the way film and television has, and therefore all its signs more obviously signal their significance within a text (Aston and Savano, 1991; Ubersfeld, 1999). To this end, everything in theatre 'acquires, as it were, a set of quotation marks' (Elam, 2002, p. 7), in which objects become representative of them-selves, rather than, as naturalism argues, being there because they just happen to be.

Such a set of quotation marks invites audiences to make sense of texts in a detached manner, consciously examining each of them as their inclusion must have some meaning-making purpose. While naturalism and realism clearly also use objects in this manner, the distinction is that theatricality acknowledges this process and may, therefore, actively use it, whereas forms of verisimilitude less consciously display the techniques used to represent the real. Comedy is often little more than a very obvious set of quotation marks, with performances which are not coded as realistic and which don't contribute towards the psychological realism of the character; instead such acting displays its purpose – to make you laugh – while simultaneously offering those gestures as comic within themselves.

For example, comic characters are often associated with the costumes they wear, the way they move, or catchphrases. Thus Naremore argues that Chaplin's costume has 'contrasts that signify he is an art object' (1988, p. 16). The ludicrousness of his suit, coupled with his moustache, cane and walk, result in a performance which signals its humorousness while simultaneously being humorous. In *Only Fools and Horses*, Del Boy's shoulder movements when he's trying to convince others (and himself) of his scams help define the character through tics which, while understandable through psychological realism, are also a signal underlining the comedy. Catchphrases – which aren't explainable through any of the major Humour Theories – are funny because their repetition puts quotation marks around them, and stops them appearing to be genuine utterances. The pleasure of catchphrases does not come from complex humour which requires an understanding of character motivation; instead, they are empty, meaningless phrases which are funny because to remove meaning from language in this way renders it empty, and therefore laughable. When Victor Meldrew says 'I don't believe it!' in *One Foot in the Grave*, we're enjoying Richard Wilson's excessive performance of the expostulation rather than it as a valid reflection of the character's exasperation. Around all such examples hover the quotation marks, which highlight the artificial performance techniques central to comic acting.

This results in 'an acknowledged exchange between performer and spectator' (Beckerman, 1990, p. 110) which foregrounds the comic intentions of the former. Naremore notes that in moments 'when deception or repression are indicated, the drama becomes a metaperformance' (1988, p. 72). That is, in naturalistic acting, when characters within a diegesis are required to perform, actors playing them – who are already performing – must signal their performance differently. If this occurs predominantly in moments of 'deception or repression', it's unsurprising that they should be so common in comedy, which is a genre often about those two aspects. Characters in sitcoms commonly have to 'play a part' within an episode's narrative, usually through some kind of comic misunderstanding; *Coupling* and *Curb Your Enthusiasm* constantly use such narratives. That is, comedy is often about characters having to perform so as not to be found out; in order for the distinction between the performance being done by the character and that being done by the actor to be distinguished, the former has to be done to excess. The theatrical way in which sitcoms are shot allows actors to display their performance to the audience, while simultaneously refusing too much character identification in the audience lest this gets in the way of the text's comic meaning. Breaking down the barrier which separates the audience from the comedy through the performer's acknowledgment of his actions and the audience itself, means that audiences are involved in 'active participation' (Tuan, 2001, pp. 161–2), rather than mere passive observation. The resulting laugh track is an obvious consequence of this participation.

It is, then, the examination of the specifics of performance which can contribute towards analysis of the ways in which comedy works. The nature of comedy performance has repeatedly distinguished itself from that of serious drama and has done so for two reasons. First, to keep the distinction between the two as clear as possible. Second, to utilise aspects of performance which highlight artificiality and acknowledge the audience, which are vital for a social phenomenon such as comedy. Performance is thus a central aspect to the nature of comedy generally; indeed, it is one of the most important signals that we're watching comedy at all.

The Origins and Development of Comedy Performance

Understanding the conventions of broadcast comedy requires an understanding of its theatrical origins and the ways in which it continues to draw on those traditions. The movement of performers from theatre and stand-up to television (often, in Britain, via radio) means that comedy actors often have a certain kind of theatrical training and are used to relying on the proximity of a live audience for response to their work. The social conventions which distinguish between comedy and seriousness in all parts of life are exemplified in the distinctions between comic and serious acting, with Naremore's definition of 'performance' far more applicable to the former than the latter. These distinctions can be seen in the history of comedy acting, which has developed a specific aesthetic and a set of physical and vocal rules which, while under constant development, remain predominantly distinct and noticeable. The most common place comedy's performance is traced to is the theatre (Elam, 2002, pp. 47–8; Mayer, 1999; Pearson, 1992), and, specifically, commedia dell'arte, and the similarities between that form's conventions and sitcom performance are clear and noticeable.

While precise definitions of commedia dell'arte are hotly disputed (indeed, the term itself is contested), it is usually used to denote a form of performance which took place in markets across Europe from about the middle of the sixteenth century and, thanks to committed theatre historians and specific theatrical troupes, continues to this day in a variety of arenas. It involved stock characters, was performed in masks, with traditional narratives, on a stage in a loud, crowded public place where the performers battled with the rest of the market's possibilities for an audience. It therefore always had an entertainment role and its comedic content functioned as a powerful way to entice audiences away from other distractions. Over time commedia developed a coherent aesthetic, which affected not only the masks, but also the characters' personalities, the roles they played within the narrative, the kinds of characters they would interact with and, more importantly, the ways in which they stood, moved and gestured. Because of this, it's possible for Rudlin (1994) to list and outline the character types on offer, describing the precise physical movements and gestures available to an actor portraying them. While this might seem like a limiting constraint, it instead demonstrates that comedy has an aesthetic tradition with its own discrete and organised conventions and expectations.

Of relevance to the debate about acting and performance is that commedia is seen less as a tradition within which individual performers could flourish and more as a set of skills appropriate to each character which are learned, as a trade, and thus passed down from generation to generation. This display of skill – which, in modern times, we might more easily apply to circus performers such as clowns – highlights the interplay within comedy performance between the individual and the traditions they work within. While it's difficult to see television sitcom acting as one which relies so concretely on the passing down of a trade, certain performers – particularly those who come to television

Absolutely Fabulous lets Jennifer Saunders and Joanna Lumley show off their mastery at physical clowning

via stand-up or theatre – talk about their work as one of learning from both the audience and other performers (Pines, 1992). This sets up a relationship between the individual star within a sitcom, and the collaborative history and aesthetic of the form in which they perform. Individual episodes of a series must both draw on the history of that programme, including all the regular characters and sets, while at the same time allowing narrative to be abandoned in places in order for a star to have a moment to display their comedic skill. The early episodes of *Seinfeld* managed this tension by including scenes from Jerry's stand-up routine and many sections in *Absolutely Fabulous* allow both Jennifer Saunders and Joanna Lumley the possibility to show off their mastery at physical clowning. Yet both these series surround their characters with ones performed in slightly less excessive manners, even if they are sometimes allowed to have their 'moments'; Jane Horrocks' performance as Bubble in *Absolutely Fabulous* is so successful it sometimes threatens to steal the show. Sitcom performance gives us more of the same at the same time as offering moments of novelty, so the notion of genre as representing 'repetition and difference' (Neale, 1992, p. 48) can be applied to performance too.

This tension is also apparent in the ways in which any actor must subsume themselves to the requirements of the role while simultaneously offering the pleasures of their own star quality to the audience. In *The Cosby Show*, there is a constant conflict between Bill Cosby playing Cliff Huxtable in as realistic and convincing a manner as possible and the audience's desire to see Cosby the performer and stand-up displaying his idiosyncratic comic skills. The narratives of *The Cosby Show* are often structured precisely to deal with this tension, repeatedly including scenes which, while a logical progression of the story, have little narrative purpose themselves, and instead allow Cosby to display his skills at riffing off an idea, often while reacting to children. While serious acting also has to negotiate the tension between moments and narrative, the pleasures of serious forms rarely rest on performance skill which has little or no narrative purpose.

Commedia's use of recurring characters, and their characterisation through masks, means that it offered character 'types' (Rudlin, 1994, p. 34) or 'personages' (Burns, 1972, p. 122) rather than ones intended to be read as psychologically complex beings. Again, though, a tension exists in how such types are realised within specific narratives and by particular performers. So, while stupid characters are common to most sitcoms, the exact ways in which these function and are performed relies on individual responses to a similar 'mask'. Thus it's perfectly logical to describe each of the characters in *Friends* as stupid, yet they are so in quite different ways, whether it be through emotional underdevelopment (Chandler), obsessive neuroticism (Monica), a lack of education (Joey), or simply a novel, emotive response to events (Phoebe). The fact that Jennifer Aniston got the part of Rachel even though she auditioned for the role of Monica demonstrates that the right interplay between performer and comic type/character is vital.

Recurring character types, which can be traced back for centuries, have significant implications for the possibilities of comedy and sitcom. That is, if commedia dell'arte repeatedly used a certain set of limited character types and presented each of them as funny in particular ways at certain times, this severely limits its representational possibilities. For Rudlin 'laugher is dependent on stereotyping' (1994, p. 35), and this has resonances with contemporary criticisms of sitcom which argue that characters can only be funny in certain ways, particularly in matters of gender and race. Yet the differences in kinds of stupidity outlined for *Friends* may also suggest that difference can exist within those stereotypes. Of course, this is not to suggest such possibilities may exist for all types of representation: however, it is worth noting that the relationship between performance and representation is one which always responds to the tension between the heritage of character types and the individual actor performing them in any particular text.

A defining aspect of the commercial and industrial nature of commedia dell'arte was that it was based around collaboration, both within the performance, and as an industrial business venture. The literal translation of 'commedia dell'arte' is 'performance for/by the artists', and thus is it a 'social rather than an artistic phenomenon, meaning above all the association of professionals' (Rudlin, 1994, p. 14). And sitcom remains a collaborative form, in a variety of ways. In America, sitcom results from collaboration between large teams of writers, a number of producers and executive producers and the development and improvisation of material by performers during rehearsal. While this collaborative process may be more muted in Britain due to the prominence of the individual writer, it can clearly be seen in sitcom written and performed by a stand-up comedian. The growth of independent television production companies in Britain in the 1980s and 90s was often a result of performers and writers seizing control of the means of production, becoming producers and sellers of a product they would have initially only had minimal commercial control over. Thus the two main independent companies producing comedy – Hat Trick and TalkBack – were set up and run by comedians who'd spent much of their previous careers as writers and performers only. The business of sitcom is a surprisingly collaborative one and while producers still have to battle with the economics and whims of the networks which broadcast their programmes, a degree of collaboration and ownership uncommon in other parts of television production is akin to that of commedia dell'arte.

Contemporary sitcom performance is derived from other histories too, particularly as the history of acting in the twentieth century was a cross-pollination between theatre, film, radio and television. Distinctions between performance are therefore far more marked between genres than they are between different media. For example, Naremore argues that 'standard postures' are apparent in comedy in every medium, for 'stereotypical expression is foregrounded' (1988, p. 63). Tim Allen's comic performance in *Home Improvement* is similar to that of his stand-up routines and his acting in films such as *The Santa Clause* (Michael Lembeck, 2002) and *Jungle 2 Jungle* (John Pasquin, 1997), and his voice skills in *Toy Story* (John Lasseter, 1995) and *Toy Story 2* (John Lasseter, 1999); the medium is less relevant than his ability to perform comically. It has already been shown that sitcom acting results from theatrical traditions and the conventions of television for its potency, and the question remains as to why it has stubbornly refused to move on from such theatricality when most television acting has.

However, while the similarities between commedia dell'arte and contemporary sitcom characters and performance are apparent, it's important to note other acting traditions which have contributed to the genre. Thus 'the techniques of Italian, Jewish and Irish humour had first been melded in the pot of vaudeville' (Rudlin, 1994, p. 7), creating an American comedy tradition which was similar to British music hall. Furthermore, Coleman (2000) argues that black comedy performance styles are so widespread within sitcom that the genre should not be understood as a 'white' form at all.

While calculating the exact influence of each of these traditions is virtually impossible, what is noticeable is that they all originate in groups seen as outsiders or minorities in society. It must be significant that such marginalised groups either turned to comedy to express themselves, or were only allowed public space to do so as comedic performers. Comedy's requirement to signal its difference from the norms of seriousness has paralleled minority groups' desire to perform in deviant ways, which itself grew out of a desire to create cultural forms capable of presenting other forms of experience. There is an inherent deviancy in sitcom performance, and this deviancy is both offered as pleasure and celebrated. Wexman argues that 'Gleason's elaborately histrionic style' (2003, p. 57) in *The Honeymooners* was a deliberate response to the failure of existing forms of performance to adequately represent the rage of the working class. A similar argument can be made for the excessive, 'in-yer-face' (Sierz, 2001) style of Alternative Comedy sitcoms such as *The Young Ones* which explicitly stated its desire to be different from the conventions of series such as *The Good Life* (BBC 1: 1975–8). Sitcom acting, then, draws on traditions which forever attempt to mark it as different, and this has significant implications not only for analysis of representation in comedy, but also for examination of the genre as a whole.

Comedy, Performance and Character Duality

The display of performance in comic acting means there is always a tension between the coherence of the character which is being acted and the person who is acting it. While this tension is what marks stars as different to mere actors generally, for comedy it functions in a different way. That is, there is a requirement within comic acting itself to present that distinction and use it as part of the performance whether an actor is a star or not; indeed, sitcom acting is a style which foregrounds its very performativity, and relies on a distance between character and actor for the performance to be read as comic in the first place. There's a parallel between this style and the kinds of characters which are common in sitcom, for comedy often results from characters pretending to be something that they're not. Performance is itself part of the makeup of many sitcom charac-ters, in a variety of ways. In *I Love Lucy*, Lucy's dream is to be a performer, and many of the plots offer the character the opportunity to act this out while simultaneously allow-ing Ball the actress to display her performance skills. The comedy of *The Larry Sanders Show* often rests on the disparity between the reality of Larry off screen and the per-formance he gives on screen when presenting his television show. The other characters in *Friends* have pointed out that Chandler's comic ripostes are his response to emotional insecurity, with him making gags to cover up his real feelings or deflect impending ridicule. The narratives of *Only Fools and Horses* regularly require Del Boy to perform, inventing patter in an attempt to sell his dodgy goods, and then making up stories to conceal the resulting problems with them. And the whole of comedy vérité rests on find-ing comedy in the ways in which people start performing once a camera is turned on them, with David Brent in *The Office* constantly checking that what he's doing is being filmed by the television crew. Comedy, then, commonly arises from this mismatch between the 'reality' of a character and the ways in which they present themselves to lovers, bosses, customers and so on. Comedy characters are often those for whom per-formance is an everyday part of life, usually used to cover up the realities of the life they lead. Comic performance, then, requires acting which expresses this duality, using pre-tence which is convincing enough for the characters within the diegesis to be fooled, but displayed enough for the audience at home to read it as such.

However, this narrative requirement of characters to perform is common in serious acting too; after all, the most famous quote from a tragedy – Hamlet's 'to be or not to be' – is one in which the character discusses how he should react and present himself to those around him. Indeed, narratives are often about characters required to be other than they are, or coming to terms with something about themselves which allows them to exist and perform in new ways. This narrative requirement is not enough, then, to explain the kinds of comic performance which are apparent. Why should it be that com-edy is performed in a way different to that for seriousness, when the characters are often part of similar narratives? The answer is twofold. First, it is representative of the social distinctions made between seriousness and comedy which commonly require the two not to be confused, and which present comedy acting as performance because it is assumed that serious acting is 'normal'. Second and more importantly, though, it's a result of the ways in which such performance attempts to construct the reaction to the fiction which is being presented by it.

While comedy often acknowledges its audience, it also keeps that audience distanced, both literally and emotionally. The 'three-headed monster' shooting style keeps the cam-eras at a distance from the performers, so that we usually see much of their bodies and not just their faces. While this is logistically necessary in two-shots, one-shots, in which we get to see a character's reaction, are framed much wider than would be the case for serious drama or melodrama. This can be seen as a hangover from comedy's theatrical origins, in which audiences are always at a distance from the performers on stage. Yet as cinema and television developed their own language and as forms of naturalism came to dominate Western media, 'the change toward psychological realism was to shorten the distance between actors and camera' (Naremore, 1988, p. 38). One of the major selling points of cinema was that it allowed massive close-ups of the face, allowing audiences the opportunity to see emotional reactions to a degree never before possible (Williams, 1972, p. 181). The vast majority of television drama, in an attempt at psychological realism, functions by using close-ups at moments of tension and emotional reaction; this is the defining shooting characteristic of melodrama and can be repeatedly seen in soap opera. The close-up is a powerful tool which, while not actually allowing us into the character's psychology, at least signals that a fiction's interests lie there. Subsequently, it demands of its actors a particular kind of performance which responds to the closeness of the camera.

By adopting a different shooting style, comedy signals that it's not particularly interested in the psychology of its characters, or in them as realistic, believable, fully-formed human beings. Of course, comedy is understood and measured against certain aspects of realism, depending on the series, yet these are dispensable in the name of humour. For comedy to be successful, and for an audience to feel comfortable in finding the misfortunes of a character they may be fond of funny, shooting and performance must combine to construct a diegesis which is understandable, but which also displays itself as fiction and doesn't allow the audience to become too emotionally involved in the characters.

It is this difficult line which *Friends* always has to tread, for, while predominantly within the sitcom mode, the series also uses the conventions of melodrama and soap opera in its narrative, and relies on audiences' involvement with the emotional lives of its characters for some of its effectiveness. The continued tribulations of Ross and Rachel's relationship, followed by Chandler and Monica's relationship and subsequent marriage, have meant that the programme has had to come to terms with how to shoot and present comedy scenes in which an audience is invited to laugh at characters with whom they may have significant emotional ties, and which relies on that empathy for much of its success. The series, then, has always required David Schwimmer and Jennifer Aniston to flit between comic and melodramatic acting, with the latter much more to the fore in the scenes they share with no other characters. Towards the end of the series, the Bings's marriage was only conceivable as a storyline because Matthew Perry's developing acting style demonstrated he could play melodrama as much as he could play the detached, wisecracking Chandler. It is perhaps significant that, of all the men, it is the character of Joey which has taken the longest to get any long-term serious storyline, with his eventual love for Rachel. Joey's comedic performance has always been different to those of Ross and Chandler, both of whom repeatedly demonstrate a crippling self-awareness and social embarrassment which means their jokes are based around performance in social situations. Joey, however, is performed differently, for his funniness rests on an unintelligence of which he's not fully aware, and which therefore hasn't required Matt LeBlanc to demonstrate a duality of character in his performance; at least, not a duality which his character is aware of. There's an irony to this, considering Joey's an actor, and the programme has made much comic potential of his inability to act well, and his ignorance of his lack of skill. The display of an emotional side to Joey, and the requirement of the actor to perform genuine heartfelt emotions, was a significant risk in the series, inviting the audience to make sense of the character in a manner which could undermine the possibility of future comic distance. The fact that, on the whole, *Friends* has been wildly successful in marrying two performance modes which could destroy the effectivity of each other has, notably, not led to a proliferation of similar series. It's significant that in the spin-off series *Joey* the character has returned to his non-melodramatic roots, and is again paired with another character – his nephew Michael – who has a self-awareness that makes it difficult for him to perform success-fully socially.

This disparity between how characters really feel and think, and how they're required to perform by social conventions, can be seen in the ways comic actors use their bod-ies. Féral (1997) argues that performance can be distinguished from acting by the ways in which it places the performer's body as the subject of the audience's attention. Much Humour Theory works from the assumption that comedy displays the physical, when it is the mental and intellectual which are prized in most societies (Bergson, 1911; King, 2002, p. 92). It was this obsession with the body which led to Aristotle finding humour a dangerous social tool (1925); wit has always occupied an elevated social position above slapstick. In comedy, the body becomes vital to performance and characters are often constructed so as to be aware of their own physicality.

The most obvious contemporary example is Homer Simpson, whose physical pleasures are expressed in his lack of health, his sheer size and his 'Mmm' responses to words with a food connotation. In series such as *I Love Lucy*, *Roseanne* and *Fawlty Towers*, it is the body which is a site of difficulty and display. This is often contextualised within the dis-course of excess and most analyses of a performer such as Roseanne examine her bodily surplus. Ball's performance rests on her character's desire to be a certain kind of per-former, even though she's not physically skilled enough to perform at a professional level (while the audience marvels at the physical skills Ball displays in demonstrating her char-acter's lack of physical skills).

The farce element in much sitcom, best exemplified in *Fawlty Towers*, is one in which all of the running around demonstrates characters' needs to cover up things they don't want to be found out and thus maintain some kind of social acceptability. But it is per-formed in a way which shows that no matter what we aim to do intellectually we're always bound by the corporeal limits of our physicality. Basil Fawlty has to run every-where because his body is incapable of moving as fast as his mind can and his plans are

Fawlty Towers demonstrates that we're always bound by the corporeal limits of our physicality

forever thwarted by the physical, whether this is cars breaking down or the customers in his hotel. The most famous scene in the series is one in which Basil's mental frustration expresses itself initially through cognitive responses, but finally through physical ones. Having been knocked out but returned to work, Basil finds it extremely difficult not to mention World War II while taking the dinner order from some German guests. The scene plays through a number of conventional comic misunderstandings, but eventually results in Basil goose-stepping out of the dining room and into the lobby, much to the horror of his now upset guests. The scene works (and has become an oft-repeated British comedy classic) because it uses performance, body and display, in two ways simultaneously. First, within the narrative it represents Fawlty's complete failure to maintain control over his body, which ends up insulting his guests in as extreme a manner as possible. Second, it offers pleasure in seeing John Cleese as a performer using his long limbs to perform physical comedy akin to that he became famous for in the *Monty Python's Flying Circus* (BBC 1: 1969–74) sketch about the Ministry of Silly Walks (Critchley, 2002, p. 44). The fact that this moment in *Fawlty Towers* gets a round of applause from the audience on the laugh track signals it is being read not just as a great joke, but also as a memorable piece of comic performance exemplifying that which the audience wants to see from this particular performer. The pleasure lies both within and outside the text, as a comic moment in which Fawlty and Cleese are one, the comic pleasure possible from each being presented simultaneously. The fact that Cleese is often requested by fans to 'do his silly walk', completely removed from the context of the episode, demonstrates how this has become a piece of performance in which Cleese's physical skill is demonstrated and his display as a performer is central to its understanding.

The performance style of sitcom is one, then, which actively displays the relationship between the audience and the performer, presenting the actor as a skilled performer demonstrating their skills in moments of comic business which, while arising from narrative, often have little narrative purpose themselves. These moments of business often rely on excess, usually physical though sometimes emotional or linguistic, and commonly rely on the audience's knowledge of the performer for their funniness. The whole is filmed within the sitcom look, which while efficiently capturing the performance within a theatrical frame, emotionally distances the audience from the action. Recent aesthetic changes in some sitcom have not led to the end of these characteristics; instead, it has resulted in the use of the conventions of other forms to achieve the same textual ends. These conventions, while developed in a particular way by sitcom to best realise its serial, narrative nature, still have significant similarities to those in other comedic forms, in any media. Comic performance is a rigidly controlled aspect of acting, in which series' purposes are signalled clearly, audience responses are cued and responded to, and the whole maintains its distinction from seriousness as clearly as possible. The consequences of the recurring theme of duality in sitcom characters will be explored below with reference to *Will and Grace*, for it has significant implications for debates about representation and stereotyping.

The Pleasures of Performance

It's impossible to understand the role performance plays in sitcom without examining the kinds of pleasures it offers and the ways in which audiences react to these. While this could be argued of any media, sitcom is one of the few genres which actively acknowledges its pleasurable intentions and incorporates their consequences. The laugh track remains, above all others, the defining aspect of sitcom, garnering much more academic interest than similar audience involvement in genres such as the quiz show and talk show. It's important in sitcom because rather than merely acknowledging the audience's existence, it functions as a record of their pleasure. We hear the audience laugh and clap, the audible signals of successful comedy. We don't hear the audience tut at badly-performed sequences or groan at poor jokes. And, as has been noted, these pleasurable responses often rely on the audience's understandings of characters and the performers who play them. The success of catchphrases in much British sitcom must work this way, as they are inexplicable through conventional Humour Theory which requires surprise. Catchphrases work in exactly the opposite way; the pleasure rests not in what is going to be said – it's always the same – but what narrative developments will result in the character uttering it. The pleasure garnered by an audience here is in seeing a performer do what's expected of them, and often that pleasure is delayed, by both script and performer, as much as possible.

Thus Victor Meldrew's 'I don't believe it' in *One Foot in the Grave* could be uttered at pretty much any point in any episode, as the series is based around the accumulation of unbelievable misunderstandings and incompetences. Episodes conventionally use the catchphrase as rarely as possible, often leaving it until the end, when the accumulation of absurdities is at its extreme. Moreover, Richard Wilson, playing Meldrew, performs the catchphrase in a manner which signals his awareness of its potential, often spluttering some incomprehensible grunts of disbelief before saying it which, while narratively explicable as the inability of a confused character to articulate his feelings, simultaneously cue an audience to the impending performance of that which they find pleasurable. Audience pleasure here is one almost of joining in and the delayed performance of the catchphrase cues an audience succinctly.

Thus the catchphrase, and the performer's delayed presentation of it, helps to bind the audience together as a common group – what Bourdon calls 'a connection of people to people' (2000, p. 534) – all of whom are interested in the same pleasures and who recognise and understand the conventions of the programme they're watching. The laugh track tries to suggest to any individual viewer that their pleasures are the same as those of others, binding together an audience in a manner which discourages alternative readings of a text, at least if pleasure is to be gained. In this way, sitcom constructs its audience and the intended reading of its text in a very active manner, clearly offering the pleasures which its audience most craves.

For this reason, the audience must be understood as part of the performance. Performers respond to the ways in which audiences react to the comedy which is performed for them, and this is more than simply allowing them time to laugh. The kinds of jokes, characters and performances which get the most positive response are likely to be more common in future episodes of any long-running series. This happens more rapidly in American sitcom where episodes are recorded as previous ones are being broadcast, and writers can therefore play up those aspects of a series which seem to be getting the most enthusiastic audience responses. The ways in which Frasier was kept on as a regular character in *Cheers*, and the occasional use of the originally non-speaking Gunther in *Friends*, demonstrate how the episodic development of sitcom relies on the interplay between the performance and the audience. While recent developments in analysis of media consumption have been keen to highlight the notion of audience power and the possibility of the meanings of texts being interpreted in a wide variety of ways by individuals, this has commonly worked from the assumption that the text is still primarily the product of the industry that produces it. So, while audiences have power of interpretation, they don't have power of production. In sitcom, this clearly isn't the case; the audience is part of the production process, an essential aspect of the recording process and an element in the text which is eventually broadcast, creating what Counsell calls 'the dialogic space' (2000,

p. 206). The sitcom therefore offers useful insights into the relationship between audience and industry, suggesting fruitful avenues of analysis on debates about that relationship.

The pleasures offered by sitcom performance are not only those involved in the momentary enjoyment of jokes. Analysis of the genre has repeatedly focused upon the ways in which the jokes work, what they say about social ideology, and why audiences should find such stuff funny. As has been noted, though, a series such as *Friends* also functions through melodrama, and therefore offer the empathic pleasures vital to that genre. Many series of *Friends* have ended on a cliffhanger, and these have usually been centred not on comedy, but on the emotional lives of the characters. The end of the first series, in which Rachel discovers Ross's love for her and goes to the airport to meet him, while the audience sees Ross get off the plane with his new girlfriend Julie, could be presented as a useful narrative twist with lots of comic potential. However, the performance of Jennifer Aniston, who, in the final shot, is given a long, slow zoom into close-up, is one in which the display of her genuine emotional feelings are made evident. The addition of music which cues the scene as 'serious' results in a scene which offers the audience pleasures often ignored by sitcom analysis; it contains not a single joke. The development of audience involvement in characters' emotional lives is also evident in *Only Fools and Horses*, with marriages, break-ups, the birth of children and, most notably, a miscarriage. And even in a series such as *The Simpsons*, conventionally analysed as cynical and gag-based, pleasures are available in the repeated examination of the emotional relationships between the family, with many episodes about the work carried out by Lisa and Homer to make sense of one another and display their mutual love. To define the sitcom as a genre fixated on comedy is certainly to pinpoint its most defining characteristic, but it's also to miss a large amount of pleasure which the genre offers. And those other pleasures arise from performance as much as the comic ones do.

So, a complexity is required in examining the comedy performance which such series present. While the majority of analyses of sitcom performance attempt to make sense of the ways in which these people are funny, the examination of comedy actors' abilities to switch between serious and comic modes has been largely ignored. Sitcom performance is not purely comic performance, just as all comic performance, in theatre, stand-up, film and radio, often uses a variety of interpretive modes. If sitcom rests on its relationship with its audience, then non-comic moments of sitcom must signal themselves as such and be performed in an appropriate manner, for them to be interpreted as desired.

It would also be useful to examine the ways in which performances are sometimes unpleasurable. That is, the majority of negative academic criticism of the genre focuses

Seinfeld: why don't I find it funny?

on its reactionary nature, as if sitcom only fails if its ideologies are inappropriate. However, it's apparent that there are other reasons why audiences don't like particular sitcoms, and one could be the way they are performed. Certainly, I find *Seinfeld* virtually unwatchable, and know I'm in a minority for saying so. Yet my problem with the programme has nothing to do with its politics, setting, characters, or any other of a number of factors; I just think it's really badly performed, with an overeager excessiveness that feels like the programme is trying too hard to demonstrate its funniness. For a series that's won so many awards and contains such fondly-remembered characters as George and Kramer, the question arises as to why I'm incapable of getting the same kinds of pleasures from those performances which are phenomenally successful with most people. Trying to make sense of, and define, 'bad' acting is virtually impossible and certainly comes down to the individual. Why *Seinfeld* should bother me so much when I marvel at similar acting in *Will and Grace*, which many people find excessive, is a question that's impossible to solve without engaging in audience studies. The bigger point is that performance is as capable of creating displeasure as its opposite, and the ways and reasons why individual audience members are incapable of enjoying acting which sends others into fits of laughter clearly demonstrate the variety of ways in which sitcom can be made sense of. And while I've repeatedly argued that sitcom can be enjoyed for reasons above and beyond its funniness, it's highly unlikely that someone who finds the comic acting of a particular series unpleasurable will ignore those bits and instead watch it for the serious stuff. So, while sitcom can be enjoyed for a range of reasons, its funniness remains its overriding attraction.

The variety of ways in which pleasure can be offered and understood by performance, and its role within sitcom, demonstrate the difficulties in making sense of what the genre is about and, more importantly, contributes to the recurrent debate about whether it's progressive or not. Gray notes that 'there is a bland assumption that the [comic] experience of both sexes is identical' (1994, p. 14); while there is work that has questioned this notion, the assumption still broadly holds that while men and women may laugh at different things, recognising the intention to be funny, as well as comedy being the main pleasure of watching sitcom, applies across the board. For Gray the variety of pleasures which sitcom offers contradict themselves, with performance vital to the acceptance of comedy as undermining social conventions. Like Mellencamp (1992), Gray maligns the narratives of *I Love Lucy* which contain Ball, while applauding the opportunities they offer her to demonstrate her comic skill. For Gray, the resulting 'embarrassment' she feels (1994, p. 50) is representative of this tension, as if finding such comedy funny is a guilty pleasure which demeans her own gender. Analysing performance becomes vital, then, for it is here where critics of the genre have managed to find vestiges of comedy's radical potential. As Goldman notes, 'Some comic effects may derive from the reduction of the human to the status of the automaton, but the comic actor is never an automaton' (1975, pp. 89–90). Similarly, performance offers useful insights into the relationship between text, industry and audience, with the examination of the laugh track and the star aspect of performers affecting how narratives and series are constructed and how they are understood by audiences. The precise radical potential of any performance, as well as the ways in which it responds to, and represents, the goal of audience pleasure, will, however, always be dependent on specific series, episodes, performers and audience members.

Will and Grace	Case Study

The variety of ways in which performance and acting can be understood, and the important relationship they have with audience readings and enjoyment are demonstrated in *Will and Grace*. This series has been read as significant in the history of sitcom because of its continued popularity despite two of its main characters being gay, particularly considering *Ellen*'s (ABC: 1994–8) ratings decline once its title character came out (McCarthy, 2001, p. 595). While American sitcom has a (limited) history of gay characters, mainstream success has eluded series whose understanding requires an empathy and understanding towards (some aspects of) gay culture. The continued success of *Will and Grace* is perhaps more startling considering it was originally scheduled among *Friends* and *Scrubs*, both of which squarely revolve around the complexities of heterosexuality. Clearly *Will and Grace* is mainstream sitcom in its setting, shooting style and narratives, all of which mark the series out as unremarkable in comparison to other series; indeed, it is *Scrubs* which looks the more stylistically progressive programme.

That *Will and Grace* has been criticised for the ways in which it represents homosexuality is discussed in the next chapter. Suffice to say that, like many sitcoms which have been lauded for successfully including sympathetic and likeable depictions of underrepresented groups, critics have argued that the requirement to appease mainstream audiences leads to portrayals which not only simplify groups or cultures, but which support the ideologies of white, male, middle-class audiences. For Battles and Hilton-Morrow the character of Will is one whose homosexuality is repeatedly signalled by his being 'effeminized' (2002, p. 90) within comic moments and stories as a whole. While they sometimes note how this works in terms of performance – most notably Will's excessive emotional outbursts in a high-pitched voice – their primary concern is the series' narrative. Here they note that while Will's masculinity is demonstrated through his career as a successful lawyer, his romantic and emotional failures, coupled with the few episodes which depict his interaction with men he fancies, forever foreground his femininity. This is supported by Will's relationship with Grace, which not only positions his heterosexual friend as more supportive than the gay community represented by Jack, but is also always narratively understood in terms of the romantic history they share. Because of this, it's possible to read the series as one whose primary narrative interest, like Ross and Rachel in *Friends*, concerns whether the two leads will ever get together, with Will's homosexuality nothing more than an extra narrative dilemma to be resolved (presumably through Grace managing to 'turn' him). By this reckoning, *Will and Grace* fails to depict homosexuality as desir-

able or unproblematic and instead repeatedly distinguishes between Will as a homosexual and Will as a person by failing to make his sexuality a 'natural' part of his character.

Battles and Hilton-Morrow similarly critique the programme's supporting characters, Jack and Karen. For them, Jack represents little more than 'the stereotype of the flamboyant gay man' (2002, p. 91), in which homosexuals who get to have sex with men are self-centred and emotionally immature; against this, Will's asexual homosexual becomes the sympathetic gay character (straight) audiences can respect. Therefore 'Will and Jack are extreme opposites on the spectrum of possible media representations of gay men' (Hart, 2003, pp. 272–3). Like Jack, Karen's cavalier attitude towards sex, drugs and alcohol is not couched within a mature adult character, and instead 'she is a screwball character not to be taken seriously' (Battles and Hilton-Morrow, 2002, p. 98). Such representation insists on a distinction between sexual activity and social maturity, meaning that while a gay character can be socially successful, this 'cannot in any way suggest that being gay has anything to do with erotic desires and practices' (Fejes, 2000, p. 116). Furthermore, it is Will and Grace who conform to idealised American ideals, by working hard and being good-looking; Jack and Karen, too self-centred and too interested in the pleasures of the flesh, are characterised by their hatred of 'proper' work and, through excessive performance and continued references to Karen's outsize breasts, are instead individuals who fail to make a proper contribution to society.

However, by examining the ways in which these four characters exist within performance rather than narrative, a quite different understanding of their meanings, the pleasures associated with them, and the broader socio-political implications of them can be outlined. As has been noted, the requirements of comic performance are ones focused on excess, in which an over-the-top display of excessive emotional response or physical absurdity not only signals a text's comic intent overall, but constitutes the specific comic moments within it. It is not hard to see that *Will and Grace* employs the pleasures of excess repeatedly and to an extent not seen in mainstream comedy for some time. This is particularly true for Jack and Karen; while the former's vocal tonal range far exceeds that which would be expected in serious drama, the latter's voice is absurd enough to be in and of itself funny.

Jack and Karen constantly move around in a bodily-excessive manner so that their physicality can never be ignored and this, in tandem with their interest in bodily pleasures, demonstrates their focus on the physical over the intellectual. While Will and Grace don't perform to these excesses, it's apparent that movement and speed are vital to the programme's humour, particularly in terms of entrances and exits. Indeed, one of the ways in which *Will and Grace* distinguishes itself from most other sitcoms is through the high-speed delivery of linguistic wit and puns. These often take place between Will and Grace, and are shot to highlight the rapidity of the banter; commonly one character is in the kitchen and the other is in the living-room, and the programme rapidly crosscuts from one performer to another as they speak. The implied difficulty for the director and editor in keeping up with the quickfire dialogue gives the impression of a skilful performance by two professional comic actors, whose theatricality is almost too quick for the mechanics of television. In

Will and Grace illustrates the recurring debates about sitcom's representation of homosexual characters

these moments, the series offers audiences the pleasures of those jokes within the programme's diegesis, as well as enjoyment of the interplay between the actors performing them. That these moments offer pleasurable performance is shown by the fact that you could remove many of them from an episode and the story and the characters would still make sense.

Sitcom is a genre which must be understood through its entertainment function, and this is often focused on moments rather than narrative; furthermore, those moments often demonstrate the performance skills of a programme's star(s). It is unsurprising, then, that so much comedy is about performance itself, and is commonly structured to give actors spaces in which to demonstrate their skills. Seidman's 'comedian comedy' (1981, 2003) suggests that comedy frequently offers the pleasures of the 'extrafictional'; that is, 'anything that interrupts the smooth exposition of a fictional universe' (2003, p. 21). Seidman demonstrates this through reference to a number of films where the comedian acknowledges the audience by deliberately looking directly at the camera. These extrafictional features are apparent in many comic forms and help distinguish them from the realist/narrative expectations of much serious fiction. For both Seidman and King (2002) comedy stars often have access to the 'extrafictional' through their performance more than anything else. While sitcom rarely allows its characters to acknowledge its viewers, the theatrical shooting style, coupled with the laugh track, allows the text to recognise the necessity of an audience; indeed, the recent trend towards comedy vérité (Mills, 2004a) is one which has allowed sitcom characters to look directly into the camera, even though within such series' diegeses the characters aren't aware of their funniness.

So, while the narratives and diegesis of *Will and Grace* don't acknowledge the audience, the programme's use of the conventional characteristics of sitcom means that the programme as a whole does. To this end it is like all sitcoms, which acknowledge and exploit their artificiality for their comic intent to function successfully. Yet *Will and Grace* takes this further, by also being about the nature of representation and performance. That is, the roles which each of the characters play within the series, coupled with the ways in which each of them is performed, clearly signals to an audience the characters' awareness of at least some aspects of their artificiality. Even more common is that their performance demonstrates their awareness that they are required to fulfil a certain social role and set of behaviour patterns.

For example, much humour in the series is derived from Jack's vocal and physical excesses. These are often coupled with dialogue which signals his refusal to conform to social norms of mature responsibility; in these instances, Jack's not aware that he's being funny, and, for the audience, he is so only in comparison to dominant ideological structures of how to behave. Yet Jack also has many lines in which he's fully aware that he's being funny and, in accordance with his excessive performance of homosexuality, these are often 'bitchy' putdowns of other characters. These are frequently about Will and Grace's sexual failures and Will's 'failure' as a homosexual, whether in sexual activity or general lifestyle. The two comedic aspects of Jack's character – one of which he's aware of, the other which he isn't – are performed differently. The former is usually much more excessive, and this demonstrates its artificiality and Jack's awareness of the role he is playing.

Jack's characterisation and performance can only be understood, then, with reference to 'the camp emphasis upon the performative aspects of everyday life' (Tinkcom, 2002, p. 122) which are demonstrated 'through a combination of irony, aestheticism, theatricality, and humor' (Cohan, 2002, p. 103). While these aspects are common within much comedy, they become camp in the character of Jack through his awareness of their artificiality and his subsequent willingness to take pleasure in deliberately inhabiting them. Jack exudes camp and he demonstrates the relationship between it, theatricality and performance, and how these may or may not be connected to homosexuality. His theatricality is clearly demonstrated in his desire to be a successful actor, and he 'stars' in his one-man show, 'Just Jack', performing excessive song-and-dance routines and (ironically) poorly executed comedy. His dialogue is littered with references to musical and iconic camp performers, culminating in the appearance of Cher on the programme; that Jack refuses to believe that he's talking to the real Cher rather than an impersonator because she doesn't look excessive enough demonstrates the camp sensibility which is about surface rather than content. Similarly, an episode which guest stars Matt Damon as Jack's secretly straight rival for a place in a gay choir tour works comically because it acknowledges camp as a performative style which can be adopted and performed by anyone, including a heterosexual. In the episode, Damon's guest star status clearly responds to his Hollywood connotations of masculinity and the audience enjoys seeing such a star performing camp. That Damon becomes a serious rival to Jack merely by wearing a tight t-shirt, 'buffing up', and singing excessively, means the comedy in the series positions Jack's campness not as a necessary result of his homosexuality, but instead merely a particular form of behaviour. Jack admonishes Damon, arguing that campness should be reserved for gays, demonstrating an awareness of his own performative choices.

By this reading Will becomes quite a different character. Battles and Hilton-Morrow outline a number of comic scenes in the series in which Will's homosexuality is equated with a lack of masculinity. Yet to argue that such portrayals suggest a limitation on the ways in which gays can be represented ignores the variety of other ways in which Will is shown, for he demonstrates a number of ways in which homosexuality can be performed, of which camp is only one. The verbal wit and high-speed banter of the series are often played through puns and the ironies of language and Will consistently demonstrates his ability at such joking. Such humour suggests a large amount of self-awareness on the part of Will, who's able to make jokes about others and himself which require him to see those gags as merely funny and not intentionally hurtful. Chandler and Joey on *Friends* are different because one of them has a lot of self-knowledge while the other doesn't, and the same distinction can be made between Will and Jack. The willingness to mock oneself – also an aspect of Grace's character – requires not only an awareness of the self's foibles, but also an emotional detachment from them which means such joking is not upsetting. That the series, like much sitcom, involves characters constantly making jokes about one another while simultaneously supplying the required emotional support network, means that the humour, within the diegesis, lacks bite. Indeed, it is difficult to understand the pleasures a television audience would get from characters being so horrible to one another if the diegesis suggested they really meant it. This kind of mockery is, then, an aspect of everyday performance which all four characters revel in as part of their normal inter-action. This can be shown by the reaction shots of joke butts in the programme, which are rarely angry but instead acknowledge the skill of the putdown.

Subsequently, Will's lack of masculinity is not an unconscious character trait but instead an accumulation of self-aware moments of camp display. That is, there are significant differences in the ways in which the character of Will is played depending on the tone and narrative function of the scene and the characters he's interacting with. Serious and emotional scenes with Grace are performed in a muted manner, with little physical movement and slower delivery, and such scenes commonly involve fewer edits and camera movements. Scenes between Will and Jack, how-ever, are performed and edited much faster, and often involve more obviously comic moments. It is in such scenes that Will is regularly portrayed – by himself and other characters – as lacking masculinity. Yet such jokes are performed in a manner which signals Will's awareness of the camp requirements of conversation with Jack; in this sense, Will is explicitly playing a role. The range of performances which makes up Will – some of which are diegetically 'truthful', and some of which are Will himself deliberately performing for the pleasure of other characters – demonstrates the range of possibilities available to this gay man, only some of which are centred on his mascu-linity. Will's lack of masculinity is an (untrue) aspect of his character which he's willing to play with and, more importantly, happily offers to the other characters for their mockery, precisely because it's meaningless. However, to refuse to partake in such camp bitchery when it arises is shown to be cutting your nose off to spite your face; the performance clearly signals that Will enjoys – now and again – such camp slanging matches with his friends. If this wasn't the case, why would he hang out with them? The series thus offers 'the unprecedented spectacle of gay subcultural interaction depicted as a practice of shared pleasure for those involved' (Castiglia and Reed, 2004, p. 163).

Battles and Hilton-Morrow's analysis which suggests the series 'emphasizes characters' inter-personal relationships rather than the characters' connection to the larger social world' (2002, p. 87) is similarly a complaint which examines only narrative and not performance. While the char-acters' interests in the series may be repeatedly inward-looking and narcissistic, the ways in which they're performed can only make sense with reference to larger social structures. That is, Jack and Will's differing uses of campness are understandable because of the social construction of homo-sexuals as camp; yet their different ways of performing this, and the self-awareness which accompanies it, renders camp as an artificial structure which can be enjoyed – both as an audience and as a performer – but which isn't a necessary aspect of homosexuality. Similarly, the series is criticised because of the ways in which it presents the gay 'conscience' as one voiced by Grace, for she 'seems to suffer the burden or consequences of Will's sexuality' (p. 100). An example is an episode in which Will's date, Matt, refuses to come out to his boss, requiring Will to pretend he's Matt's brother. After coaxing from Grace, Will eventually forces the issue, and the relationship ends. Battles and Hilton-Morrow argue that this simple moment suggests coming out is easy and doesn't acknowledge the difficulties likely to be faced by gay characters. Yet the fact that the sto-ryline is treated – narratively and performatively – as an 'issue', culminating in a speech by Will in which he states he can't go on lying, and the whole is acted in a very serious manner, clearly implies some sort of social convention which makes such decisions difficult. Indeed, the fact that the episode still 'makes sense' even though it doesn't acknowledge and examine the possible homophobic consequences must surely suggest that such difficulties are assumed by an audience, and therefore don't need to be explicitly stated.

In these ways, *Will and Grace* highlights the difficulties in examining the meanings on offer in sitcom, the ideologies they rely on for their jokes and the problems inherent in ignoring aspects of performance. Through a display of performance, *Will and Grace* makes links between the artificial presentation style of conventional sitcom and the performative excesses of camp. The ways in which the series moves from comic moments and scenes to serious ones often mirrors its shift from those in which the characters are aware of their own foibles and are willing to play with them, and those where they are not. As comedy so often requires such artificiality of performance, it seems the perfect mode in which to present, and explore, the nature of performance and representation within society, particularly in American sitcom which commonly centres on self-aware, wisecracking, comedians as characters. The lack of critical vocabulary examining performance and acting is a significant barrier to examining sitcom and the avoidance of the investigation of it has led to readings of sitcom which ignore this fundamental role. This has resulted in a history of analysis of sitcom, and comedy as a whole, focused on narrative without an understanding of how such narratives are presented to viewers. It is therefore unsurprising that one aspect of sitcom which has been repeatedly maligned is its representational strategies, which are explored in the next chapter.

Chapter 4 | Sitcom and Representation

Negative equity is when your mortgage is more than your house is worth . . . Not funny, if you've got it, but it might make you see the funny side of Edward and Priscilla's dilemma. Or, to put it another way, watching their farcical trials and tribulations might make you feel better about your negative equity, especially as the episode ends with the Springfields reconciled to staying where they are. I often feel that sitcom has that kind of therapeutic social effect.

David Lodge, *Therapy* (London: Secker & Warburg, 1995), p. 104.

All in the Family led to heated debates about sitcom and humour, representation, offence and acceptability

In January 2005 the BBC broadcast the most complained about programme in the history of British broadcasting. The content of *Jerry Springer – The Opera* included multiple swear words, Springer trying to solve the conflict between God and the Devil, and jokes about Jesus' stigmata. Led by a group called Christian Voice, the BBC was swamped with over 60,000 email complaints and pickets outside its offices. Security guards were posted at the houses of senior management, and at least one BBC producer resigned. The opera had been running in a London theatre for quite some time without much complaint, but its appearance on television led to a furore whose consequences, at the time of writing, were not clear. While not a sitcom, *Jerry Springer – The Opera* demonstrates the difficulties in incorporating particular ideas and characters within comedy and is only the latest in a long line of comic television programmes which have ignited debates about humour, representation, offence and acceptability. In America, major debates have centred on programmes such as *Amos 'n' Andy* (CBS: 1951–3), *All in the Family*, *Mary Hartman, Mary Hartman* (syndicated: 1976–7), *Murphy Brown* (CBS: 1988–98), *The Simpsons*, *South Park*, *Beavis and Butt-head* and *Ellen*; in Britain, similar discussions have focused on *Till Death Us Do Part*, *Love Thy Neighbour* (ITV: 1972–6), *Mind Your Language* (ITV: 1977–9), *'Allo 'Allo!* (BBC 1: 1982–92), *The Young Ones*, *Rab C. Nesbitt* (BBC 2: 1989–99), *Brass Eye*, *The Crouches* (BBC 1: 2003–) and the yet to be broadcast animated sitcom, *Popetown* (BBC). These programmes all demonstrate that for large sections of the audience the content of sitcom is highly significant and how it represents the world can be extremely important.

More than anything else, sitcom has been examined in terms of its representational strategies. While representation has been a major force in the analysis of media for some time, the fact that it has dominated analysis of the sitcom to an extent unseen for other genres demonstrates certain assumptions. It assumes that comedy has a particular relationship to representation. It is argued that as comedy is more likely to fail if it requires too much thought to work the jokes out, it has to draw on a range of simplistic character types which are easily understandable. While sitcoms may develop more fully 'complex' characters over a number of series, the characters within it must be easily recognisable in the first instance in order for audiences to find them funny at all. This is unlike other serious fictional forms, where the gradual revelation of character psychology and motivation can be a vital part of narrative development and sometimes the driving force behind the programme as a whole. However, it's also argued that such character types aren't insignificant and instead they must draw on wider social assumptions about people for their effectiveness. That is, the six character types on show in *Friends* are not only funny solely because of the way they act in the programme, but because they relate to dominant social assumptions about rich Jewish daughters (Rachel), new-age hippies (Phoebe), actors (Joey), university lecturers (Ross) and so on. Sitcom can, then, be read as an indicator of the ways in which the audience it's produced for feels about individuals and groups.

This gives sitcom a much more significant social role than it is commonly afforded. As the analysis of genre and the social position of comedy showed, sitcom is commonly seen as a form with less social significance than 'factual' television and 'serious' fiction. In terms of representation, however, the genre has been read as a useful reflection of general social attitudes, with the growth and reduction of certain character types over time mirroring broader attitudes within society (or, perhaps more accurately, within the television industry which produces the series and the institutional bodies which regulate them). Indeed, the histories of American sitcom outlined by Hamamoto (1989), Marc (1989) and Jones (1992) see the genre as serving little purpose other than reflecting attitudinal developments in American society. The sitcom has remained the main television genre to be analysed this way in America because of its ratings dominance there for a number of decades; in Britain, however, the soap opera is usually seen as the genre most accurately representing the *Zeitgeist*.

Examining sitcom's representational strategies is not confined solely to the worlds of academia. The assumption that sitcom's representations have some sort of significance has led to a whole raft of institutional bodies, regulations, audience pressure groups and campaigning bodies which focus much of their work on it. In America, organisations such as GLAAD (Gay and Lesbian Alliance Against Defamation), NAACP (the National Association for the Advancement of Colored People) and the Jewish Anti-Defamation League monitor and report on the frequency and type of representations which broadcasting offers, relative to 'real world' percentages (see Dow, 2001; Zurawik, 2003, p. 3; Montgomery, 1989). For such organisations, the numerical breakdown of characters on television should mirror that of society as a whole. These bodies also produce reports examining the ways in which characters are represented, again comparing them to some kind of 'truthful' or 'acceptable' representation. In Britain, there is a long history of regulatory bodies – the Independent Television Commission, the Broadcasting Standards Commission and, more recently, OfCom – who are publicly funded to adjudicate on public complaints about the ways in which individuals, social groups and organisations are represented within broadcasting. Yet measuring media representations against the 'real world' is highly problematic because it fails to take into account the specifics of any particular genre or form. For sitcom this is a complex matter, as its need to be funny is seen as calling into question some of the boundaries which are assumed for serious programming. So, the Broadcasting Standards Commission granted comedy a 'special freedom' (1998, p. 24) without explicitly stating what that means or how it functions within specific series. Complaints about unfair or offensive representations are often greeted with the response that the complainer has no sense of humour, which is a damning criticism in British society. Certainly adjudications made by regulatory bodies about television sitcom attempt to take into account its funniness, even though many would argue that it's the comic aspects of some programmes which are precisely the problem.

Such debates are complex and unlikely to be resolved to the satisfaction of all parties. What disagreements do signal, however, is the assumption that how sitcom represents people and groups is important and that comedy isn't a licence to say or do anything. This is a battle over content which is resolutely public and has an institutional legitimacy. So, while there aren't organisations battling over the generic boundaries of sitcom, there are ones battling over its representations. And even though this is apparent for broadcasting as a whole, assumptions about the relationship between society and comedy generally, plus the dominance of the genre in America, make sitcom a ripe battleground. In that sense, it is within representation that sitcom is seen to actually *matter*. And while this is partly because comedy is conventionally read as reflecting social attitudes, broader assumptions about media effects – even though these are still hotly contested by researchers – mean that it is presumed that 'incorrect' representations within sitcom could have far-reaching consequences. As will be shown, the ways in which this debate is structured, and how it is applied to sitcom, demonstrate the complex arguments about representation as a whole, of which sitcom is only a part.

Debates about Representation

If the ways in which representation takes place matter, it's only because there is seen to be some disparity between the ways media characterises people and how they 'really' are. In most cases, problems occur because it's felt that media portrayals conform to limiting and outdated assumptions about people, based on such characteristics as race, age, gender, nationality and sexuality. This is the process known as stereotyping. In individualistic Western societies, stereotyping is criticised for two reasons. First, it is simplistic, merely reproducing representations borne out of previous ones, and failing to take into account the variety of ways in which people live, think and behave. Second, it is seen as feeding into understandings of people outside media, so that society makes assumptions about groups and individuals which fail to account for their complexity. The first criticism is an aesthetic one, the second a social one. While stereotyping is a process connected to a broad range of media and cultural products, its relationship to the sitcom works in particular ways, demonstrating the specific characteristics of the genre and comedy.

This is because comedy is commonly examined, in its social context, though its relationship to social power, and stereotyping more generally has connections to power too. For many, one of the ways in which power exerts itself socially is through comedy. It is those who are powerful who often have the authority to make the move from serious to comic discourse, as well as signalling what can and can't be joked about. Certainly Riggs's statement that the 'list of unproductive stereotyping [of elderly people] is voluminous, especially in comedies' (1998, p. 7) is seen to demonstrate that group's general lack of social power. Similarly, bosses have a certain legitimacy in telling jokes which subordinates must acknowledge, even if the jokes themselves aren't funny; much of the humour of *The Office* comes out of the embarrassment expressed by the staff at their boss's jokes, and they are powerless to question his inappropriate humour. Brent has to be the boss for his comedy to be (consciously) unchallenged and it's telling that, in the second series, when he becomes subordinate to another, his use of humour changes radically. *The Office* is a comedy about humour and power, where the latter is expressed through the former. Much of Brent's humour works through the application of stereotypes, often about gender and the inclusion of a wheelchair-using character in the second series results in his internal battles as he attempts to include her in his jokes while struggling not to stereotype her in an obviously offensive manner. As the series shows, the wheelchair-using character can do little to fight back against Brent's unavowed stereotyping precisely because her lowly status in the office doesn't give her the legitimacy to invoke any comic power she might have.

Yet there is a distinction to be drawn between the ways in which comedy might work in terms of power within society and within sitcom. First, and most pertinently, sitcom is a fictional dramatic form, existing within a discourse quite different to that of social comedy. The ways in which sitcom represents characters arise out of the conventions and history of the genre and these must be understood and accepted for the jokes to be pleasurable. Second, comedy is seen to express power through the relationship between the joke-teller, the audience and the butt. In social comedy, this relationship can be an extremely close one and jokes which could be deemed offensive by certain audiences can be rendered acceptable because of the intimacy between everyone involved in the joke exchange. For example, a joke which stereotypes men for their sexual inadequacy could be rendered inoffensive if told between long-term friends for whom the joke has little meaning other than its comic value; told by a woman it may be rendered threatening, just as it would be if told by a man unknown by the joke's butt. Here, then, the possible meaning of the joke, and its resulting acceptability, is affected by the context of its consumption. This becomes problematic for the sitcom, though, because the context is quite different. For a start, jokes told on sitcoms are being presented to a mass audience whose possible reactions are various. By reaching a much larger audience, the potential offensiveness is multiplied. This is exacerbated by broadcasters' inability to control the context within which a text is consumed; a programme benign when watched with friends may become offensive once it's watched with parents, for example. Social comedy usually knows exactly who its audience is and designs its jokes precisely in response to that audience; while different channels and different parts of the broadcasting schedule allow broadcasters some control over the audience, this is not a watertight process.

Power and stereotyping are also affected by the nature of broadcasting. Unlike much social comedy, broadcast sitcom allows little opportunity for audiences and butts to respond to the kinds of comedy presented to them. That is, an audience or butt in social comedy has the opportunity to 'get their own back' by telling a joke as a comeback, or simply informing a joke-teller that their material is unacceptable and this can usually take place in the same arena, at the same time, as the original joke. Yet while broadcasters and regulatory bodies have systems set up to receive complaints about offensive representations, the fact that these take months to investigate, plus the fact that the resulting adjudication is unlikely to reach as large an audience as the original joke, renders the audience or butt for a joke relatively powerless. Similarly, the oft-invoked argument that anyone offended by television material can simply turn their set off is of little help, for offended viewers are aware that not only have they failed to prevent the material existing, but that it's still likely to be consumed by large audiences. It is, then, the mass audience of television as a whole which means that debates about the nature of comic representation matter.

The existence of such material on television also lends it a connotation of acceptability. For example, the BBC's remit to broadcast material representative of British society and function as some kind of uniting force, means that its programming has an implication of authority which legitimises its portrayals. The kinds of humour offered by broadcasting therefore tell us the ways in which the media see the audience, or, the kind of audience the broadcaster wishes us to be. The movement away from certain 'stereotyped' representations of race and gender which were acceptable in comedy in previous decades suggests that broadcasters no longer legitimise certain kinds of jokes and that other forms of comedy should now be acceptable to an audience. The ways in which niche audiences signal their difference by using kinds of comedy clearly unacceptable on more mainstream channels – such as *South Park* on Comedy Central in America and Channel 4 in Britain – help define the kinds of audience which those channels are trying to attract. There is, then, still a significant relationship between joke-teller, audience and butt, and channels and scheduling are two of the ways in which broadcasters attempt to work within these constraints.

Yet there is a difficulty here, because the concept of a joke-teller becomes problematised within broadcasting. In social comedy if someone tells me a joke I find offensive, it's easy to pinpoint the perpetrator and tell them what I think of them. For television sitcom, however, pinpointing the actual teller of the joke is more difficult. While most jokes are performed by an actor playing a role – that is, they are voiced by an individual in a manner identical to that of social humour – it is not as if that performer is the joke-teller. Instead, the teller is the broadcaster even though the joke would not have been written by that broadcaster, but by a writer employed by it. There are, then, many parts of the joke-telling process, which are normally conflated in social humour. Locating where power lies becomes, therefore, a difficult issue, with the nature of broadcasting dismantling conventional social comedy formats. Of course, in certain instances performers have been seen as the joke-tellers and criticised as such; Warren Mitchell's repeated legitimisations of Alf Garnett's racist and sexist outbursts in *Till Death Us Do Part* have centred on him justifying why he, as an actor, should find it acceptable to perform material which he'd never utter outside of the performative frame. In this case, who is 'responsible' for material read as offensive because of its stereotyping: the actor Warren Mitchell; the character Alf Garnett; the writer Johnny Speight; the broadcaster the BBC? Regulations certainly lay the blame at the feet of the broadcaster, even though it's clear offended audience members might sometimes target writers and performers instead. This means that the nature of responsibility in television sitcom becomes difficult and this is because it doesn't function in the traditional manner of social comedy in which the teller of a joke is unambiguous and easily reachable.

Till Death Us Do Part offers further insight into the difficulties of examining sitcom and representation. While it's difficult to argue that none of Garnett's speeches are sexist or racist, it is much more difficult to pinpoint the ways in which the text attempts to position the audience relative to him; that is, whether we're invited to sympathise or not with Garnett's views. This exemplifies a long-standing issue of comedy, of whether we laugh *with* or *at* something. Speight's recorded intention in the programme, as well as Mitchell's justification for his portrayal, was that Garnett is meant to be a parody of certain attitudes and that, within the programme, the audience is clearly meant to find his views ridiculous. Indeed, the comedy works precisely through Garnett's outbursts being rendered nothing more than funny, and his tortured logic and uninformed opinions con-

In *Till Death Us Do Part*, do we laugh *with* or *at* Alf Garnett?

nect into centuries-old Superiority Humour Theories (Aristotle, 1925). We are, then, meant to laugh *at* Garnett. However, the ways in which audiences actually interpreted the series were quite different, with many viewers explicitly supporting Garnett's opinions and laughing *with* him as he mocked other races, religions and lifestyles (Husband, 1988; Mills, 2004b). The sound on the laugh track at the end of one of Garnett's speeches could be laughter endorsing what he's just said, or laughter at the stupidity of the mind which would believe such stuff, and it's impossible to know why and how audiences are laughing at something merely from listening to their reaction. The lack of studies examining audience response to comedies has seriously hindered making sense of this dilemma. Certainly, arguments insisting that a sitcom has a particular, unarguable meaning – whether it's an offensive one or not – are moot, saying more about the reader than they're ever able to say about mass audiences as a whole.

Furthermore, it's problematic to always see the *with* and *at* dichotomy as mutually exclusive, which is how it's normally discussed. Surely it's possible to enjoy Garnett's racist statements about 'coons' at the same time as getting pleasure from laughing at the absurdity which results in his logic. Similarly, the supposed post-modern irony of series such as *South Park* and *The Simpsons* is double edged. While *South Park* may attempt to present Cartman as laughable because of his racist views (particularly towards Kyle's Judaism), he has ended up as the series' most popular character because of the variety of ways we're invited to identify with him. Such characters are ones we laugh *with* and *at* simultaneously, taking pleasure in the venom of their views and their reiteration of offensive stereotypes at the same time as feeling such opinions are offensive, unacceptable outside comedy and the result of flawed and misinformed logic. Indeed, Freud's (1960) Humour Theory rests entirely on this process and he argues that it's a necessary one in order for people to release repressed feelings. The meaning of any particular joke, what it says about the teller who told it, and the implications for the audience that laughs at it, may be complex and contradictory notions, in which offensive processes such as stereotyping can occur simultaneously with more positive, progressive ones. It is this complexity within humour and the ways in which audiences make sense of it which require much fuller understanding.

Another problem is that the majority of analysis of sitcom which finds its representations offensive or stereotyped usually focuses on a particular programme's jokes and doesn't examine the genre's narrative aspects. While a specific joke may rest on stereotypes and may be told by a character who supports such stereotypes, the narrative within a specific episode, or that stretched across the series as a whole, may suggest a very different reading. This is clearly the case in the representation of Alf Garnett, in which the jokes may give him a comic voice, but he is repeatedly shown to be a fool by the narrative. Feminist analysis of *I Love Lucy* makes this distinction, for the possible liberating aspects of her performance, rendering her in control of the jokes, are undermined by the narrative structures of the series which never allow her to break away from her domes-

tic situation and so she is eventually rendered merely laughable (Mellencamp, 1992). Deciding which bits of a sitcom to examine is an important factor in making statements about the kinds of representations it offers, and the conflict between comic moments and overall narratives is indicative of the ways in which sitcom works as a whole, offering specific instances of pleasure which are subsumed within overarching stories.

Debates about whether representations within sitcom are progressive or not are indicative of one of the primary assumptions about comedy; that one of its main social roles is the subversion of authority. Certainly, anthropological and sociological analyses of social comedy demonstrate how humour is used as a tool for subversion (most obviously, see Bakhtin, 1984), as demonstrated by comedians' threatened position within many dictatorships (Jenkins, 1994). It seems that to be laughed at is to acknowledge mistakes as the Superiority Theory argues and so the banishment of mockery is a way to assert power. Grote's (1983) main criticism of the sitcom is that, in conforming to the industrial and commercial requirements of broadcasting, the sitcom has abandoned this role and instead presents worlds in which nothing ever changes. This results in two assumptions about comedy and its relationship to power, which are contradictory. First, comedy is used by the powerful to demonstrate their power and thus to maintain social relationships: second, that comedy is used by the powerless to mock the powerful and thus to undermine social relationships. These two arguments feed into debates about representation within sitcom, yet are complicated by the difficulty in deciding who the 'teller' of the joke is within sitcom.

Also, examining sitcom's representations is complicated because, just as we have to take into account the narrative conventions of the form, so we need to examine the conventions of content. So, while it's not that hard to read the camp portrayal of Jack in *Will and Grace* as a stereotype of homosexuality, this has to be understood within the traditions of camp and excessive performance in comedy generally and the sitcom specifically, which are notably different to those for other forms. Of course, this doesn't necessarily legitimise them; because a representation has antecedents doesn't automatically render it acceptable. However, the ways in which comedy is signalled to audiences, conventionally through performance excess, mean that such a camp performance has a different meaning in a comic context from that which it might have in a serious drama. The comic intent of the performance, and its role within a comic narrative, are all parts of the ways in which the representation is constructed and the kinds of pleasures it offers audiences. Because of this, reports published by audience groups which include statistical accounts of the number of times groups and individuals are portrayed in certain ways are flawed, as they fail to make the distinction between the genre conventions and expectations within which any portrayal must exist.

Lucille Ball's liberating performance in *I Love Lucy* may be undermined by the domestic restrictions of the narratives

This heritage of comic representations means that there can also be a difficulty in making the distinction between stereotypes and archetypes. It's certainly the case that the kinds of personality traits found within comic characters are repetitive, and have striking similarities with comedy of the past. Butsch (1995), for example, finds notable similarities in the characters of Ralph Kramden, Fred Flintstone, Archie Bunker and Homer Simpson, even though they are from series made decades apart set centuries apart, and two of which are animated. And it's not difficult to make a connection between *Frasier*'s Frasier, *Keeping Up Appearances*'s Hyacinth Bucket and Shakespeare's Falstaff, in their concern for social standing and rampant snobbery. Comedy clearly cannot exist without certain kinds of characters; at least, it would certainly be made very difficult, and would lead to audience confusion. Funny characters have often been stupid, ignorant and self-deluded, and to condemn such portrayals as stereotypes and unacceptable is not only to rely on unproven assumptions about how audiences make sense of such stupidity, but also to abandon a large part of comic heritage. Again, this is not to justify all kinds of portrayals; however, it is to ask why some comic archetypes continue to be used with little complaint, while others come to be defined as stereotypes and are seen to be feeding into broader social problems concerning representation and social power. Indeed, this chapter will examine the representations on offer in sitcoms with reference to race, gender and sexuality; why no analysis of age, class or intelligence? The arguments that certain representations feed into social injustice not only make unproven assumptions about the relationship between media and society but also, by extension, inevitably argue for the outlawing of virtually all comic representation.

And the notion of stereotyping is itself a complex one. The ways in which individuals or groups are stereotyped are often contradictory, meaning that, while the process is understood as the reduction of individuals to repetitive types, the exact ways in which this is done are often quite complex. Thus homosexuality is stereotyped by either a lack of conventional masculinity or an excess of it; either the weedy, ineffectual, limp-wristed poof, or the body-building, sexually voracious, good-looking Adonis. Similarly, women in comedy have repeatedly been stereotyped in terms of their sexual appetite, either non-existent (the crabby, frigid spinster or mother-in-law) or voracious (the young, pouting, big-breasted nymphet). Now, the existence of a number of stereotypes for any portrayal does not mean that any portrayal is possible; instead it shows that stereotypes can often work in contradictory ways, and that distinctions between them and archetypes are often based on subtle differences of degree.

To make sense of sitcom in terms of representation, then, is to engage with a complex debate which, unlike much analysis of the genre, has a life outside the academic world. The analysis of representation is a large and significant area within the study of media and assumptions about the powerful effects of the social role of comedy mean that the ways in which sitcom represents its characters are seen to be significant. Yet, representations within sitcom are hard to pin down, precisely because of the nature of humour and its relationship to particular series, episodes, narratives, jokes and performances.

Gender

When debates about the representation of gender are raised, what is usually discussed is the portrayal of women and femininity. The last decade has seen a rise in the examination of the depiction of men and masculinity, which is a result of the rise of the feminist movement in which assumptions about gender as a whole began to be questioned. Furthermore, analyses of masculinity have often been justified as a development of the analysis of femininity, in which the role of men needs to be examined in order for the patriarchal pressures which exist for women to be understood. While each gender can only exist within the context of the other, the patriarchal nature of society means that, while masculinity may be seen as a problem, it is so primarily because of how that impacts upon women. The main way this takes place is through the normalisation of masculinity and masculine concerns, in which the male position within society is so all-pervasive that it requires subtle interrogation to be understood.

There is, then, surprisingly little work on the relationship between sitcom and masculinity specifically, even though the 'male crisis' is evident in series such as *Men Behaving Badly* and *Home Improvement* (McEachern, 1999). Similarly, while sitcom has a history of male characters, Butsch (1992) finds that the roles they fulfil are limited, particularly in terms of class. The examination of comedy generally and the sitcom specifically are useful starting points when exploring the depiction of masculinity for 'The great tradition of British situation comedy has centred around men' (McQueen, 2001, p. 58). While this is partly due to the male dominance of all aspects of the comedy industry (female stand-ups are still notably uncommon; see Cook, 1994), it also arises from the ways in which humour as a whole has been co-opted as a male trait.

Gray points out, 'a truth universally acknowledged: Women have no sense of humour' (1994, p. 3). That is, social differences include a distinction between the relationship between gender and comedy, and sociological and psychological studies demonstrate the different ways men and women use humour. Because of this, Fraiberg argues that 'it is important to place *comedy* at the center of a discussion of *women* because it has been done too rarely' (1994, p. 317). For Grotjahn 'Kidding is almost a male prerogative' (1966, p. 35), for he finds that in mixed company it is men who communicate through a comic mode, and who are authorised by the group to make jokes about other members. This is seen to be a part of social upbringing, in which 'women are neither expected, nor trained, to joke in this culture' (Pollio and Edgerly, 1976, p. 225), and the presence of a female telling jokes is a significant disruption to social norms. Furthermore, the kinds of jokes which men and women tell are quite different, with studies finding that 'females indulge in self-deprecatory humor to a greater extent than do males'

(Levine, 1976, p. 174). Studies show that men commonly use humour to mock others, thus reasserting their dominant role within communication, whereas women are only allowed by social convention to joke if they use the opportunity to mock themselves, contributing to their subordinate position. Of course, these studies are nearly thirty years out of date, and changes within social structures may have led to different opportunities for women (Auslander, 1997, pp. 108–25). However, the kinds of treatment experienced by contemporary female comedians – as shown by Cook's (1994) interviews with Jo Brand, Jenny Eclair and Donna McPhail – suggest that not much has changed.

This inevitably has consequences for the opportunities women have within sitcom and the ways they are represented. If society is unused to seeing women performing comedy and, when women do tell jokes, certain kinds of material are expected, it's difficult to see how programmes diverging from such content will be made or, if they are, how they will be intelligible enough to an audience to become popular. The vast majority of major sitcom characters are male and sitcom content, as a whole, has developed in response to changes in social conditions for men. In America, the preponderance of eponymous male series – *Seinfeld*, *The Bernie Mac Show*, *The Drew Carey Show* (ABC: 1995–2003) and so on – results from the dominance of men in the stand-up industry which is the traditional breeding ground for sitcom stars. In Britain, in which sitcom is developed by writers rather than performers, the general male dominance of the television industry means female writers pitching ideas have to work much harder. Perhaps more significant is that the concerns of masculinity are ones which society generally discusses through humour and it is the male voice which is seen as appropriate for comic discourse. Thus even a programme like *I Love Lucy*, which has been examined by a number of critics for its feminist meanings, has a title in which the audience is asked to identify with Desi, not Lucy.

This is indicative of the ways in which women are represented in media and society generally. Since Mulvey, analyses of women in media have acknowledged how they're positioned as objects, in which they are significant for their 'to-be-looked-at-ness' (2001, p. 397). Audiences, whether male or female, are required to adopt a masculine reading position to make any sense of a text, with this ideological construct normalised to the extent that it is no longer seen as a creative process, but just 'how things are'. This is apparent within sitcom, which 'positions the woman not simply as the object of the male gaze but of the male laugh – not just to-be-looked-at but to-be-laughed-at' (Gray, 1994, p. 9). While it remains difficult to ascertain whether audiences are indeed laughing *with* or *at* characters, Gray argues that the dominant ideological position offered to audiences in sitcom remains one in which they are asked to identify with the male in order to enjoy the pleasures the comic moments, and the series as a whole, may have to offer.

Doty (2003), however, argues that sitcoms can be read in very different ways to this. He explores the ways in which male and female viewers make sense of series with predominantly female casts such as *Sex and the City* and *Designing Women* (CBS:

1986–93), and in which the external threats which serve as the impetus for most episodes' narratives are virtually always men. For Doty this offers viewers a very different set of pleasures and a particular relationship to the characters and the programme, a relationship which he calls 'lesbian' (p. 189). It may be significant that both of these series have connotations of 'quality' and are understood for their dramatic and melodramatic content as much as their comedy. There's still a difficulty in uniting the overall comedic tone common to sitcom with a feminine or lesbian viewpoint, and instead those series whose primary and unashamed aim is humour require a masculine perspective in order to accept that it's okay to laugh at the content on offer.

Many of the ways in which men and women are portrayed in sitcom relate to comedy's obsession with sex, and how this affects male–female relationships. A contemporary sitcom such as *Friends*, for example, while narratively about relationships and the desire to find a partner for life, has a lot of jokes about sex, rather than love or relationships. More importantly, in the series sex is seen primarily as a male goal, with Chandler and Joey's constant references to their interest in porn, and the women they've (successfully or not) attempted to sleep with. Furthermore, their relationships with the female characters are ones in which they constantly sexualise them, making sly passes or referring to their bodies in a manner which the series rarely allows the female characters to do. The female characters are much more concerned with marriage and long-term love, with the initial narrative drive of the series centred on Rachel's jilting her groom on her wedding day, which the series presents as a significant emotional choice for a woman.

The ways in which comedy constructs the relationship between masculinity, femininity, sex and love, seriously limit the opportunities for characters. Joey, for example, is the most sexually active of the male characters and is therefore defined as the most male; it has also meant that, until the latter series where he developed an understanding of the difference between love and sex in his crush on Rachel, he was the male character with the least narrative development or long-term storylines. Ross, on the other hand, who has been married three times and repeatedly suppresses his masculine sexual desires in order to demonstrate an emotional development, is portrayed as feminine and laughably unmasculine. Similarly, Chandler's consistent inability to attract the women he's interested in renders him laughable because of his failed masculinity. Throughout the series, then, successful masculinity – or, at least, masculinity which isn't mocked – is one which treats women as sex objects and denies any emotional core.

This is reiterated in the depiction of the women. While Rachel and Monica are feminine in slightly different ways, there's a clear link between their femininity and their relationships with the opposite sex. Both Rachel and Monica work through a number of significant relationships in the series, with Rachel's relationship with Ross the main narrative driving force for the series as a whole, and this is only supplanted by Monica's affair with, and eventual marriage to, Chandler. Throughout this, Rachel and Monica's femininity is clearly signalled through Monica's obsession with domestic correctness and Rachel's interest in clothes and shopping. Their jobs are avowedly feminine, even though the series attempts to offer them some kind of gender empowerment. While Monica may be in charge, her career as a chef signals her domesticity and role as provider. And though Rachel makes an empowered move in giving up waitressing and eventually getting a high-powered office job in fashion, the series makes explicit links between her feminine desire to shop and her career. The difficulty in sitcom characters breaking out of such roles and remaining funny and intelligible is shown by Phoebe, the one female character who makes repeated reference to her own sexuality and refuses to conform to a number of standard feminine traits; for Phoebe to be depicted as such without threatening gender norms too much, the series makes her the 'oddball' character, interested in unconventional philosophies and constantly questioning the other characters' beliefs. The series, therefore, depicts a sexually active and desiring female character as somewhat deranged, in a manner remarkably similar to Dharma in *Dharma and Greg*, Roz in *Frasier*, Jane in *Coupling* and Patsy in *Absolutely Fabulous*.

Unruly Women

Yet, this depiction of women can also be read as having some kind of radical feminist potential. All the characters cited above not only function as main agents within a comic narrative, they do so by refusing to conform to accepted notions of feminine behaviour. This may be unsurprising, considering comedy functions, particularly in its Incongruity and Relief forms, through representing that which is deviant, and it is the deviant which is funny. It may be for this reason that Gray argues that sitcom 'is one of the few comic narrative forms in which women performers have played an important part from its inception' (1994, p. 14). Sitcom is able to incorporate female characters to a greater extent than many other television narrative forms precisely because its focus on the deviant allows them more scope; women can be more than housewives.

For Rowe (1990, 1995) this is best represented by *Roseanne*. The series, which clearly draws on Roseanne Barr/Arnold's stand-up character and public persona, represents a significant comic interlude in the representation of women, motherhood, femininity and domesticity. Roseanne Conner is funny because she refuses to conform to the standard feminine conventions in terms of her appearance, the way she treats her children, the responsibilities she has towards her family and how she interacts with others generally. Primarily, and inescapably, Roseanne doesn't look like sitcom mothers, and it is 'Arnold's *fatness* . . . and the *looseness* or lack of personal restraint her fatness implies, that most powerfully define her and convey her opposition to middle-class and feminine standards of decorum and beauty' (Rowe, 1995, p. 60, italics in original). In a society which has 'a long tradition of the fat female body as a site of comedy' (Hole, 2003, p. 315), the feminine body is one which is intended to consume commodities but remain as unnoticeable as possible, unless acting as an object for male gratification. Therefore

Roseanne is a significant comic interlude in the representation of women, motherhood, femininity and domesticity

Roseanne's fatness becomes a powerful tool for continually reminding audiences of female desires.

In the programme it's clear that Roseanne and Dan have a healthy, loving and lustful sex life, something not only radical for a female character, but almost inconceivable considering much fiction suggests it's only conventionally thin and attractive people who can possibly enjoy sex or be attractive to others. *Roseanne* thus manages to present a female character which, while refusing to conform to the standard presentations of femininity, is not presented as oddball, goofy or deranged. Instead, the programme's insistence on its resolutely working-class setting and long-term storylines about economic hardship and menial jobs places it in a more 'realistic' context than much sitcom, meaning that it's harder to explain away the Roseanne character as fantasy. Of course, there's another way in which this diegesis can be read; Roseanne's interest in sex could merely be seen as part of her working-class lout-ness, conforming to class stereotypes in which uneducated workers have to indulge in sex as they don't have the cultural capital to enjoy much else (Kirkham and Skeggs, 2000, p. 312). Similarly, the fact that the series remains in a domestic setting means it could be seen as presenting merely 'yet another form of media's romanticized working-class matriarch' (Press, 1991, p. 42).

Yet British sitcom has actively engaged with the contradictions within being a housewife and mother. Andrews argues that *Butterflies* found humour merely within the absurdities of being a housewife, meaning that it 'was seen as suitably ridiculous to be

Butterflies finds humour within the absurdities of being a housewife

the situation for a comedy' (1998, p. 60). The main character, Ria, loves her family but hates being a housewife and while the programme finds humour in her inability to cook, she is not punished for her lack of culinary skills and instead the series questions why it's assumed that she should be able to make food in the first place. The writer of *Butterflies*, Carla Lane, has repeatedly tackled this theme, continually situating humour in the gap between society's expectations of women and their disenfranchisement from these, and, significantly, finding the former to be the problem. *Solo* depicted the assumptions society makes about any woman not in a long-term relationship; *The Mistress* invited the audience to empathise with a woman having an affair with a married man; *Screaming* depicted three female friends all in love with the same man. Andrews calls such series 'housewives comedy' (p. 60) and argues that they are powerful because they render certain aspects of femininity as ridiculous. It's certainly the case that there are now many more sitcom depictions of women unhappy with the domestic social roles assigned to them and which show housewifery to be ridiculous, such as *2point4 Children* (BBC 1: 1991–9), *Absolutely Fabulous* and *According to Bex*.

Rowe, Mellencamp (1992), Auslander (1997) and McCracken (2002) place *Roseanne* in this rich tradition of comic women in sitcom, relating it particularly to Lucille Ball in *I Love Lucy* and Gracie Allen in *The Burns and Allen Show*. For these authors, while all these series present the 'unruly woman' (Rowe, 1995), 'grotesque woman' (Russo, 1986)

or 'female grotesque' (Waddell, 1999) for comic effect, *Roseanne* represents a significant development because it doesn't offer a male point of identification for the audience
through which such radical feminist unruliness is rendered merely laughable. Instead,
Roseanne represents a '*woman's* point of view' (p. 82, italics in original), requiring audience identification with Roseanne for the comic pleasures the programme offers. The
programme does so by taking more time to allow Roseanne's responses to events to be
foregrounded, and in giving her more narrative space in which to express herself. Thus
Roseanne's sister Jackie is a significant diegetic character for she allows the scriptwriters
the opportunity to write scenes in which the two discuss their lives and, as the series
developed, their family history and relationships with their parents. It is this which distinguishes it from series such as *The Mary Tyler Moore Show*, which, while seen as radical
and feminist by contemporary critics, instead presented a new representation of women
which still implied that 'compliance produces more happiness than resistance' (Dow,
1990, p. 269).

Similarly, Roseanne's various jobs – on a factory line or waitressing – always set her
working with a number of other females, allowing more all-female scenes. While Dan
also has male friends in the series, his workplace was predominantly solitary and his
friends much less important to the programme overall. Furthermore, Roseanne's point
of view was expressed through her own responses to the events in her family, events
which she had the comic ability to mock, make fun of and laugh at. This is another way
in which this representation was a significant step forward, for 'Lucy endured the bore-
dom and demanding routine of housewifery by transforming it into physical comedy;
Roseanne endures by turning domesticity into wit' (Mellencamp, 1992, p. 347).

Body, Violence and Gender

There is a contradictory stance being adopted here, though. As has been argued, one
of the primary ways in which funny women can express dissatisfaction with patriarchal
structures is by behaving in a physically comic manner which not only places the female
form as a ripe site for comedy, but also refuses to conform to the convention of the
female body as needing to take up as little space as possible, and only to be looked at
for male sexual pleasure. For this argument, Ball's physical comic mastery is the ultimate
feminist stance, for it places gender politics at the physical level. Roseanne, however,
rarely indulges in physical humour for, while the sight of the character stomping around
the set and sitting heavily on the sofa is contrary to conventional female movement, her
body is rarely used for comic effect itself. Instead, Roseanne is a character who lives by
her wits and is funny because of what she says rather than what she does. There is,
then, a distinction to be made between physical humour and verbal humour, and
women's appropriation of each of these modes has quite different meanings. And considering Bergson (1911) argues that much humour arises from laughing at the physically
inadequate, it is arguable that Roseanne's refusal to be laughed at for her body, no mat-

ter how unconventional that body is, may in fact be a more radical gesture than Ball's unruly physicality.

The body, its functions and, in particular, its secretions, are vital to much humour (Limon, 2000), and it is noticeable how these aspects are employed differently by each gender, particularly in a mass audience form like the sitcom. Punishment to the male body is forever funny, and is at the core of slapstick (Dale, 2000). It is taken to its extreme in *Bottom*, which consists of narratives conceived to allow as much physical abuse between the characters as possible and whose title clearly signals the programme's obsession with physicality. In animated sitcom there is a long history of funny physical violence, resulting from a combination of sitcom slapstick conventions and animation's absurd possibilities. The eponymous characters from *Beavis and Butt-head* regularly pound one another; it is a rare episode of *The Simpsons* which doesn't involve Homer being injured in some way; the regular death of Kenny in *South Park* demonstrates how the extreme and ritualistic slaughter of a main character can be a source of pleasure in sitcom. All of this is taken to its logical conclusion, and parodied, in *The Simpsons*'s cartoon-within-a-cartoon, 'The Itchy and Scratchy Show', which presents nothing other than almost un-narrativised extreme violence as comedy, which Bart and Lisa howl in enjoyment at.

It is noticeable that all of these characters are male and that the comic violence which occurs to them is at the hands of others. This is different to the kinds of physical comedy performed by women, in which pain is much less apparent and the cause of physical discomfort is most likely the woman herself. Lucy's physical comedy is rarely physically painful and is instead funny because it demonstrates someone unable to achieve their goals. Far more excessive physical hardship befalls Patsy and Edina in *Absolutely Fabulous*, with many falls and injuries; yet the narrative makes it clear that the cause of such pain is usually the pair's intoxication from drink and drugs. Violence towards women, enacted by another character, is rarely presented as funny, and certainly not an inoffensive comic staple in the way it is for men. In an episode of *Men Behaving Badly* ('In Bed with Dorothy'), in which Gary nurses a recuperating Dorothy after an appendix operation, he wakes her up by deliberately prodding her wound; the audience's response on the laugh track is one in which hilarity is clearly mingled with sounds of shock and sympathy. It's probable that the joke is only acceptable because the rest of the episode demonstrates Gary's caring nature, that previous series of the programme have prepared the audience for such jokes and, more importantly, that episode narratives nearly always result in the men being punished for any transgressions they make and Dorothy achieving the upper hand. When the series was transferred to America and the same episode was recorded, that particular joke was removed, suggesting that American audiences may be more sensitive than British ones to comic violence against women.

The comic topics available to men and women, and deemed acceptable by mainstream audiences, therefore differ greatly. Gray (1994, p. 110) notes that

No female character in a British sitcom has yet been given the dramatic licence of a Hancock or an Old Steptoe to be rude, disruptive, dirty or aggressive; for that matter, no female character has been gay, or poor, or a full-blooded spinster without regrets. (1994, p. 110)

While this was written before the mainstream success of *Absolutely Fabulous*, it's arguable that that series increasingly presents its main characters without any attempt at the emotional depth or social longing managed with Steptoe and Hancock. That is, while male comic characters can be both foul and emotional, and therefore both repulsive and attractive to an audience, the development of repulsive female characters doesn't allow for similar audience identification. It may be for this reason that *Roseanne*'s humour is one resolutely not about physicality, for this would disallow the emotional involvement in the family's lives which the humour of the series requires. *Absolutely Fabulous*'s jokes about the nature of female physicality, including comic reference to such things as the menopause, female contraception and hormone replacement therapy, represent an acknowledgment of the realities of the female body in a manner rarely found elsewhere. Because of this, the series 'can be vaguely disconcerting for a man to watch' (Ellis, 2002, p. 88). Even though references to male physicality, with jokes about penis size and masturbation an age-old comic staple, are common, *I Love Lucy* told the whole story of Lucy's pregnancy without using the 'p word' once (Kisseloff, 1995, p. 302). Porter argues that humour on such issues 'essentially marginalises men' as they construct 'a specific female address' (1998, p. 81), though whether this is actually empowering or merely marginalising is moot. Examining film comedy, King notes that while contemporary films such as *American Pie* (Paul Weitz, Chris Weitz, 1999) and *There's Something about Mary* (Bobby Farrelly, Peter Farrelly, 1998) include examples of male excreta for comic effect, 'it is hard to imagine a mainstream gross-out comedy of the near future including projectile menstrual bleeding among its comic attractions' (2002, p. 77). In mainstream comedy, semen is funny but periods aren't, even if stand-ups like Jenny Eclair and Paula Poundstone have attempted to prove otherwise.

This embarrassment about the female body and its functions is at the core of comic performance which explicitly acknowledges gender differences and the ways in which they're performed: drag. If gender is nothing more than a set of performed characteristics then it's possible to transgress these boundaries, yet such gender confusion is, in mainstream media, merely laughed away as a comic transgression. It is, after all, in Shakespeare's *comedies* that the characters dress as the opposite sex; a scene in which Hamlet soliloquises while wearing a miniskirt would reduce its tragic weight. And what is generally regarded as the funniest film of all time – *Some Like It Hot* (Billy Wilder, 1959) – works from the assumption that such Hollywood masculine men as Tony Curtis and Jack Lemmon appearing in drag is enough to maintain an entire comic narrative, even if Marilyn Monroe's own excessive performance of femininity is not funny enough in itself. Men dressed as women are funny because masculinity is read and presented as a 'neutral unmarked norm' (King, 2002, p. 141), and drag is a deviance from this. The fact that a man in a dress is funny in itself, without any necessary narrative contextualising and justification, shows how ingrained and normalised masculinity is. It is the position which masculinity occupies which continually makes feminine comic performance and content a matter of contestation and debate; for if comedy results from the deviancy from accepted norms, how can a woman be funny if femininity is in and of itself seen as deviant?

Sexuality

Heterosexuality is a social and media norm just as masculinity is. Sitcom's recurring interest in relationships between the sexes, with many programmes centred on 'traditional' families, means that certain versions of home life are far more common than others, and the majority of these are about heterosexual relationships. For McCarthy, 'narrative development in sitcom was something of a hetero privilege' (2003, p. 92), in which the threats to normality which are at the core of many sitcom narratives position heterosexual relationships as not only normal, but desirable. In looking at the history of comedy in theatre, Nicoll notes that it 'habitually balances and contrasts what might be called the eternal masculine and the eternal feminine' (1962, p. 121). While there has been a trend in the last couple of decades for series about the surrogate (consisting of

Coupling finds comedy in the conflict between a desire for heterosexual relationships and the inability to understand the opposite sex

housemates or work colleagues) rather than the biological family, these still often use the attainment of a stable heterosexual relationship as their major narrative hook. This is clear in Ross and Rachel, and Monica and Chandler, in *Friends*, Niles and Daphne in *Frasier*, Sam and Diane in *Cheers*, and everyone in *Coupling*. Many sitcoms use the conflict between the desire for a stable heterosexual relationship and the inability to understand the opposite sex as major comic forces, as shown by *Men Behaving Badly*, *Seinfeld*, *Marion and Geoff* and *Scrubs*. The happy ending necessary for much classical comedy is based around a wedding, with this narrative event often the only criteria used by critics to define comedy. The British series *To the Manor Born* (BBC 1: 1979–81) and *Just Good Friends* (BBC 1: 1983–6) constructed their entire narrative drives around the 'will they/won't they' nature of their protagonists' relationships, with the longed-for marriage in their final episodes. Indeed, Scodari notes that the coming together of suitors must end a comedy, for it removes the 'thrill of the chase' (1995, p. 23) which is often the narrative's primary driving force.

The ways in which gay and lesbian characters are represented have a particular significance in sitcom, as comedy is one of the few places in which homosexuality has a long and distinguished heritage, with the topic referred to more often, and earlier in broadcast history, than is the case for many genres. This is particularly the case in the United Kingdom, where homosexual performance styles were common in music hall which sitcom grew out of. Why this should be the case is moot, though many have

Ellen demonstrates the difficulty in maintaining regular appearances of homosexual characters in mainstream sitcom

noted that there's a willingness to present homosexuality (in certain ways) in British culture missing from that of many other countries (Medhurst and Tuck, 1982, pp. 49–52; Healy, 1995; McCarthy, 2001, p. 616); fittingly, the international comedic stereotype of British people is that they are gay (Davies, 1990).

This is not to suggest that gay comic characters don't exist in American sitcom; however, it is to note that these are much rarer and their portrayal has always been a site of struggle. While gay characters existed as one-offs in a number of series, the first regular gay character in an American sitcom was Jodie in *Soap*, and it may be no coincidence that such a character found a space on a series full of excessive personality types and absurd, extreme storylines. The difficulty in maintaining regular mainstream appearances of homosexual characters in sitcom is shown by the battles – whether in production and/or reception – over *Ellen* and *Will and Grace*, as examined by many authors (Battles and Hilton-Morrow, 2002; Budd, Craig and Steinman, 1999, pp. 20–1; Dow, 2001; Feuer, 2001; McCarthy, 2001, 2003). However, Shugart (2003) and Arthurs (2004) find that there has been an increase in gay characters in American cinema and television in recent years, even if the way they're portrayed is limited and repetitive. As with all issues of representation, the possible positive connotations of the prevalence of such characters can be undermined by noting the stereotyped and limited roles they're required to fulfil.

The Thin Blue Line attempts to combine the pleasures of traditional sitcom with contemporary 'politically correct' humour

Camp

The desire to present sympathetic homosexuals in contemporary British comedy is further confused by the heritage of characters which, if not explicitly gay within their series' diegeses, instead draw on the conventional ways in which homosexuality has been represented. These have consistently coded homosexuality through campness, to the point where the two are indistinguishable and the former only exists in relation to the latter; indeed, the majority of gay characters are shown to be homosexual not through any kind of sexual activity, but instead by their being camp.

In Ben Elton's *The Thin Blue Line*, for example, there is clearly an attempt to distinguish between homosexuality and campness in the character of Constable Goody. The series is an obvious attempt to recreate the pleasures of 1970s, mainstream, ensemble sitcom while incorporating post-political correctness politics, showing that the ideologies associated with that movement had moved from the fringe and into the mainstream. Indeed, as Elton is the person who most 'epitomises that fast-talking brew of anti-racist, anti-sexist banter which characterised the salad days of Alternative Comedy' (Cook, 1994, p. 40), the fact that his series was broadcast on prime-time BBC 1 shows the politics which had begun to pervade all forms of sitcom in the 1990s. *The Thin Blue Line* concerns the fairly inept workers at a local police station, meaning plenty of traditional comic banter about 'truncheons' while also allowing Elton to make political statements about policing and the nature of criminality. That the series wasn't particularly successful – seemingly failing to please both Elton's alternative audience and the BBC's mainstream one – highlights the difficulty in placing progressive representations in mainstream fare.

This is most obvious in the character of Constable Goody, who is heterosexual but camp. Within mainstream sitcom conventions, it's almost impossible not to read him as gay. This campness is signalled through traditional codes, such as 'flamboyant mannerisms' (Sontag, 1994, p. 281), which litter the portrayal and result in much laughter from the studio audience. Yet Elton attempts to signal Goody's heterosexuality frequently, with his attraction for the female Constable Habib one of the programme's prominent narrative driving forces and a major source of humour. But there is a conflict here between Elton's character construction and the generic conventions of British comedy in which homosexuality and campness have a strictly defined role and meaning, which reached its apotheosis in *Are You Being Served?*'s (BBC 1: 1973–85) Mr Humphries. And while Alternative Comedy strove to define such representations as homophobic stereotypes, the failure to replace these portrayals with any other kind of gay or camp characterisation simply meant that such characters ceased to exist rather than being redrawn in another way. Because of this, gay characters are caught in a representational 'trap' (Dyer, 1992, p. 146).

The removal of such characters from sitcom's repertoire also removes the possibility for the kinds of jokes that can be gleaned from them. The history of comedy means that

In *Gimme Gimme Gimme*, James Dreyfus plays a character who is both camp *and* gay

camp characters have significance within humour which rests on campness's supposed synonymy with homosexuality, and homosexuality is funny because it deviates from a male, heterosexual viewpoint. To attempt to distinguish between homosexuality and campness within mainstream sitcom is to refuse to offer audiences the comedic pleasures which the other genre characteristics suggest. For audience members applying the traditional generic rules that the rest of *The Thin Blue Line* invokes, Goody has to be laughed at because he's gay/camp, particularly as that campness is actively foregrounded in James Dreyfus's portrayal of the character.

Indeed, in Dreyfus' subsequent series – *Gimme Gimme Gimme* (BBC 2, BBC 1: 1999–) – he plays a character who is camp *and* gay, and it's virtually impossible to see any representational difference between this character and Constable Goody. Dreyfus's association with homosexuality is so clear that the BBC's defence against complaints about his portrayal in *Gimme Gimme Gimme* rests entirely on the connotations he holds. They say he is 'well-known to viewers in other television comedy roles which could reasonably have been expected to indicate the nature of the comedy to much of the potential audience' (Broadcasting Standards Commission Complaints Bulletin 21, 1999, p. 17). It's obvious that even the BBC has forgotten that Dreyfus has never played a gay character before, just a camp one: either that or to them, as to much of the audience reading sitcom, the two are one and the same.

So, gay characters in sitcom (and much humour generally) are only signalled as such by their campness and, most significantly, are only funny *because* of their campness. In British comedy campness is funny, not homosexuality; the latter hardly exists. So Goody is funny when doing mincing walks, when talking in a conventionally camp voice and when overreacting to any situation; all of these are sitcom codes for campness, not homosexuality, unless – as in sitcom – the rules used to make sense of them are one and the same. As Dyer notes, both the media and audiences 'never seem to realize that camping is only one way of being gay' (1992, p. 137).

The relationship between campness and homosexuality in comedy had begun to be redrawn in Britain in the 1990s due to the rise of a number of homosexual stand-ups whose routines explicitly drew on their sexuality, such as Rhona Cameron and Donna McPhail. Most obvious in this movement was Julian Clary, whose use of double entendres was so explicit that the joke stopped being about the hidden possibility that he might be gay and instead made it quite clear that he was. If stand-up had begun to question the ways in which homosexuality and comedy were related, why is *The Thin Blue Line*'s Constable Goody so problematic? There's a difficulty in transferring the content of stand-up to sitcom because audience expectations for the two forms are quite different. Sitcoms use stereotypes in a way that stand-up doesn't, as the codes and conventions of the genre require them. Or, to be more precise, one of the generic factors of the sitcom is its use of easily identifiable characters in which characterisation is foregrounded because of the tension within its 'dual-reading focus' (Cook, 1982, p. 18). Stand-up can foreground its artificiality in a way that sitcom can't because it doesn't rely in the same way on character, situation and narrative, to the point where it is uncommon to hear of the former being discussed in such terms. The conventions of the forms are different, and so the ways in which readers make sense of them are different too; by extension, this also means that the constraints that exist for the two forms differ too.

So, part of the reason that sitcom deals in stereotypes in a manner dissimilar to some contemporary stand-up is that large sections of the audience aren't interested in that kind of stand-up, and don't have access to the strategies required to make sense of it in the manner intended by its creators. The sitcom, if it is to be a popular, mass audience product, must somehow attempt to incorporate as many different kinds of audience as possible and remain easily intelligible to them all. This is likely to be done through adherence to conventional forms and representations that are easily understood by those with experience of them. Elton's Constable Goody can be seen as a compromise between the requirements of the sitcom (the easily identifiable characterisation) and the form of comedy which is his heritage (Alternative Comedy's refusal to stereotype homosexuals in a traditional way). However, by doing so, the representation straddles two opposite forms of reading and fails to make any sense to readers using either of the strategies to interpret it. Clary himself was a victim of this tension, as his stand-up routine failed to make a successful transfer to sitcom, as the responses to *Terry and Julian* (Channel 4: 1992) showed.

The constraints upon the portrayal of the homosexual, then, result from sitcom's humour occupying a mass social position in a society which is still prejudiced towards gays, and in which one of the generic factors of the sitcom is that homosexuality is laughable. While it has yet to be proven (either here or anywhere else) that comedy is capable of constructing or upholding regimes of control, it's unsurprising that critics of the genre see a relationship between such portrayals and homophobic prejudices in society. Considering contemporary comic representations of homosexuals – in series such as *Gimme Gimme Gimme* and *Will and Grace* – repeatedly draw on camp in order to be funny, there's little to suggest that any attempts at progressive portrayals have been successful. Since the 1990s there certainly has been a growth in the number of sitcom characters who are openly gay, compared with previous decades where the joke was always about camp characters who might or might not be gay. Whether this is a positive move is debatable; while it could be argued that the rise in numbers is simply a good thing, questions still need to be asked as to why this groundswell in openly gay characters has done nothing to undermine the recurring use of campness as an indicator of homosexuality.

Jewish Comedy

In comparison to debates concerning the representation of gender, race and sexuality, the nature of Jewish representation has received comparatively little discussion. This may be partly due to the differing histories which each of these groups has had to contend with. It's more likely, however, that the 'constructed and highly contested nature of Jewish identity generally' (Brook, 2001, p. 269) has meant that internal discussions concerning it have prevented as unified an approach towards the analysis of its representation. Furthermore, belonging to a Jewish group is a far less 'visible' matter than is the case for race and gender, which has meant that, historically, Jews in America (and in Europe and throughout history) have spent much time attempting successful assimilation by, for example, changing family names. The complicated and contested nature of Jewishness results in a more obvious range of possibilities for representation, even if this hasn't always actually resulted in a variety of representations being broadcast.

Yet Jewishness occupies a significant role in the history of America's entertainment industries, with Hollywood virtually a Jewish invention. Similarly, contemporary television comedy production is noticeably over-represented by Jewish staff, whether as producers, writers or performers. Indeed, this 'Yiddishization of American humor' (Krieger, 2003, p. 395) means that in many ways Jewish comedy *is* American comedy and the 'embarrassingly rich crop of American Jewish comedians defies common sense' (Epstein, 2002, p. x). In this way, the self-aware neuroses of Chandler in *Friends* mean that, in many ways, the comedy he offers is Jewish, even though the character himself actually isn't.

One of the difficulties in 'spotting' Jewish characters is that, like camp, Jewishness in comedy is a performance style which can be successfully (if not completely) recreated by Gentiles, at least enough for the humour to work. This 'normalisation' of a specific group's stereotypical characteristics demonstrates the ways in which white culture is capable of appropriating other groups; a process which, through fear, Jews have historically taken part in.

Both Brook (2003) and Zurawik (2003) outline an astonishing rise in the number of openly Jewish characters in American sitcom in the last decade, as well as those characters appearing in programmes in which a Jewish sensibility is central to the comedy. Brook states that 'thirty-three sitcoms with Jewish protagonists made their way onto America's television screens form 1989 to 2001' (p. 3) and notes that, in the previous five decades, only seven such series had appeared in total. Moreover, such explicitly Jewish series were massive, mainstream hits, including *The Nanny*, *Dream On* (HBO: 1990–6), *Mad About You*, *Dharma and Greg*, *Will and Grace* and the series that started it all, the 'dominant cultural force' (p. 6), *Seinfeld*. Brook outlines three phases in this sitcom development, seeing *The Nanny* as a programme which altered subsequent series because of its display of excessive Jewishness. Furthermore, Brook (2003) makes it clear that he doesn't see this trend as abating and its influence can also be seen in the growth of Jewish characters in serious forms. By this reading, American television as a whole has seen an outburst of Jewish representations in less than a decade, suggesting a much broader cultural and representational shift than the 'one-off' breakthroughs such as *The Cosby Show* and *Roseanne*.

Yet the ways in which these series present Jewishness have been criticised because they fail to offer comedy from a meaningful Jewish point of view. Thus '*Seinfeld* stigmatizes Jews who are not assimilated enough to Anglo-American norms of being in the public world' (Krieger, 2003, p. 389) because 'a large part of the audience prefers its Jews Gentile' (Berger, 1996, p. 100). Indeed, Pierson argues that *Seinfeld* is a 'modern comedy of manners' (2000), in which the humour rests on an understanding of acceptable social behaviour and mocks those who fail to conform; the parallels to Jewish responses to a turbulent history are apparent. So, even though contemporary American sitcoms are more willing to admit that both their characters and the actors playing them are Jewish, their Jewishness rarely informs comedic content and it's extremely uncommon for aspects of Jewish cultural and religious life to be presented positively, if at all. The fact that Jewish comedy is virtually synonymous with American comedy means that such Jewish characters have been assimilated by the dominant culture, and contemporary sitcom not only demonstrates this, but helps to perpetuate the process. This results in 'the bitter irony of the Jewish sitcom trend … that just when Jews have arrived at the point where they are confident enough to portray themselves openly, they are finding precious little that's distinctively Jewish left to portray' (Brook, 2000, p. 299).

However, the significance of such debates is altered once non-American audiences consume Jewish programmes. Certainly, for the majority of British audiences the notion of Jewishness and Jewish comedy is virtually meaningless, because of the different histories of that country coupled with a much less visible Jewish community, which means that Jewish concerns have rarely had a 'voice' in Britain (Stratton, 1998). This has significant implications for arguments about the assimilation of Jewish comedy and performance, for the fact that British audiences can happily consume and enjoy American sitcoms like *Seinfeld* without requiring an understanding of the Jewishness of its content demonstrates how Jewish comedy has become a performance style disassociated from its ethnic, religious and cultural roots.

The Cosby Show	Case Study

The Cosby Show is the most examined sitcom in the history of television. Considering the lack of analysis of popular forms and the paucity of work on sitcom generally, the fact that at least two books (Jhally and Lewis, 1992; Fuller, 1992) are dedicated to it demonstrates the significance which is attached to the series. The programme is more than just meaningful for academics though; one of the main reasons that *The Cosby Show* has become a 'media landmark' (Barnouw, 1990, p. 515) is its relationship with its intended audiences, and the effect it had upon both broadcasting generally and sitcom in particular. Because of changes in the broadcasting landscape, with multiple channels serving increasingly small and specific audiences, *The Cosby Show* 'is likely to be the last

The Cosby Show is the most examined sitcom in television history because of its representation of middle-class Black America

of television's prime-time programs to achieve a blockbuster audience' (Staiger, 2000, p. 141), managing to unite disparate audiences and maintain its ratings dominance for at least five of the eight years it was broadcast in America.

What is all the more significant is the factor which has resulted in all the academic interest in the series; that it was centred on a middle-class, successful African American family. The debates about *The Cosby Show* demonstrate the continued difficulty in portraying characters in comedy who aren't white, particularly considering the heritage of such portrayals and the reluctance of mainstream Western audiences to watch in their masses any series which doesn't have white characters as its central focus. What this highlights is that series about ethnic characters will always be the focus of such scrutiny because of the 'burden of representation' (Daniels and Gerson, 1989, p. 9) they bear, that any black character often has a social responsibility forced upon it to somehow coalesce the range of possible black experiences, lifestyles and ideologies, in a way which no white character or series must do. This in itself is pointless, for it's absurd to talk of any group – whether based on race, age, nationality, sexuality or whatever – as having a unified viewpoint which all its members can relate to (Cripps, 2003). Indeed, Kothari, Pearson and Zuberi note how the complex and multicultural nature of New Zealand means that series such as *Goodness Gracious Me* (BBC 2: 1998–2000) and *The Fresh Prince of Bel-Air* (NBC: 1990–6) 'constitute a field of competing ideas about race and ethnicity' (2001, p. 136), which affects their popularity and the ways in which they're read. That such series are open to this scrutiny succinctly highlights the ways in which white representations are normalised in much culture.

The Cosby Show is seen as significant because it attempts to acknowledge black culture while simultaneously moving on from traditional American sitcom portrayals of African Americans, resulting in a series which was progressive and aspirational. In this way, 'the show quite intentionally presented itself as a corrective to previous generations of television representations of black life' (Gray, 1995, p. 80). American sitcom has a much richer heritage than Britain of black characters, particularly as one of the main ways in which television broadcasters attempted to entice audiences away from radio and onto television was through the transfer of ethnic comedies such as *Amos 'n' Andy*, *The Goldbergs* (NBC: 1949–54) and *Beulah* (ABC: 1950–3). Coleman argues that because the development of television sitcom in America was a result of such series, not only should Black sitcom be seen as a separate genre in the same way as comedy drama, but that the term 'situation comedy' should refer only to Black series with 'white situation comedy' a developmental offshoot from it (2000, p. 68). Indeed, that terms such as 'Black comedy' or 'Black sitcom' exist whereas the white equivalents don't demonstrates the ways in which whiteness is culturally normalised. It also shows how, like many aspects of music and performance, white cultures assimilate and eventually dominate cultural forms which are, in origin, black.

Coleman argues that Black sitcom defines more than simply a series which has central black characters; it is also one in which much of the production team are black, and the series uses black experience, as understood and explored by blacks, as the focus of its humour. In this way, *The Cosby Show* clearly follows the lineage that she outlines. Indeed, considering television sitcom began with many black portrayals, it's a little surprising that, with notable exceptions, it took another thirty years or so for a series to come along which managed to be so successful and appeal to a broad range of audiences.

Along with that success came both acclaim and criticism. The debates which the series raises represent those which constantly plague the sitcom, but are focused here predominantly on matters of race. There were three broad ways in which the content of *The Cosby Show* was examined; 'the Huxtable family as a black middle-class family, the program's humor, and the fiction's realism' (Staiger, 2000, p. 144). Of these, it is the first and last which have received the most attention and which clearly interact with one another. It may be unsurprising considering the history of analysis of the sitcom that the kinds of jokes which exist in *The Cosby Show* are rarely explored, nor are the ways in which they are performed often theorised. As usual, the role of comedy within sitcom is downplayed and the consequences of comic representation are examined as if they are the same as those for serious programming.

That Bill Cosby wanted the series to be aspirational, with weekly moral and familial lessons learned by characters, is well documented, as is the fact that his educational qualifications were highlighted in the series' credits, and scripts were examined by developmental psychologists for their 'truthfulness' (Fuller, 1992). In this way, the series clearly attempted to make some kind of representational claim, though whether this was to an actual truth or a possible one is of some debate. So, while the series is often criticised for its lack of realism, the fact that its narrative continually portrayed a family who emotionally and ethically progressed every week (even if the sociocultural situation they were in remained the same) could suggest a form of realism which is emotionally, not economically, based.

However, critics of the series have repeatedly focused on the failure of the series to accurately reflect the economic and social hardships of the majority of black people living in America, and how therefore it wasn't 'realistic' (Joyrich, 1996, p. 118) or 'authentic' (Bodroghkozy, 2003, p. 405). More importantly, while it portrayed a comfortable, middle-class black family, the series neither demonstrated how it had achieved this position nor, other than brief nods towards the parents' legal and medical careers, how it remained there. The Huxtable family appears to be rich and comfortable simply because it is, a status which is not born of struggle. The series, it is argued, presents such a lifestyle as within the grasp of everyone, as readily attainable, and the result purely of the achievements of those within the family. That such a representation exists at a time when whites maintain their dominance – culturally, ideologically and economically – in America, is seen to be of concern.

Furthermore, the series rarely goes outside the confines of the Huxtable house, both geographically and ideologically. Like the majority of sitcom, the action occurs predominantly within the few sets which make up the family's home, which is unsurprising considering sitcom has repeatedly used a domestic setting. That the family in *The Cosby Show* should see their house as a safe haven from the complexities of the outside world is once again a recurring sitcom trope; many series position the home as one which is not only secure structurally, but also familialy. Sitcom repeatedly says that while most of the problems which result in comedic narratives are ones centred on the family, when push comes to shove families will always come together to repel disruptive outside forces. This is most clearly seen in *One Foot in the Grave*, where Victor Meldrew, housebound against his will due to enforced retirement, finds even his home is not protection from the outside forces of incompetent workers and antisocial neighbours. In sitcom, then, the home is a significant unifying element.

To criticise *The Cosby Show* for its small focus may be failing to recognise the heritage of sitcom. The problem is that *The Cosby Show* came along at precisely the point at which American sitcom producers had managed to work out how to use the genre to demonstrate the links between the domestic and the social and political forces which structure daily life and the problems which individuals encounter. That is, series such as *All in the Family/Till Death Us Do Part* and *M*A*S*H* had managed to exhibit the relationship between politics and daily existence, even though both of them rarely ventured out of the tiny locale in which they were set. By placing characters with different political and ideological beliefs in an inescapable familial relationship, *All in the Family /Till Death Us Do Part* forced the Archie Bunker/Alf Garnett character to face alternative lifestyles and modern politics which he not only hoped to keep outside the family and home, but which began to undermine those beliefs which he'd normalised. Similarly, *M*A*S*H* rarely ventured outside the tents of the hospital in which it was set, and could be read as a metaphor for war generally, particularly as its broadcast coincided with the latter years of America's involvement in the conflict in Vietnam. By making the series' narratives a result of broader political decisions made by those in power, it managed to powerfully demonstrate how 'ordinary' people have to deal with the messes made by politicians. At this point, sitcom, if not avowedly political, had begun to use its recurring inside/outside conflict as something other than a useful way to make comedy and, in doing so, started to demonstrate the possibilities of mainstream comedy with a political message. Significantly, *All in the Family* repeatedly centred such debates on race and the success of this led to the spin-off series *The Jeffersons* (CBS: 1975–85).

The possibility of a successful mainstream sitcom, centred on a black family, but which comically examined the nature of race and its relationship to economics and culture, was not that remote then. It is within this context that the reception of *The Cosby Show* must be understood. In presenting a successful black middle-class family who 'are never represented in situations where their racial identity matters' (Gray, 1989, p. 383), it failed to take advantage of the possibilities of using such a successful family to examine their lack of representativeness or the struggles which financial success cannot eradicate. Furthermore, any difficulties which did exist were presented as purely personal, rather than a result of broader social attitudes. So, while many of the characters did at some point encounter racism, this was always seen to be the prejudice of a group of individuals and didn't examine the ways in which such social conflicts come into being. It's possible to argue then that, in representing middle-class black existence as one free from the strife of working-class black experience (constantly seen in news programmes and documentaries), the series suggested that the difficulties facing the majority of black people in America were a result of their economic hardship, rather than a result of race. By presenting the Huxtables as hard-working, successful people who maintain their middle-class existence comfortably and not pointing out the difficulties in becoming wealthy if you're black, the suggestion is that failure to be so successful is purely a personal matter. That is, by embodying the American Dream, the Huxtables imply failure is nothing more than an individual trait.

Because the programme rarely acknowledged that its characters' race was an area of debate, it has also been criticised for its 'colorblindness' (Fuller, 1992, p. 120). That is, the success which the Huxtables have achieved is one which not only elevates them into the middle class but also defines such success as white. So, while there are brief acknowledgments to black culture (Cliff's love of jazz, his grandchildren being named Winnie and Mandela), the Huxtables live a life which can be read as normal simply because, in American society, white equals normal. In examining audience responses to the series Jhally and Lewis (1992) repeatedly demonstrate the ways in which white audiences see the Huxtables as 'normal' or successful through criteria which position whiteness as if it is neutral. Therefore, white audiences are invited by the series to like the Huxtables as it demonstrates that black people can be 'just like us' (p. 48), if only they abandon much of their culture and, more importantly, if they're rich. In this way, the series does nothing to make other aspects of black culture either acceptable or mainstream; nor does it in any way undermine the assumption that certain kinds of culture are simply dominant, and not normal or neutral at all.

Yet the majority of this analysis doesn't examine the ways in which individual moments of humour work within the series. That is, it would be possible for the series to be conventional in its setting and narratives, yet allow for new forms of black experience within the jokes it contains. Performance has been shown to be a significant force within the ways in which texts offer meanings to audiences. *The Cosby Show*'s comedy arises primarily out of its eponymous star, who dominates its opening titles and who brings with him the associations of decades of television work. The series' narratives are clearly constructed to allow Cosby the most time on air, and, as often as possible, to interact with children, a comedic skill he continued to employ in *Kids Say the Darndest Things* (CBS: 1996–2002). Quite often the funniest scenes are ones with little narrative drive at all and merely require Cosby to display his comic skills, particularly in response to the other characters; the framing and editing of the series repeatedly positions Cosby as central, giving him a (theatrical) space in which to perform. Cosby's performance is highly physical, in which his body and expressive face often supply the humour rather than the dialogue; similarly, his use of pauses and reactions to other characters not only results in laughs, but allows his comedic presence to dominate that of the other characters. A reading of Cosby could, then, highlight the positive qualities of his portrayal, which presents a funny character to an audience and doesn't conform to the heritage of black, stupid stereotypes which litter the history of comedy.

However, the possibilities of other readings demonstrate the difficulties in controlling audiences' reactions. So, while highlighting the possible positive implications of the preponderance of black characters in comedy, Coleman notes that 'The permanence of the buffoonic has been particularly troubling' (2000, p. 7). In looking at the heritage of black comedy characters, Coleman, King (2002) and Bodroghkozy (2003) find repetitive performance styles which suggest that comedy and blackness are often understandable in limited terms. The performance stereotype of the 'coon' is 'a harmless, little screwball creation whose eyes popped, whose hair stood on end with the least excitement, and whose antics were pleasant and diverting' (Bogle, 1994, p. 7). That this could serve as a definition of comedic performance generally supports Coleman's thesis that sitcom as a whole grew out of 'black sitcom'. Indeed, Chaney argues that the fact that white comedy characters are capable of adopting such techniques when parodying black culture shows how black people are defined by their 'static identity' (2004, p. 173).

In societies which value intelligence and reason, comedy performance is excessive because it demonstrates the ways in which funny characters are over-the-top, unintelligent and incapable of thinking before speaking. That Cliff Huxtable in *The Cosby Show* should perform in a similar manner not only makes him intelligible in a manner which undermines his supposed intelligence, it also renders him readable within the history of black sitcom performance. It's noticeable that it is precisely those aspects of Cosby which conform to the 'coon' stereotype which make him funny and, therefore, function within the sitcom genre; the other aspects of his character – his relationship with his family, his class, his education, his job – don't exist comedically, only diegetically. So, while the series may present a character and a family who undermine conventional ways of portraying black families, they don't manage to make any of this funny. Instead, the comedic moments in the series are ones which, depoliticised as they are, could exist within any setting.

Such portrayals are apparent in much black sitcom, regardless of its country of origin and those black comedians who have made the move from television to global film success predominantly employ an excessive performance technique. An examination of stars such as Whoopi Goldberg, Eddie Murphy, Martin Lawrence and Chris Rock demonstrates the similarities in their comedic performance style (Bogle, 1994; King, 2002; Leab, 1975; Musser, 1991; Winokur, 1991). The fact that it is these black stars who have not only managed to move from stand-up to television, but then from television to film, point to the limited opportunities available to black performers. Clearly Will Smith could be added to the list, as could Bernie Mac; indeed, the fact that Mac's performance as Bosley in *Charlie's Angels 2: Full Throttle* (McG: 2003) should be so excessive in comparison to his more subtle portrayal in *The Bernie Mac Show* – and particularly in comparison to Bill Murray's noticeably more muted performance as the same character in the first *Charlie's Angels* (McG: 2001) film – could suggest that the demands for such performances become stronger once the move is made from national television to global film.

However, little of this actually begins to make sense of the ways in which audiences actually understand such material. Certainly the global popularity of *The Cosby Show* suggests the programme's ability to remain intelligible and pleasurable across a range of cultures (Havens, 2000). Most notably, *The Cosby Show* was a minor success in Britain, broadcast on the minority channel Channel 4, and not achieving the same cultural awareness as other imported series (Ross, 1996, p. 100). For Havens, 'white Britons resisted *The Cosby Show* because the family was black' (2000, p. 377). It's certainly the case that Britain has repeatedly failed to produce successful, long-running black sitcom, and the only major, mainstream black comedy star at all is Lenny Henry, who starred in the first British black sitcom *The Fosters* (ITV: 1976–7). Instead, black sitcom characters have a history of being understood only in terms of white norms and as such have been criticised for their 'potentially damaging effect on race relations' (Daniels, 1994, p. 67). The only other notable black comedy series in Britain are *Desmond's* and its spin-off, *Porkpie* (Channel 4: 1995–6), both, again, on Channel 4, and *The Crouches*, unbelievably the BBC's first sitcom centred on a black family and roundly criticised in its first series not only for being unfunny, but mainly for being written by a white man (Asafu-Adjaye, 2003, p. 18). Because of this, *The Crouches* is seen as lacking the 'authenticity' (Bodroghkozy, 2003, p. 405) by which such representations are often judged. More successful in Britain has been Asian comedy, in series such as *Goodness Gracious Me* and *The Kumars at No. 42*, and films like *East Is East* (Damien O'Donnell, 1999), *Bend It Like Beckham* (Gurinder Chadha, 2002) and *Anita and Me* (Metin Hüseyin, 2002). Despite all this, 'British television comedy remains dominated by the cult of the alternative White comedian' (Malik, 2002, p. 102). Debates about race have always had a less visible presence in Britain than those of gender and class, and media portrayals of social inequality have always been filtered through those concerns, rather than, as in the US, race.

What is most significant here is the continuous manner in which comedy and sitcom are repeatedly examined (and criticised) for the representational strategies they employ. This persistence not only rests on an assumption about the social effects and role of media, but also the specificities of comedy and the role it can play in questioning, or supporting, social structures. *The Cosby Show* is of much concern precisely because it failed to offer representations which undermined widespread stereotypes and is therefore seen as a missed opportunity. The question still remains, though, as to what effect a truly radical programme would have on social structures, representations in other texts, and audiences. After all, progressive comedy 'serves liberal progress but does not directly threaten any of the protected interests of super media ownership and the dominant class' (Real, 2003, p. 245). The fact that critics constantly call on comedy and sitcom to be threatening for precisely these reasons not only assumes something about what comedy should be for, but also what viewers are able to do with it. Yet while audiences must employ the required strategies to make sense of the humorous material presented to them, the ways in which they distinguish between narrative, diegesis and jokes have significance for examining the possible effects of such comedy. How audiences consume, make sense of and enjoy sitcom must be examined in order for assumptions about the importance of sitcom representation to be relevant, and this is an area in which there's a significant lack of research.

Chapter 5 | Sitcom Consumption

'This is sitcom we're talking about, not fucking Ibsen.'

David Lodge, *Therapy* (London: Secker & Warburg, 1995), p. 171.

Debates about the content of sitcom – whether these examine its generic aspects, its performance or its representational strategies – become meaningless unless audiences and consumption are examined. The industrial nature of sitcom production, coupled with the commercial concerns which help inform its content, are capitalist responses to the desires of consumers and governmental broadcasting structures. While this is true of all media, the role of the audience is more readily apparent in sitcom because of the genre's primary aim to make its viewers laugh. As has been noted, the use of the laugh track means that sitcom is one of the few genres to actively acknowledge its audience and to use them as part of the text. In addition, the fact that sitcom's goal is so straight-forward and 'measurable' in contrast to other genres means that audience response is central to it. This means sitcom is a genre which invites audience response in a much more transparent way than the vast majority of media forms, and so understanding that audience helps make sense of all aspects of it.

Yet it's noticeable how rarely analysis of the sitcom has attempted to come to terms with the people who consume it. The debates about representation which infringe on virtually everything written about the sitcom are usually removed from the experiences of its viewers. Even though there are pressure groups that monitor and examine sitcom representation, coupled with individuals who may be offended by particular series or episodes, the majority of people who watch sitcoms probably prioritise the genre's enter-tainment function over its representational strategies. Sitcom's longevity rests far less on the possible progressiveness of any individual series and far more on whether audiences find them funny or not. Of course, critics such as Grote (1983) and Marc (1989) see this as precisely the point; the genre's prioritisation of entertainment over the social role of comedy demonstrates the commercial and industrial strategies which have neutered the anarchic and subversive power of humour, particularly as sitcom is the widest reaching comedy form.

There are a couple of problems with this. First, it assumes that debates about how a form should be are more important than examination of how they are; it seems a little presumptuous to call for changes in sitcom's form and content when so little work has been carried out on it, particularly as there's a lack of understanding of the ways audiences make sense of it. Second, it ignores the other possible pleasures associated with comedy's humour. While comedy may have been a powerful tool for social critique historically, it has always offered a simultaneous entertainment function. The pleasures which comedy and sitcom can offer are complex and important; indeed, it can be argued that this is the primary aspect of comedy. That the sitcom has rarely been examined in terms of why people enjoy it not only says something about the biases of much media analysis, it also highlights the fact that the natures of pleasure and enjoyment have received scant attention as a whole.

This arises from a suspicion of entertainment generally, which renders analysis of it too entertaining to be meaningful or significant. I've lost count of the number of times I've been criticised for spending my time watching and analysing sitcoms because it's an entertaining thing to do, when colleagues who do the same with documentaries, art or literature don't receive such censure. It is also difficult to make generalised statements about the nature of entertainment and enjoyment. The extremely personal nature of an individual's sense of humour means that 'When it comes to what amuses us, we are all authorities, experts in the field' (Critchley, 2002, p. 2). This possible range of responses to comedy results in the vast majority of television sitcoms failing with audiences and being hauled off the air. If comedy did function in a uniform way and audience responses to it were predictable, the television industries would be far more successful in tempering their output to audience desires. But the history of sitcom is littered with the failed output of writers, producers, directors and actors whose previous comedy efforts have entertained millions, such as John Sullivan's *Heartburn Hotel* (BBC 1: 1998–2000), Simon Nye's *The Savages* (BBC 1: 2001), Caroline Aherne's *Dossa and Joe* (BBC 2: 2002), Susan Harris's *The Golden Palace* (CBS: 1992–3), Norman Lear's *704 Hauser* (CBS: 1994) and Chris Morris's *Nathan Barley*.

The nature of entertainment and pleasure is made more complex by the fact that enjoyment of sitcom can often contradict 'politically correct' readings of it. It's certainly possible to enjoy a 'racist' or 'sexist' joke while simultaneously being offended by it, meaning there's a contradiction between ideologies held outside humour and the lure of pleasure. Enjoyment of such material can function as some sort of 'guilty pleasure', in which the transgressive nature of humour is itself part of the satisfaction; indeed, the very nature of comedy – particularly in a Freudian (1960) sense – means that it is such transgressive pleasures which lie at its heart. Perhaps the nature of enjoyment in comedy has been so often ignored, then, because it powerfully undermines those very ideals which the majority of analysts want comedy to fulfil. This personal and contradictory aspect of the pleasures of comedy is best summed up by Brook: 'I come to praise *Will and Grace* as a liberal, but to critique it as a progressive. As a radical, I have no business watching it at all' (2003, p. 10).

Audience Research

However, there has been useful work carried out on the ways in which audiences make sense of sitcom. Significantly, the majority of such work examines audiences to determine the ways in which their responses conform to assumptions about the stable and regressive nature of sitcom content. There has been quite a bit of work done on the ways in which black audiences respond to black sitcom characters and whether such readings demonstrate an unquestioned or assumed racism. For example, Bodroghkozy (1995) analyses the letters and phone calls NBC received when they broadcast their sitcom *Julia* (1970–3). This programme portrayed the life of a black, working-class widow, looking at the topic of race in only a very muted form and was produced by Norman Lear, a man with a history of provocative and radical sitcoms to his name. While the programme received little widespread attention and was neither censured nor applauded for its portrayal of a black character, Bodroghkozy still finds a large disparity in the readings of the programme by different ethnic groups.

So, black viewers appeared to wish to participate more actively in the construction of the programme. That is, 'while white viewers offered criticisms of the program, only the black viewers took it upon themselves to offer their assistance in improving the show' (p. 421). Bodroghkozy suggests that black viewers were much keener to make the programme 'meaningful', for they felt that it was a chance to construct representations different to those in most sitcom. To white viewers the programme was a sitcom which just happened to have a black actress in the main role; black viewers wished it to be a statement about their lives and wanted Julia to represent the black way of life. The problem for black viewers was that *Julia* is a programme about black people but from a white point of view and the fact that the majority of the production staff was white only reinforced this unease. For white viewers, conversely, this is precisely what made the programme acceptable. In addition, white viewers were more likely to see the programme as progressive, for it portrayed a black person living a 'normal' life and the humour and situations did not rely on Julia's blackness for their meaning. However, to black viewers, this was also a problem, as the programme portrayed a black person living a normal *white* life and not what would be common for a black widow. The representation the programme offered to the black audience was that 'black people were "just people" to the extent that they conformed to an unexamined white norm of representation' (p. 416).

Jhally and Lewis (1992) find similar audience responses to *The Cosby Show*. White viewers saw the programme as progressive because if the characters were white they'd be the same, whereas for black audiences that was precisely the problem. This feeds into unexamined assumptions about 'the normal' which, in Western cultures, centre predominantly on white-ness (Dyer, 1997), and so for a white audience a positive black portrayal is one which renders black characters the same as 'us'. Jhally and Lewis call this 'enlightened racism', for white audiences condone a particular version of racism towards blacks, while simultaneously failing to see that acknowledging cultural differences between races, nations and ethnicities is vital to understanding and acceptance. As has been shown, there's a significant disparity between the number of black sitcoms in Britain and America, which suggests that British audiences find black sitcom characters more problematic.

While these analyses attempt to demonstrate the problematic ideologies sitcom's pleasures rest on, an alternative response could be to celebrate the variety of ways in which it's possible for audiences to make meanings from the genre. Recent ethnographic audience research has focused squarely on the variety of ways in which audiences make sense of what they watch and sitcom seems a logical genre for this to be applied to. So, Gillespie demonstrates the alternative readings London Asian audiences make of a range of television programmes including sitcoms (1995). Elsewhere, she shows how white–British and Asian–British audiences make different readings of the Asian sketch show, *Goodness Gracious Me* (2003). Similarly, Doty (1993, 2003) outlines how a vast number of sitcoms – such as *Bewitched*, *I Dream of Jeannie* (NBC: 1965–70) and *Sex and the City* – have alternative readings which recast characters as gay, or are seen to offer camp pleasures which are enjoyed by gay and lesbian viewers. That such readings are rarely explored, and that instead examination of the sitcom commonly adopts a white middle-class, male approach, not only demonstrates the backgrounds of those doing the analysis, but also downplays the variety of ways sitcom can be enjoyed.

Rarely in such analyses is the notion of pleasure – and, in particular, comic pleasure – explored. While Jhally and Lewis find that white audiences take pleasure in their assumed progressive understandings of *The Cosby Show*, this is demonstrated through examination of character representation and narrative development. Yet *The Cosby Show* is a series which offers many pleasures in its performances and particularly in that of Cosby himself. This is obviously apparent in the series in those moments where, as previously discussed, the narrative halts while Cosby carries out some kind of comic riffing, most commonly with a child. And understanding the pleasures of such moments is important because it may be here that positive, progressive aspects of sitcom may be found. That is, while it's possible to read the series' diegesis as one which fails to foreground significant aspects of black culture, the comic pleasure of the series is an almost extra-diegetic one centred around the actor Bill Cosby rather than his character Cliff Huxtable. The pleasures of the comic moments of *The Cosby Show* may be quite different to those associated with either its narrative or diegesis and Cosby's performance may demonstrate aspects of 'black-ness' which the rest of the series doesn't. While these two parts of the programme may contradict one another, it's surely the case that audiences watch the programme far more for the comic pleasures it offers than any amount of narrative development, and so what needs to be examined is why such large audiences enjoy the comic performance of this particular actor and character.

Other audience research has shown how audiences understand the role of sitcom within broadcasting. For example, Hargrave questioned audiences over their expectations of television, and discovered that 'the key indicator of the likely content of a programme was its timing' (1995, p. 6). She goes on to demonstrate audiences' awareness of the relationship between genre and scheduling, and to show that viewers are able to transfer this theoretical knowledge onto their expectations for particular series and episodes. While Hargrave doesn't explore the notion of audience pleasure, the fact that audiences are able to recreate the scheduling strategies of broadcasters demonstrates their understanding of the relationship between pleasures and scheduling, which has implications for the ways in which viewers seek out particular programmes for the implied pleasures they offer.

Overall, though, there is a notable lack of examination of sitcom audiences and the ways in which they make sense of series, episodes, comic moments and performance. This is unfortunate, particularly as Media Studies' and Cultural Studies' recent use of ethnography to examine the ways in which women gain pleasure from soaps has not only demonstrated the complex and personal ways in which audiences function, but has also undermined many negative assumptions about soaps and their effects on those who consume them. Furthermore, ethnography has demonstrated the active nature of audiences; considering the nature of humour and laughter is one which itself consistently demonstrates active audience response to comic material, it would seem that analysis of audiences is the next logical step in understanding sitcom.

Pleasure

Herbert argues that definitions and divisions of what makes people laugh are nowhere near as important as creating an overarching theory which incorporates the enjoyment offered by humour. That is, comedies have no purpose other than their 'primordial fixation upon pleasure' (1984, p. 402). Yet there are particular ways in which pleasure functions in the sitcom distinct from those of humour and comedy within society because of the conventions of broadcasting and the effect of narrative. The pleasures of sitcom oscillate between those of comic moments and narrative development, with both of these aspects partly reliant on one another for their effects. The pleasures of sitcom can also be non-comic and instead involve either intense character identification or the enjoyment of tragedy or melodrama. *Friends* certainly offers emotional pleasures which don't rely on comedy. While *Soap* mocked the conventions of the genre it parodied, it also offered the possibility of enjoying the melodramatic twists and turns which befell its characters. *Only Fools and Horses* developed an intense relationship between its audience and the developing family relationships of its characters, in particular in those scenes based around Rodney and Del Boy's love lives. And Morreale notes that final episodes of sitcoms often offer different pleasures from other episodes precisely because they acknowledge the massive investment viewers have made in series and their characters, especially as 'sitcoms rarely say goodbye' (2003b, p. 274).

Curtis notes that the audience position offered by the sitcom 'is manifestly one of the satisfaction of watching sitcom' (1982, p. 9). That is, when audiences watch sitcoms a large part of what they enjoy comprises precisely those things which most transparently define the genre. In terms of the ways in which genres offer 'repetition and difference' (Neale, 1992, p. 48), this is the comfort of repetition. However, Curtis goes on to suggest that the audience's position for sitcom is one in which the deviancies which occur are seen to be deviant precisely because the audience is offered a 'normal' position from which it is marked (1982, p. 9). Indeed, examination of humour has usually assumed that 'One of the pleasures offered by comedy is the freedom vicariously to enjoy departures from the norm' (King, 2002, p. 7), without the radical social implications such departures may inspire. Therefore, it's argued that sitcom merely recreates the subversive pleasures of comedy in a manner which is ultimately unthreatening; that the media industries manage to make money out of this demonstrates the success of consumer capitalism in appropriating the very aspects of society which could most effectively threaten it. Pleasure, then, becomes merely a commodity and while the sitcom may offer enjoyment in disruption of social norms, it does so within a medium which distances that disruption from anything outside it.

MPs saw *Yes, Minister* as a celebration of their working environment, contrary to the intentions of the programme's production team

But this does not necessarily imply a staid conventionality in the form. As Curtis notes, 'Ignorance, lack of sympathy with or enthusiasm for the transgressions involved can fail to generate a comic response, and, in that case, deny the "meaning" of the comedy' (1982, p. 9). This acknowledges the fact that, as Hall's (1980) encoding/decoding model points out, audiences are capable of constructing negotiated and oppositional readings of programmes. A series which is intended to offer an audience position in line with a dominant ideology by using humour to mock deviancies can instead be repositioned by those whom it is ridiculing, and read as a celebration. This can be seen in the readings made of *Yes, Minister* by members of the civil service; while the programme was intended as a scathing satire on the excesses of government, it ended up being the favourite programme of many Members of Parliament because they read it as a celebration of their environment (Oakley, 1982, p. 69). While the pleasures of the jokes in the programme may be the same for a variety of audiences, the consequences of those pleasures differed significantly from what was intended.

Audiences are offered a 'dual reading focus' (Cook, 1982, p. 18) for sitcom. That is, audiences are offered pleasures common to most narrative television (a story well told; likeable, recurring characters; enigmas and solutions; and so on), but these exist in common with those of comedy itself, which do not necessarily coincide with those of narrative drama. Goddard argues that the dual reading focus is born out of the nature of comedy itself. For sitcom to find humour in the disruption of norms and expectations, it is necessary for it to present those norms so that there's something for the disruption to be measured against (1991, p. 80). An audience's reading of a sitcom depends on their ability to understand the norms presented by the programme while simultaneously finding pleasure in their destruction. And, because that which often disrupts – such as absurd narrative and deliberately comic performance – is usually presented in a manner incongruous to those aspects which construct the programme's diegesis, the audience is required to simultaneously accept the 'realism' of the programme and maintain distance from it. So the naturalism presented by sitcom is based on an audience 'suspending disbelief in return for pleasure' (ibid.). It is necessary to 'believe' the diegesis of any particular sitcom only to the point that the comedy which contradicts it begins to make sense. While sitcoms such as *M*A*S*H*, *One Foot in the Grave*, *The Mary Tyler Moore Show* and *The Office* may be lauded for being in some sense realistic, it's actually quite apparent that they're not, and they all contain characters and events which don't happen in the 'real world'. In sitcom, realism instead points to a suitability between the diegesis created by the programme and its humour, so that series are commended because it appears as if the comedy arises 'naturally' out of character and situation. The reading strategy required for sitcom is one which prioritises the pleasures of humour, and audiences are willing to ignore a whole host of implausibilities and coincidences if the jokes are good enough.

What this suggests is that the pleasures relevant to the sitcom differ to those for other genres and forms, and are a significant part of defining it. Zillmann (2000) finds that a desire to enjoy the pleasures of humour not only has a range of physical and psychological properties, but that comedy is often deliberately sought out by individuals because of the benefits it offers. The pleasures of sitcom, then, are ones which audiences know are different to those of other genres, and which they might sometimes actively try to find. Such pleasures don't reside purely within the text; the social nature of watching sitcoms as a family or a group – as demonstrated by the massive audience ratings for Christmas specials of sitcoms in Britain – shows that the pleasures of sitcom can also come from the context of consumption. Comedy's social role is often assumed to be that it critiques and examines social systems; yet it can also be one which binds groups together at the moment of consumption. The laugh track is a device which attempts to remind audiences that they're not laughing at this stuff alone, and therefore the pleasures of comedy – as demonstrated by people quoting funny lines and catchphrases – are often social. Indeed, Gauntlett and Hill find that *The Simpsons* functions as a 'communal viewing event' (1999, p. 37) for families and people living in shared houses.

Yet the pleasures offered by particular series can vary, depending on particular audience members and moments of consumption. Hartley outlines the different readings he and his daughters make of *Clarissa Explains It All* (Nickelodeon: 1991–3), finding that the pleasures they get from it are affected primarily by age and gender (1999, pp. 181–5). Elsewhere he similarly outlines the very personal meanings of *Whatever Happened to the Likely Lads?* (BBC 1: 1973–4), in which the series connects into nostalgic memories of his past. In these ways, the pleasures of sitcom are bound up in very personal matters of identity and memory, and the commercial success of 'classic' sitcoms on DVD demonstrates how people are willing to rewatch comedy from their past. Watching sitcom can function as a re-enactment of earlier pleasures and the joy in laughing at jokes you've already heard is quite different to that for new ones.

To understand pleasure, then, is to attempt to make sense of a broad range of complex phenomena, which can be personal and social, momentary and enduring, progressive and reactionary, physical and mental. The precise reasons why audiences seek out comedy, and gain pleasure from it, are inadequately understood. To merely say 'because it is funny' not only ignores a variety of other possibilities, but also downplays the complexity of funniness itself. Discussions about pleasure inevitably become mired in a theoretical trap in which every aspect of sitcom can only be applauded for what it demonstrates about recurring debates about representation. That is, by arguing that, for example, the pleasure of Bill Cosby's performance in *The Cosby Show* may be progressive, I'm still prioritising the notion of progressiveness over that of pleasure. Cultural Studies as a whole seems unable to come to terms with pleasure, for it repeatedly assumes that enjoyment is a tool used by the powerful to satiate the public, and is only meaningful and worthwhile if it in some way subverts dominant ideologies. This is not to deny that the vast majority of entertainment may have little radical force; however,

I'm arguing that pleasure may in and of itself be significant. Indeed, considering the academy's mistrust of pleasure, it's unsurprising that Cultural Studies has so much difficulty examining popular forms on their own (and their audiences') terms. That analysis of media has failed to make sense of pleasure as a whole highlights a significant gap in understanding audiences' relationship with media, as well as revealing why it is that sitcom – as a form built on the promise of pleasure – has been inadequately theorised.

Offence

Pleasure is not the only possible response to sitcom and comedy. While it's perfectly possible to sit stony-faced through a sitcom and reject the comedy it has on offer, refusing to accept the humour of a joke can also result in offence. It's noticeable that sitcom has been discussed far more during those times when it has caused offence and is therefore far more visible as a genre when it constitutes some kind of social problem. Offence is an aspect of all communication and the regulatory bodies which govern media – certainly those responsible for television – oversee decisions and resulting punishments when audiences complain. Television comedy is a form which is seen to require regulation and this is done because of the social role broadcasting fulfils generally. While it's perfectly possible for social jokes to be understood as offensive, it's rare for such offence to result in legal proceedings or the adjudication of regulatory bodies. The nature of sitcom offence, then, is inextricably bound up with assumptions about broadcasting, which means that there are aspects of comic content which, while acceptable in social communication, become problematic once on television. Offence is useful for critics keen to highlight the active nature of audiences because it demonstrates that viewers not only construct readings which probably weren't intended by programme-makers, but also define themselves as arbiters of what is socially acceptable in broadcasting. That Perren can recount the 'letter-writing campaign' (2003, p. 110) which called for the removal of the lewd and crude *Married . . . with Children* shows the responsibility and power audiences feel they should have, and how this can be evoked by offensive comedy material. Of course, the fact that the series continued, successfully, unabated, for many years may say something about the ways in which broadcasters see their viewers.

While the fear of offence is a logical one for a television industry which will lose audiences and revenue if it offends its viewers, the debate, particularly in Britain, is rarely couched in commercial terms. Instead, offence is seen as something unacceptable in broadcasting merely because of the effect it has upon those who are offended. Such assumptions also work from the belief that there is a relationship between media portrayals and social inequality more broadly, which is why offence is commonly bound up in issues of portrayal. Certainly the debates about *Till Death Us Do Part* and *All in the Family* often revolved around the offensive language used by the series' main character to describe minority groups and other cultures, and the possibility that this might support or incite racial hatred in society.

Indeed, the whole debate about the nature of representation in comedy is one which, while rarely acknowledging audience offence, certainly sees reactionary and regressive portrayals as offensive. Yet the relationship between comedy and offence is different to that for other modes, particularly as comedy is assumed to function as an arena in which the unsayable can be voiced. For Freud, it's vital that it does so, for venting 'psychical energy' (1960, p. 199) through offensive comedy releases repression which might otherwise express itself through violence. There's certainly pleasure to be gained from particular kinds of offensive material (depending on your sense of humour), and humour can be seen to function as 'permitted disrespect' (Radcliffe-Brown, 1952, p. 91). The ways in which stand-up comedians treat their volunteers and audience members would be unacceptable outside comedy and the pleasures on offer here are often ones of shock as much as funniness. The ways in which stand-ups alter their act once they appear on television show that what may be fine in a comedy club is problematic once transferred to the social arena of broadcasting.

Yet there has been much sitcom which has deliberately attempted to offend its audience; or, at least, specific subsections of it. Taylor argues that *The Young Ones* was meant to be seen as disgusting and alienate certain audience groups in the process. As the programme saw itself as undermining and redrawing both sitcom structure and content – as part of Alternative Comedy's aims – it was inevitable that, in its use of language, violence and humour about bodily functions, it would offend some people. Similarly, McArthur (1998) argues that *Rab C. Nesbitt's* use of Scottish vernacular and slang was

Is *Rab C. Nesbitt* a hoary old stereotype or a progressive display of linguistic subversion?

read as retreading a hoary old stereotype by some but, for him, was instead a progressive display of linguistic subversion. Concerns over the representation of national identity are also explored by Free (2001), who notes the range of responses to the portrayal of Ireland and the Irish in *Father Ted*, which deliberately attempted to play around with stereotypes in a manner which may not have been read as such by all of its viewers.

Comedy and violence have had a long-standing relationship, and there's a whole range of violent acts that are acceptable in sitcom but which would draw censure if a part of serious forms. However, this hasn't stopped concerns over the possible effects of comic violence leading to complaints and campaigns. This has been particularly apparent in the recent trend in adult animation, with many series condemned amid fears of copycat behaviour. Thus *Beavis and Butt-head* was criticised from its very first episode, in which the two main characters use a frog as a ball in a game of baseball (Kellner, 2000). Such concerns moved beyond individual audience complaints, and were seized upon by government figures, for 'Former US Attorney General Janet Reno said that shows like B+B were causing the decline of youth in the Western Civilization' (Kozintsev, 2002, p. 425). Such criticisms echo those for *The Simpsons* a few years earlier, in which Bart's unswerving 'underachiever and proud of it' attitude coupled with his parents' lax attitude towards their familial responsibilities led to then President George Bush stating that America needed less families like the Simpsons, and more like the Waltons (Flew 1994, p. 14). In this way, fears arose that

> animated narratives constructed from the perspective of the fourth grade hellion Bart were sure to produce a new generation of rebellious underachievers who are 'proud of it, man', and not about to back down in the face of proper authority. (Glynn, 1996, p. 63)

Similar concerns over the effects of animation have been voiced for both *Ren and Stimpy* and *South Park*, particularly as the latter's main characters are children (Larsen, 2001).

While all these debates rest on assumptions about the nature of media effects, it's significant that the most feared series on television seem to be cartoons. This is because while these series clearly offer what are conventionally defined as adult pleasures, their 'double coding' (Wells, 1998, p. 225) means that they can be enjoyed by children too; indeed, Western assumptions about animation mean that they're coded as children's media first and foremost. For sitcom this represents a new phase in debates about offensiveness, in which assumptions that the kinds of comedy acceptable for children and adults should be kept separate have fallen apart.

Offence, just like pleasure, is a phenomenon which, while clearly influenced by social and cultural norms, can often be predominantly personal. Riggs finds that elderly viewers' responses to *Roseanne* often defined the character as 'revolting' and 'vulgar' (1998, p. 54) precisely because she failed to conform to those notions of femininity which other critics have repeatedly maligned. She also recounts one male elderly viewer who responded very negatively to *The Fresh Prince of Bel-Air* who 'finally noted that his own prejudice against African Americans probably motivated him to feel this way' (p. 135). While such responses latch into lifelong ideologies, it's clear that comedy can also be offensive because of an unfortunate coincidence between its content and contemporary events, which wouldn't matter only a few weeks or days before. From my own experience, a scene about a funeral which involved all manner of slapstick misadventures befalling the coffin in *If You See God, Tell Him* (BBC 1: 1993) didn't go down too well in my family's home the day after my Dad died. Comedy always carries the risk with it of offence; indeed, it's this possibility, and the success when comedians and sitcoms manage to skirt it, which is one of its pleasures.

And Finally . . .

This debate about the possible offensive nature of sitcom rests on the assumption that, first, the content of sitcom says something about the society which it is made for and which consumes it, and second, that it is capable of having some kind of effect – whether in terms of change or reinforcement – upon that society. Yet it has been demonstrated that to make statements about this role that are neither too generalised nor too specific is extremely problematic. Ethnography has been one method which Media Studies has employed in an attempt to overcome making broad theoretical statements that fail to acknowledge the complexities of media consumption. However, this hasn't stopped a whole range of sitcom critics repeatedly exposing the genre as reactionary, conservative, and contrary to the radical history of comedy as a whole, even though there's still no evidence to prove that comedy either upholds or creates social understandings. The debate concerning the conservative nature of the sitcom has to acknowledge that while there are methodological concerns in demonstrating the effects or consequences of comedy, the repeated assumption that this is a fundamental aspect of the way in which it works cannot be merely denied and instead must be confronted. My main point is that it has been the failure to acknowledge sitcom's complexities which has resulted in serious flaws within existing analysis of it, and this book has aimed to, if nothing else, broaden out the ways in which it can be thought about. This doesn't, however, render the debate of sitcom's social role as redundant; it instead offers extra ammunition in interrogating it.

Television exists, on the whole, to offend as few people as possible. Because of the mass nature of the medium, it is likely that ideologies which are seen to be representative of the majority of viewers are those which are most common. It is this which has led to many critics maligning sitcom for its repetitive and stable nature, even though, if this is true, it must also be so for broadcasting generally. This means that sitcom is forever plagued by 'constraints' (Mills, 1998) whose cause may be specific to the genre, applicable to all media or related more broadly to the social role of comedy. The implication in this viewpoint is that comedy is currently neutered by the commercial and homogenising nature of broadcasting, and therefore what it gets to say is severely limited.

Yet the argument criticising sitcom's limitations is usually not one that says constraints should not exist at all. Critics who malign the genre's repetitiveness do not do so from a position that supports unquestioned free speech; the argument is that certain kinds of representation, which currently don't exist, should. In addition to this, the argument runs that those representations currently prevalent feed into, and come out of, social structures which legitimise certain voices. Thus the portrayals of African Americans in *The Cosby Show* are deemed acceptable by the institution of television in ways which a whole range of other possible African American representations aren't. And while the television industry can argue about the 'truthfulness' of its portrayals as much as it wants, the construction of the broadcasting institutions means that the 'acceptable portrayals' are given a preponderance of airtime, whereas the latter are ghettoised or denied entirely.

In this way, accessibility to a public space is seen to uphold a range of power structures:

> one of the most effective ways a group has of reducing people to silence is by
> excluding them from the positions from which one can speak. Conversely, one of the
> ways for a group to control discourse consists in filling the positions from which one
> can speak with people who will only say what the field authorizes and calls for.
> (Bourdieu, 1993, p. 92)

It is this notion of 'authority' which is seen to uphold these structures and voices which appear on television and are authorised by their being broadcast. Furthermore, by denying some groups access to this public forum the legitimacy of television is seen to be upheld; the fact that there is a selection process means that audiences are expected to assume that those voices which do appear are in some way authorised over those which don't. After all, if everyone gets to speak, how will we know who to believe? This is what Bourdieu and Passeron term 'the magisterial discourse' (1990, p. 109), and it supports a system which can only be questioned by those with authority that the system itself bestows, resulting in a repeated reiteration of the known.

This system's existence is enshrined within the construction of the television institutions, and feeds into reading strategies employed by audiences. It supports, critics argue, broadcasting which fails to conform to Habermas's 'public sphere' (1989). Because of this, 'The public service claim to representativeness is a defence of *virtual* representation of a fictive whole, a resort to programming which *simulates* the actual opinions and tastes of only *some* of those to whom it is directed' (Keane, 1995, p. 263). The criticism, then, is one that not only argues that television is unrepresentative of its audience's demographic makeup and opinions, but also that it is structured in such a way as to convince the audience that this is not the case. This imbalance is seen to be a consequence of the editorial processes within the television industry, which upholds its own legitimacy by that very selection.

A solution to this may be the eradication of any form of editorial process within the television industry, but it is difficult to see how this could be achieved to the satisfaction of all members of a society. Littlewood and Pickering note the dilemma inherent in such a proposition; the removal of that process would indeed give access to a wider range of voices and opinions, even though this means that sexist or racist material – or other forms seen by those in power as unacceptable – would be an inevitable result (1998, p. 294). They argue that more groups should be given access to television as long as they're 'the right' ones, however these are defined. The problem that remains highlights the complex nature of attempting to construct a broadcasting industry which doesn't discriminate against any group unfairly while working out which groups this actually means. It is these complexities which the regulatory bodies would argue they are trying to find some compromise between.

The most visible debates in terms of this revolve around gender, race and sexuality, precisely because there are specific pressure groups working to raise awareness around these topics. So, the anti-racist and anti-sexist ideologies which some Alternative Comedians argued were intrinsic to their comedy (Wilmut and Rosengard, 1989, pp. 2–3) were a result of social shifts and public campaigns to alter attitudes towards these groups generally, even though these debates are nowhere near a resolution either in comedy or anywhere else.

However, those within the television industry are now so concerned about the possibility of criticism concerning representations of these groups, coupled with increased audience sensitivity to the political implications of comedy, that this has resulted in a lack of such portrayals overall. By making the representation of, say, race, an extremely problematic phenomenon, comedy's effectiveness, which relies on easily understood texts and instances, is undermined. Viewers have yet to discover *how* they're meant to laugh at blacks, females or gays in contemporary comedy without inadvertently supporting power structures which keep these groups subordinate, precisely because the comedy industry has yet to offer concrete alternative reading strategies. Of course, I'm not arguing that we should go back to sexist, racist and homophobic comedy; the point is that there is a conflict between the requirements of effective mainstream television comedy and complex portrayals, especially for mass audiences. The difficulty in solving this conflict has resulted in the banishment of such portrayals either to minority channels or off television altogether, and it's difficult to see this as a positive step.

Such statements become more problematic when considering the notion of class, partly because there aren't visible groups fighting for the better depiction of social classes. Wagg works through the last five decades of broadcast comedy, finding that, with a few notable exceptions – *Steptoe and Son* and, in particular, *Till Death Us Do Part* – working-class life has been repeatedly ignored by British sitcoms, and, when it has appeared, it has usually focused on domestic aspects of it rather than the workplace (1998, pp. 4–21). He argues that this is particularly apparent in the 1990s, where sitcom has become very middle-class and, if workplaces are presented, they are likely to be those associated with the media and are thus middle class (p. 23). This dichotomy is clear in *The Royle Family* which, while drawing on British soap opera traditions for representing the working class, never moves out of the confines of its domestic setting. Wagg suggests that contemporary comedy doesn't so much fail to represent the working class sympathetically or accurately as much as it fails to acknowledge that it even exists. The implied criticism is that this reinforces power structures in which not only are such people denied access to the medium, but that the content of their lives is not deemed worthy of broadcast through it. It is suggested that this is a result of the demographics of the television industry whose staff are overwhelmingly middle class.

Yet working-class sitcoms have begun to appear, and this may be in response to the success of *The Royle Family*. *Early Doors* (BBC 2: 2003–) is similar to *The Royle Family* in that it has very little action and places itself within the other traditional British soap opera setting, the local pub. BBC 3 has certainly attempted to represent working-class lifestyle because it seems to presume it's synonymous with the youth audience it's aiming for, in series such as *Two Pints of Lager and a Packet of Crisps* and *Ideal*. Peter Kay, in both *Peter Kay's Phoenix Nights* and *Max and Paddy's Road to Nowhere* (Channel 4: 2005–), draws on his Northern working-class background and it came as no surprise when he appeared in a comic cameo role in *Coronation Street* (ITV: 1960–). Common themes, such as Northern settings, alcohol, accents and a focus on the ordinariness of everyday life occur within all these series, and so it could be argued that comedy draws on particular versions of working-class life in order to be funny. Rowbotham and Beynon (2001) argue that working-class depictions often draw on understandings of the past and traditions, and there's certainly little in any of these series which means they couldn't be set any time in the last thirty years.

There is also the question of genre here. There are working-class portrayals on television, but they are far more likely to be within docusoaps, reality television and, in Britain, soap operas. Why this should be the case is moot, but to argue that there aren't sympathetic working-class portrayals on British television ignores its most popular genre. The answer may simply be, then, that the codes and conventions of each of these genres are ones in which the depiction of certain social classes are expected by audiences, and programmes are read in terms of these. However, this doesn't undermine the contradiction that the working class are visible in British soap opera but often missing from sitcom, and that comedy's potential for social analysis is one which some critics would argue should be focused on all people. Working-class characters are even less apparent in American sitcom, mirroring the lack of such characters in American television as a whole.

A possible response to the problem of the lack of representation is that, 'There can be no significant context-shift until members of subordinated groups are the ones who are telling the jokes, regardless of their content. Indeed, in such cases the material may be similar to "politically incorrect" comedy' (Littlewood and Pickering, 1998, p. 308). However, such a solution is surely simplistic, even if it would offer currently unrepresented groups access to the 'public sphere'. While a joke's teller affects its reception and can alter meanings which are made from it by a variety of audiences, not all audiences will consume jokes in the manner intended. Indeed, subordinate groups telling jokes could, instead, merely serve to reinforce those assumptions which individual audience members have already made about them. So, while *Goodness Gracious Me* is an obvious attempt by its writers and performers to offer representations not seen elsewhere, and to reposition the Asian in comedy as not merely a butt, this is not the only reading which can result in comic pleasure. *Goodness Gracious Me* makes jokes about Asians' arranged marriages and working in corner shops, and while this is an attempt to offer such jokes from a particular perspective, it is perfectly possible for them to be read as merely confirming stereotypes. And, as comedy often relies on butts, *Goodness Gracious Me* has to present pathetic, inadequate, laughable Asians in order to be funny. Of course, the programme also offers these butts as funny from an Asian perspective but, to someone unwilling to read it as such, this could just be funny per se. It is simply impossible for programme-makers to completely control the readings which audiences make of their programmes, and this is even more problematic when the content differs from the audience's expectations for comedy, when they fail to employ the required reading strategies.

Littlewood and Pickering argue that it would be acceptable to excuse comics from subordinated groups telling jokes which are 'politically incorrect' because the fact that they are a different kind of comedian is more progressive than a standard comedian adopting a 'politically correct' stance (1998, p. 308). Yet such an argument endorses black and African American comedians making a range of jokes about their colour, and offering the black comedian as butt. Furthermore, they see this as more progressive than a number of Alternative Comedians attempting to refuse to conform to such stereotyping, and instead trying to pursue a more progressive line. Bernard Manning or Andrew 'Dice' Clay's racist, sexist and homophobic humour, then, would be progressive as long as someone black, female or gay performed it. This argument suggests that people from under-represented groups are incapable of reinforcing the assumptions made about that group no matter what they do; this is doubtful, particularly as it ignores the range of possible readings which audience members are likely to make. Furthermore, it might actually do the opposite; a black person telling racist jokes surely offers powerful legitimisation above and beyond a white person telling such jokes.

It is this difficulty in containing meanings made by audiences which is at the heart of many of the constraints that exist for the sitcom. By conforming very firmly to genre expectations and structures, sitcoms signal clearly the manner in which their creators wish them to be understood. By undermining these in an attempt to create new, progressive comedic forms, large sections of the audience will either find programmes incomprehensible, or create oppositional readings that undermine authors' intentions. It is this problem which, after all, led to the range of various and conflicting readings concerning Constable Goody in *The Thin Blue Line*. Because of this, it is difficult to see how different forms of comedy can be created which encompass new ideas and ideologies but which simultaneously draw on comedic traditions which are understandable to those who bring conventional reading strategies to them. The history of Alternative Comedy proves the point, for its small audience figures on minority channels meant that it remained unintelligible – or, at least, unpleasurable – to the majority used to conventional comedic forms. And there seems to be little point in concocting 'radical' comedy that is not consumed by those who don't conform to its ideology, as it ends up simply preaching to the converted.

Furthermore, it's also been argued that audiences' understandings of comedy are now so complex that humour exists as a discourse utterly removed from the ways in which we interpret the world outside of it. Limon argues that 'what the audience is finding funny is that it finds this funny' (2000, p. 18), demonstrating that it is the notion of seeking out the pleasure of humour which is itself ridiculous, but enjoyable nonetheless. Olson (2001) suggests that this is a response to the post-modern condition, in which humour's refusal to conform to standard understandings of the world renders it simultaneously powerful and meaningless. For Auslander, comedy is so removed from the seriousness of life that 'there is nothing left to laugh at except the idea that someone might try to make us laugh' (1992, p. 137). In this sense, the political content of comedy – whether progressive or not – is pointless, for anything which is truly radical will probably be read as so only within the realm of comedy, and is therefore inapplicable to the serious matter of everyday life. While this suggests that comedy is incapable of changing anything for the better, it also argues that it's not responsible for things being bad in the first place.

Despite this, the question concerning who should be allowed access to broadcasting, and which representations are deemed acceptable, refuses to go away. Littlewood and Pickering's argument also rests on the assumption that members of a certain group have the overriding right to determine whether representations of them are acceptable or not. This is likely to result in 'the truth' being defined in terms of the positive. It would also uphold the requirement for those with racist, sexist and homophobic views to have their say concerning the portrayal of characters with such views on television, and this is likely to result in the insistence of positive portrayals of them too. Here the attempt to undermine a more widespread authority simply replaces it with a range of conflicting, infinite authorities, in which it would become impossible for any kind of portrayal to be constructed. More problematic for the sitcom, it would also make many conventional comedy structures unavailable, as it is unlikely that many people would allow themselves to be represented in ways which invite audiences to laugh at them. As comedy rests on exploring conflicts within the social order it also requires that conflict to be presented in ways which are unlikely to be positive about everyone within it.

Instead, the content of the humour is paramount and is the factor that must change if progressive humour is to be developed. The relationship between teller and audience affects the reception of humour greatly, but the range of possible interpretations is still bound by the content of the joke. As semiotics argues, language is polysemic, but it isn't open to an infinite number of readings. To be sure, progressive humour would best be achieved by the combination of new kinds of jokes being told by tellers who previously didn't have access to the form, but it is the content of humour which is most capable of redefining humour content; the tautology, at least, proves the point.

However, it is still difficult to see how this can be successfully carried out considering the mass audience nature of television, where texts must attempt to unite disparate audiences within understandable comedy formats. The mass nature of the sitcom is responsible for the impressive social effect it can have, while simultaneously constraining its possibilities. That is, new forms of comedy can only occur between small groups, where the joke-teller can rely on the audience's assumed knowledge to be as specific and as natural as his/hers, and where the audience can ask for clarification if this is not apparent. If new forms of comedy do occur, they are likely to be on minority or niche channels, as it is there that programmes don't have to reach large audiences so they don't have to be homogenous. However, what this does is marginalise any progressive comedy, associating it with the 'youth', 'weird', 'alternative', 'minority' connotations of those channels. The television industries are not, on the whole, constructed in a manner which can promote radical comedy, and while this is partly because the nature of broadcasting requires large audiences, it is also a result of the regulations and commercial requirements for each station, in which 'experimental' programming is lumped together on specific channels so that those who want to can easily avoid it.

Comedy of all kinds must conform to mass, traditional structures if it is to remain intelligible to large audiences. However, such a criticism is not to single out comedy or the sitcom; television as a whole has to conform to traditional structures to remain intelligible. While this could be seen as a damning criticism of the medium, it must be accepted that this conventionality may only refer to the industrial nature of the medium and the readings that are intended by broadcasting. These conventional forms in no way ensure that all audiences consume texts in a similar manner, whether it be individual episodes, whole series, or throughout television. This is a conflict which many Media Studies methodologies have failed to fully account for, mainly because it is an impossible thing to do. While ethnography has explored in detail the precise meaning-making processes of specific individuals and has recorded seminal and worthy findings, transferring this to a wider, social understanding is a dangerous and flawed procedure. The question remains then – particularly for those who criticise the structures of television for reinforcing dominant ideologies – as to how this hypothesis can be proven.

More importantly, the debate concerning sitcom and social power rests on the assumption that it *matters* that the genre conforms to power-based social structures, a concern far disproportionate to the social position which sitcom itself is seen to occupy by audiences and regulators; after all, it's only sitcom. The epigraph for this chapter highlights the low cultural status of the genre succinctly, with clear distinctions made between the social importance of the work of Ibsen and television sitcom. It also reminds us that, even to many people who work within the television industry, sitcom doesn't really matter. The television industry's departmental structure clearly shows that broadcasting in Britain sees drama, news and documentaries as 'more important' than the sitcom, if judged in terms of budget. The dominance of sitcom on American television can be explained away as a commercial phenomenon in a country where little television makes claims to 'high' culture or social relevance. It is easy to malign this distinction, and in a sense I do; however, it has to be accepted that not only is the sitcom a low cultural form, but that society as a whole, and the industry which produces it, is quite happy to see it that way.

The reasons sitcom has this cultural position come about from its main elements. Television is seen to be a low cultural form compared to, say literature and art, and the same holds true for comedy; combine the two and you're left with one of the most maligned cultural forms. And while it is easy to dissect such an argument, the point is that, on the whole, this is an accepted response, whose existence feeds into expectations for, and constraints upon, the genre.

Furthermore, the sitcom is seen as a low cultural form precisely because it is popular. Bourdieu, exploring the ways in which tastes are constructed and categorised, notes that, 'all the goods offered tend to lose some of their relative scarcity and their distinctive value as the number of consumers both inclined and able to appropriate them grows. Popularization devalues' (1993, p. 114).

Thus, the increase in amounts of comedy on television in the last couple of decades (Wagg, 1998, p. 21), as well as the introduction of a range of satellite and cable channels devoted entirely to comedy, undermines the very distinctiveness of the form which existed when comedy was a rarity on television. Furthermore, the availability of a variety of comedy splinters audiences into their specific tastes, resulting in the loss of the mass social function which earlier comedies were more likely to have. In this sense, the sitcom is devalued partly because its popularity undermines comedy's social function, but also because, currently, popularity equates with a low cultural status anyway. As Bourdieu notes, part of the 'authority' with which a range of cultural forms and institutions are invested is often based around scarcity.

There is an automatic assumption within Cultural Studies that such low status is intrinsically a bad thing and that, as someone writing a book on the subject, my desire would be to reposition the sitcom as a valuable cultural form. Yet there is a problem here, precisely because the sitcom actually relies on its low cultural status for the pleasures it offers. And while this may constrain the genre in a number of instances, it doesn't undermine its ability to speak to, and be accepted by, a range of audiences which other, highly valued cultural forms could only wish for. Put simply, lots of people watch sitcoms and that creates a valuable public space which, significantly, the mass is likely to feel belongs to them in a manner unlikely for Dennis Potter plays, documentaries and arts programmes.

Of course, I'm not arguing that the ability to reach large audiences is in itself a progressive thing, but what it does is create a forum in which anything that is progressive is able to have a far-reaching effect. Furthermore, the role of humour is likely to make any such novelty accepted by the majority of audiences. Which is actually more progressive: Victor Meldrew's frequent comic tirades against a range of social problems in *One Foot in the Grave*; or an iconoclastic, seditious piece of performance art above a pub in, say, Swindon? I don't want to base an argument purely on populist structures, but surely, in terms of the masses, it's often easy to overlook the power of television's reach. Sitcom, surely, can challenge social structures without being a high cultural form; my argument is that it may achieve this aim more powerfully precisely because it's not a high cultural form.

To create sitcom which performs functions other than those standard for the genre would require a complete repositioning not only of its cultural value, but also of television and comedy as whole, and of audiences' reading strategies for it. While this is extremely unlikely, it is, more importantly, difficult to see how this could be achieved while retaining the pleasures which sitcom can offer. The pleasures associated with comedy and television rely quite squarely on their very specific social position and function. Is it possible, then, to create comedy which is simultaneously simplistic enough for the jokes to work while also performing functions different to those which are the norms for it? And, fundamentally, how can it be ensured that audiences would consume such texts in the intended manner; that is, if they didn't get confused and bored and so not bother to consume them at all?

So, to change the nature of sitcom would require a complete repositioning of all cultural forms, which would result in categorisations between the popular and the elite being destroyed. If this occurred, then all comedic butts would be removed; if comedy relies on the existence of 'the other', it is difficult to see how it could be created in a society with no categorisations, as this would offer nothing to laugh at. As Bazalgette, Cook and Medhurst argue, the complex nature of comedy is 'too slippery to be pinned down on any altar of political correctness' (1989, p. 14) and this is because the denial of some kind of power structure removes the subject matter of comedy. After all, social humour seems to produce its most powerful and funny examples within societies with restrictive social stratifications (Draitser, 1989, p. 124; Jenkins, 1994; Olson, 2001, p. 11).

And while the popular nature of the sitcom devalues its cultural standing, what does this actually mean? To whom does it matter that the sitcom is a low cultural form? By remaining as it is, the sitcom continues to occupy a social position in which it appeals to, and speaks to, large audiences and, when it does have things to say, it manages to reach that large number of people. Furthermore, it offers pleasures not associated with what are seen to be higher cultural forms and so, by extension, those pleasures must be of a type which is not acceptable to those who uphold such distinctions. The fact that the sitcom is seen to be a low cultural form means it must already be doing something contrary to the criteria which would elevate its status.

So Nuttall and Carmichael note that there are pleasures in comedy available to the working class which work precisely because of the fear it generates in those in power. This is humour which works as social force, that 'rests heavily on the perpetual celebration of common factors' (1977, p. 24). While they view this in terms of club and music hall comedy, it is clear that the sitcom now plays this role and does so to a much wider audience. And while the sitcom may be an extremely watered-down, constrained version of the comedy that preceded it, its ability to bind together audiences on such a massive scale is unrivalled. The assumption that sitcom needs to be regulated demonstrates the fear which those in power have for the possible subversive effects of comedy.

Furthermore, Nuttall and Carmichael note that the working class don't want comedy which binds them with those from other social groups, that the whole point is that 'their' comedy excludes those from higher social classes from the pleasures it offers (p. 24). In this way, just as the working class don't have access to a range of forums, so those from the elite don't have access to *My Family*; and if they do, they don't understand it, or get certain kinds of pleasure from it. Comedy does serve to highlight and maintain social stratifications but, in terms of pleasure, this is as restrictive for those in power as it is for those who are powerless.

Whose loss is more significant here, then; the working-class rejection of Ibsen or the upper-class inability to comprehend *My Family*? The condemnation of power structures on this inequality uses value judgments based precisely around those structures being condemned. So, while those concerned with such structures might complain that sitcom isn't 'fucking Ibsen' (Lodge, 1995, p. 171), plenty of people – myself included – would say, 'Thank fuck it isn't'.

Bibliography

Abercrombie, Nicholas, *Television and Society* (Cambridge: Polity Press, 1996).

Alberti, John (ed.), *Leaving Springfield: The Simpsons and the Possibility of Oppositional Culture* (Detroit, IL: Wayne State University Press, 2004).

Anderson, Christopher, *Hollywood TV: The Studio System in the Fifties* (Austin: University of Texas Press, 1994).

Andrews, Maggie, 'Butterflies and Caustic Asides: Housewives, Comedy and the Feminist Movement', in Stephen Wagg (ed.), *Because I Tell a Joke or Two: Comedy, Politics and Social Difference* (London: Routledge, 1998).

Aristotle, *Ethica Nichomachea*, trans. W. D. Ross (London: Humphrey Milford, 1925).

Arthurs, Jane, *Television and Sexuality: Regulation and the Politics of Taste* (New York: Open University Press, 2004).

Asafu-Adjaye, Jacqueline, 'Why Television Has to Change', *Broadcast*, 24 October 2003, pp. 18–19.

Aston, Elaine and George Savano, *Theatre as Sign-System: A Semiotics of Text and Performance* (London and New York: Routledge, 1991).

Attallah, Paul, 'The Unworthy Discourse: Situation Comedy in Television', in Joanne Morreale (ed.), *Critiquing the Sitcom: A Reader* (Syracuse, NY: Syracuse University Press, 2003).

Auslander, Philip, *From Acting to Performance: Essays in Modernism and Postmodernism* (London and New York: Routledge, 1997).

Auslander, Philip, *Liveness: Performance in a Mediatized Culture* (London and New York: Routledge, 1999).

Badsey, Stephen, '*Blackadder Goes Forth* and the "Two Western Fronts" Debate', in Graham Roberts and Philip M. Taylor (eds), *The Historian, Television and Television History* (Luton: University of Luton Press, 2001).

Baker, M., 'Transatlantic Transplants', *Broadcast*, 19 January 1996, pp. 24–5.

Bakhtin, Mikhail, *Rabelais and his World* (Bloomington: Indiana University Press, 1984).

Barber, Nick, 'Laugh? I Nearly Stayed at Home', *The Independent on Sunday*, 7 July 1996, Real Life Section, p. 15.

Barish, Jonas, *The Antitheatrical Prejudice* (Berkeley and Los Angeles: University of California Press, 1981).

Barnouw, Eric, *Tube of Plenty: The Evolution of American Television,* 2nd edn (New York and Oxford: Oxford University Press, 1990).

Barr, Tony, *Acting for the Camera* (New York: HarperCollins, 1997).

Bathrick, Serafina, 'The Mary Tyler Moore Show: Women at Home and at Work', in Joanne Morreale (ed.), Critiquing the Sitcom: A Reader (Syracuse, NY: Syracuse University Press, 2003).

Battles, Kathleen, and Wendy Hilton-Morrow, 'Gay Characters in Conventional Spaces: Will and Grace and the Situation Comedy Genre', Critical Studies in Media Communication vol. 19 no. 1, 2002, pp. 87–105.

Bazalgette, Cary, Jim Cook and Andy Medhurst, Teaching TV Sitcom (London: BFI, 1989).

BBC, 'Speech Given at the MediaGuardian Edinburgh International Television Festival 2004 – Defining Public Value', at<www.bbc.co.uk/pressoffice/speeches/stories/thompson_edinburgh04.shtml>, 2004.

Beckerman, Bernard, Theatrical Presentation: Performer, Audience and Act (London: Routledge, 1990).

Berger, M., 'The Mouse That Never Roars: Jewish Masculinity on American Television', in N.Kleebat (ed.), Too Jewish? Challenging Traditional Identities (New Brunswick, NJ and London: Rutgers University Press, 1996).

Bergson, Henri, Laughter: An Essay on the Meaning of the Comic, trans. C. Brereton and R. Rothwell (London: Macmillan 1911).

Bignell, Jonathan, An Introduction to Television Studies (London and New York: Routledge, 2004).

Bishop, L., 'Jokes for the Boys', Television: the Journal of the Royal Television Society vol. 33 no. 7, 1996, pp. 22–3.

Block, Alex Ben, Outfoxed: Martin Davis, Barry Diller, Rupert Murdoch, Joan Rivers, and the Inside Story of America's Fourth Television Network (New York: St Martin's Press, 1990).

Bodroghkozy, Aniko, 'Is This What You Mean by Color TV?: Race, Gender and Contested Meanings in NBC's Julia', in Gail Dines and Jean M. Humez (eds), Gender, Race and Class in Media: A Text-Reader (Thousand Oaks, CA: Sage, 1995).

Bodroghkozy, Aniko, 'The Smothers Brothers Comedy Hour and the Youth Rebellion', in Lynn Spigel and Michael Curtin (eds), The Revolution Wasn't Televised: Sixties Television and Social Conflict (London and New York: Routledge, 1997).

Bodroghkozy, Aniko, 'Good Times in Race Relations? CBS's "Good Times" and the Legacy of Civil Rights in 1970s Prime-Time Television', Screen vol. 44 no. 4, 2003, pp. 404–28.

Bogle, Donald, Toms, Coons, Mulattoes, Mammies, and Bucks: An Interpretive History of Blacks in American Films, 3rd edn (Oxford: Roundhouse, 1994).

Bonila, Paul C., 'Is There More to Hollywood Lowbrow Than Meets the Eye?', Quarterly Review of Film and Video vol. 22 no. 1, 2005, pp. 17–24.

Bordwell, David, Janet Staiger and Kristin Thompson, The Classical Hollywood Cinema: Film Style and Mode of Production to 1960 (New York: Columbia University Press, 1985).

Bourdieu, Pierre, Sociology in Question, trans. R. Nice (London: Sage, 1993).

Bourdieu, Pierre and J. Passeron, Reproduction in Education, Society and Culture, 2nd edn, trans. R. Nice (London: Sage, 1990).

Bourdon, Jérôme, 'Live Television Is Still Alive: on Television as an Unfulfilled Promise', *Media, Culture and Society*, vol. 22 no. 5, 2000, pp. 531–56.

Broadcasting Standards Commission, *Codes of Guidance, June 1998* (London: Broadcasting Standards Commission, 1998).

Broadcasting Standards Commission, *Complaints Bulletin 21* (London: Broadcasting Standards Commission, 1999).

Brook, Vincent, 'The Fallacy of Falsity: Un-"Dresch"-ing Masquerade, Fashion, and Postfeminist Jewish Princesses in *The Nanny*', *Critical Studies in Media Communication* vol. 17 no. 3, 2000, pp. 279–305.

Brook, Vincent, 'Virtual Ethnicity: Incorporation, Diversity, and the Contemporary "Jewish" Sitcom', *Emergences* vol. 11 no. 2, 2001, pp. 269–85.

Brook, Vincent, *Something Ain't Kosher Here: The Rise of the "Jewish" Sitcom* (New Brunswick, NJ and London: Rutgers University Press, 2003).

Brooks, T. and E. Marsh, *The Complete Dictionary to Prime Time Network TV Shows 1946–Present,* 2nd edn (New York: Ballantine Books, 1981).

Bruzzi, Stella, *New Documentary: A Critical Introduction* (London and New York: Routledge, 2000).

Bruzzi, Stella, 'Docusoaps', in Glen Creeber (ed.), *The Television Genre Book* (London: BFI, 2001).

Budd, Mike, Steve Craig and Clay Steinman, *Consuming Environments: Television and Commercial Culture* (New Brunswick, NJ and London: Rutgers University Press, 1999).

Buonanno, Milly (ed.), *Shifting Landscapes: Television Fiction in Europe* (Luton: University of Luton Press, 1999).

Buonanno, Milly (ed.), *Continuity and Change: Television Fiction in Europe* (Luton: University of Luton Press, 2000).

Burns, Elizabeth, *Theatricality* (London: Longman, 1972).

Buscombe, Ed, 'The Idea of Genre in the American Cinema', *Screen* vol. 11 no. 2, 1970, pp.33–45.

Butler, Jeremy G., *Television: Critical Methods and Applications* (Belmont: Wadsworth, 1994).

Butsch, Richard, 'Class and Gender in Four Decades of Television Situation Comedy: Plus Ça Change . . .', *Critical Studies in Mass Communication* vol. 9 no. 4, 1992, pp. 387–99.

Butsch, Richard, 'Ralph, Fred, Archie, and Homer: Why Television Keeps Recreating the White Male Working-Class Buffoon', in G. Dines and J. M. Humez (eds), *Gender, Race and Class in Media: A Text-Reader* (Thousand Oaks, CA: Sage, 1995).

Cantor, Muriel G., 'Prime-Time Fathers: A Study in Continuity and Change', *Critical Studies in Mass Communication* vol. 7 no. 3, 1990, pp. 278–85.

Cantor, Paul A., *Gilligan Unbound: Pop Culture in the Age of Globalization* (Lanham, MD: Rowman and Littlefield, 2003).

Carlson, Marvin, *Performance: A Critical Introduction* (London and New York: Routledge, 1996).

Casey, Bernadette, Neil Casey, Ben Calvert, Liam French and Justin Lewis, *Television Studies: The Key Concepts* (London and New York: Routledge, 2002).

Cashmore, Ellis, *. . . And There Was Television* (London and New York: Routledge, 1994).

Castiglia, Christopher and Christopher Reed, 'Ah Yes, I Remember It Well: Memory and Queer Culture in *Will and Grace*', *Cultural Critique* vol. 56, Winter, 2004, pp. 158–88.

Caughie, John, 'Adorno's Reproach: Repetition, Difference and Television Genre', *Screen* vol. 32 no. 2, 1991, pp. 127–53.

Chaney, Michael A., 'Coloring Whiteness and Blackvoice Minstrelsy: Representations of Race and Place in *Static Shock*, *King of the Hill*, and *South Park*', *Journal of Popular Film and Television* vol. 31 no. 4, 2004, pp. 167–75.

Charney, Maurice, *Comedy High and Low: An Introduction to the Experience of Comedy* (New York: Oxford University Press, 1978).

Cherniavsky, Eva, 'Karmic Realignment: Transnationalism and Trauma in *The Simpsons*', *Cultural Critique* vol. 41, Winter, 1999, pp. 139–57.

Clarke, Mike, *Teaching Popular Television* (London: Heinemann Educational Books, 1987).

Cohan, Steven, *Hollywood Musicals: The Film Reader* (London: Routledge, 2002).

Coleman, Robin R. Means, *African American Viewers and the Black Situation Comedy* (New York: Garland, 2000).

Cook, Jim (ed.), *B.F.I. Dossier 17: Television Sitcom* (London: BFI, 1982).

Cook, William, *Ha Bloody Ha: Comedians Talking* (London: Fourth Estate, 1994).

Corner, John, *Television Form and Public Address* (London: Edward Arnold, 1995).

Corner, John, 'Afterword: Framing the New', in Su Holmes and Deborah Jermyn (eds), *Understanding Reality Television* (London and New York: Routledge, 2004).

Counsell, Colin, 'Signs of Performance', in Lizbeth Goodman with Jane de Gay (eds), *The Routledge Reader in Politics and Performance* (London and New York: Routledge, 2000).

Creeber, Glen (ed.), *The Television Genre Book* (London: BFI, 2001).

Creeber, Glen, '*News at Ten*', in Glen Creeber (ed.), *Fifty Key Television Programmes* (London: Arnold, 2004).

Cripps, Thomas, '*Amos 'n' Andy* and the Debate over Racial Integration', in Joanne Morreale (ed.), *Critiquing the Sitcom: A Reader* (Syracuse, NY: Syracuse University Press, 2003).

Critchley, Simon, *On Humour* (London and New York: Routledge, 2002).

Cunningham, Stuart and Elizabeth Jacka, *Australian Television and International Mediascapes* (Cambridge: Cambridge University Press, 1996).

Curtis, Barry, 'Aspects of Sitcom', in Jim Cook (ed.), *B.F.I. Dossier 17: Television Sitcom* (London: BFI, 1982).

Dale, Alan, *Comedy Is a Man in Trouble: Slapstick in American Movies* (Minneapolis: University of Minnesota Press, 2000).

Daniels, Thérèse, 'Programmes for Black Audiences', in Stuart Hood (ed.), *Behind the Screens: The Structure of British Television in the Nineties* (London: Lawrence and Wishart, 1994).

Daniels, Thérèse and J. Gerson, *The Colour Black: Black Images in British Television* (London: BFI, 1989).

Davies, Christie, *Ethnic Humor Around the World* (Bloomington: Indiana University Press, 1990).

Davies, Christie, *The Mirth of Nations* (New York: Transaction Publishers, 2002).

Dent, Eric B., '*Seinfeld*, Professor of Organizational Behavior: The Psychological Contract and Systems Thinking', *Journal of Management Education* vol. 25 no. 6, 2001, pp. 648–59.

Dobson, Nichola, 'Nitpicking *The Simpsons*: Critique and Continuity in Constructed Realities', *Animation Journal* vol. 11, 2003, pp. 82–9.

Donnelly, Kevin, 'Adult Animation', in Glen Creeber (ed.), *The Television Genre Book* (London: BFI, 2001).

Doty, Alexander, *Making Things Perfectly Queer: Interpreting Mass Culture* (Minneapolis and London: University of Minnesota Press, 1993).

Doty, Alexander, 'I Love *Laverne and Shirley*: Lesbian Narratives, Queer Pleasures, and Television Sitcoms', in Joanne Morreale (ed.), *Critiquing the Sitcom: A Reader* (Syracuse, NY: Syracuse University Press, 2003).

Double, Oliver, *An Approach to the Traditions of British Stand-Up Comedy* (Unpublished PhD thesis: Sheffield University, 1991).

Double, Oliver, 'Teaching Stand-Up Comedy: A Mission Impossible?', *Studies in Theatre and Performance* vol. 20 no. 1, 2000, pp. 14–23.

Dovey, Jon, 'Reality TV', in Glen Creeber (ed.), *The Television Genre Book* (London: BFI, 2001).

Dow, Bonnie J., 'Hegemony, Feminist Criticism and *The Mary Tyler Moore Show*', *Critical Studies in Mass Communication* vol. 7 no. 3, 1990, pp. 261–74.

Dow, Bonnie J., '*Ellen*, Television, and the Politics of Gay and Lesbian Visibility', *Critical Studies in Media Communication* vol. 18 no. 2, 2001, pp. 123–40.

Draitser, E., 'Soviet Undergound Jokes as a Means of Popular Entertainment', *Journal of Popular Culture* vol. 23 no. 1, 1989, pp. 117–26.

Durham, Kim, 'Methodology and Praxis of the Actor within the Television Production Process: Facing the Camera in *EastEnders* and Morse', *Studies in Theatre and Performance* vol. 22 no. 2, 2000, pp. 82–94.

Dyer, Richard, *Only Entertainment* (London and New York: Routledge, 1992).

Dyer, Richard, *White* (London and New York: Routledge, 1997).

Dyer, Richard, *Stars,* 2nd edn (London: BFI, 1998).

Easthope, Antony, 'The English Sense of Humor', *Humor: International Journal of Humor Studies* vol. 13 no. 1, 2000, pp. 59–75.

Eaton, Mick, 'Television Situation Comedy', in Tony Bennett, Susan Boyd-Bowman, Colin Mercer and Janet Woollacott (eds), *Popular Television and Film* (London: BFI, 1981).

Eco, Umberto, 'Semiotics of Theatrical Performance', *The Drama Review* vol. 21, 1977, pp. 107–17.

Elam, Keir, *The Semiotics of Theatre and Drama,* 2nd edn (London and New York: Routledge, 2002).

Ellis, John, *Seeing Things: Television in an Age of Uncertainty* (London and New York: I. B. Tauris, 2002).

Epstein, Lawrence J., *The Haunted Smile: The Story of Jewish Comedians* (Oxford: Public Affairs, 2002).

Evans, Peter William and Celestino Deleyto (eds), *Terms of Endearment: Hollywood Romantic Comedy of the 1980s and 1990s* (Edinburgh: Edinburgh University Press, 1998).

Fejes, Fred, 'Making a Gay Masculinity', *Critical Studies in Media Communication* vol. 17 no. 1, 2000, pp. 113–16.

Féral, Josette, 'Performance and Theatricality: The Subject Demystified', in Timothy Murray (ed.), *Mimesis, Masochism, and Mime: The Politics of Theatricality in Contemporary French Thought* (Ann Arbor: University of Michigan Press, 1997).

Feuer, Jane, 'Genre Study and Television', in Robert C. Allen (ed.), *Channels of Discourse, Reassembled: Television and Contemporary Criticism* (London and New York: Routledge, 1992).

Feuer, Jane, *Seeing through the Eighties* (London: BFI, 1995).

Feuer, Jane, 'The "Gay" and "Queer" Sitcom', in Glen Creeber (ed.), *The Television Genre Book* (London: BFI, 2001).

Feuer, Jane, Paul Kerr and Tise Vahimagi (eds), *MTM: 'Quality Television'* (London: BFI, 1984).

Fisher, John, *Funny Way to Be a Hero* (St Albans: Paladin, 1976).

Fiske, John and John Hartley, *Reading Television,* 2nd edn (London and New York: Routledge, 2003).

Flew, Terry, '*The Simpsons*: Culture, Class and Popular TV', *Metro*, no. 97, 1994, pp. 14–19.

Fraiberg, Allison, 'Between the Laughter: Bridging Feminist Studies through Women's Stand-Up Comedy', in Gail Finney (ed.), *Look Who's Laughing: Gender and Comedy* (Langhorne, PA: Gordon and Breach, 1994).

Free, Marcus, 'From the "Other" Island to the One with "No West Side": The Irish in British Soap and Sitcom', *Irish Studies Review* vol. 9 no. 2, 2001, pp. 215–27.

Freud, Sigmund, *Jokes and Their Relation to the Unconscious* (London: Penguin, 1960).

Fry Jr, William, 'The Appeasement Function of Mirthful Laughter', in Anthony Chapman and Henry Foot (eds), *It's a Funny Thing, Humour* (Oxford: Pergamon Press, 1977).

Fry, William F. and Melanie Allen, *Creating Humor: Life Studies of Comedy Writers,* new edn (New Brunswick, NJ and London: Transaction Publishers, 1998).

Fuller, Linda K., The Cosby Show: *Audiences, Impact and Implications* (Westport, CI: Greenwood Press, 1992).

Furniss, Maureen, *Art in Motion: Animation Aesthetics* (London: John Libbey, 1998).

Gardiner, Judith Kegan, 'Why Saddam Is Gay: Masculinity Politics in *South Park –*
Bigger, Longer, and Uncut', *Quarterly Review of Film and Video* vol. 22 no. 1, 2005,
pp. 51–62.

Gauntlett, David, *Broadcasting Standards Council Research Working Paper 10: A*
Profile of Complainants and Their Complaints (London: Broadcasting Standards
Council, 1995).

Gauntlett, David and Annette Hill, *TV Living: Television, Culture and Everyday Life*
(London and New York: Routledge, 1999).

Gillespie, Marie, *Television, Ethnicity and Cultural Change* (London and New York:
Routledge, 1995).

Gillespie, Marie, '*Goodness Gracious Me*, British Television Comedy, and
Representations of Ethnicity', in Michael Scriven and Emily Roberts (eds), *Group*
Identities on French and British Television (New York and Oxford: Berghahn Books,
2003).

Gitlin, Todd, *Inside Prime Time,* rev. edn (London: Routledge, 1994).

Glynn, Kevin, 'Bartmania: The Social Reception of an Unruly Image', *Camera Obscura*
no. 38, 1996, pp. 61–90.

Goddard, Peter, '*Hancock's Half-Hour*: A Watershed in British Television Comedy', in
John Corner (ed.), *Popular Television in Britain* (London: BFI, 1991).

Godkewitsch, M., 'Physiological and Verbal Indices of Arousal in Rated Humour', in
Tony Chapman and Henry Foot (eds), *Humour and Laughter: Theory, Research and*
Applications (London: John Wiley, 1976).

Goffman, Erving, *The Presentation of Self in Everyday Life* (Garden City, NY:
Doubleday, 1959).

Goffman, Erving, *Frame Analysis* (Cambridge, MA: Harvard University Press, 1974).

Goldman, Michael, *The Actor's Freedom: Toward a Theory of Drama* (New York:
Viking 1975).

Gray, Frances, *Women and Laughter* (Basingstoke: Macmillan, 1994).

Gray, Herman, 'Television and the New Black Man: Black Male Images in Prime-Time
Situation Comedy', *Media, Culture and Society* vol. 8 no. 2, 1988,
pp. 223–42.

Gray, Herman, 'Television, Black Americans, and the American Dream', *Critical Studies*
in Mass Communication vol. 6 no. 4, 1989, pp. 376–86.

Gray, Herman, *Watching Race: Television and the Struggle for 'Blackness'*
(Minneapolis: University of Minnesota Press, 1995).

Grote, David, *The End of Comedy: The Sit-Com and the Comedic Tradition* (Hamden,
CT: Archon, 1983).

Grotjahn, Martin, *Beyond Laughter: Humor and the Subconscious* (New York:
McGraw-Hill, 1966).

Habermas, Jürgen, *The Structural Transformation of the Public Sphere*, trans. T. Burger
(Cambridge: Polity Press, 1989).

Hall, Stuart, 'Encoding / Decoding', in Stuart Hall, Dorothy Hobson, Andrew Lowe and
Paul Willis (eds), *Culture, Media, Language* (London: Routledge, 1980).

Hamamoto, Darrell, *Nervous Laughter: Television Situation Comedy and Liberal Democratic Ideology* (New York: Praeger, 1989).

Haralovitch, Mary Beth, 'Sitcoms and Suburbs: Positioning the 1950s Homemaker', in Joanne Morreale (ed.), *Critiquing the Sitcom: A Reader* (Syracuse, NY: Syracuse University Press, 2003).

Hargrave, Andrea Millwood (ed.), *Broadcasting Standards Council Annual Review 1992: Sex and Sexuality in Broadcasting* (London: John Libbey, 1992).

Hargrave, Andrea Millwood (ed.), *Broadcasting Standards Council Annual Review 1995: The Scheduling Game* (London: John Libbey, 1995).

Harries, Dan, *Film Parody* (London: BFI, 2000).

Hart, Kylo-Patrick R., 'Representing Gay Men on American Television', in Toby Miller (ed.), *Critical Concepts in Media and Cultural Studies: Volume 2* (London and New York: Routledge, 2003).

Hartley, John, *Tele-Ology: Studies in Television* (London and New York: Routledge, 1992).

Hartley, John, *The Uses of Television* (London and New York: Routledge, 1999).

Havens, Timothy, 'The Biggest Show in the World: Race and the Global Popularity of *The Cosby Show*', *Media, Culture and Society* vol. 22 no. 4, 2000, pp. 371–91.

Hayman, Ronald, *Techniques of Acting* (London: Methuen, 1969).

Healy, Murray, 'Were We Being Served? Homosexual Representation in Popular British Comedy', *Screen* vol. 36 no. 3, 1995, pp. 243–56.

Henry, Matthew, 'The Triumph of Popular Culture: Situation Comedy, Postmodernism, and *The Simpsons*', in Joanne Morreale (ed.), *Critiquing the Sitcom: A Reader* (Syracuse, NY: Syracuse University Press, 2003).

Herbert, C., 'Comedy: The World of Pleasure', *Genre* vol. 17 no. 4, 1984. pp. 401–16.

Hilmes, Michelle, 'Where Everybody Knows Your Name: *Cheers* and the Mediation of Cultures', in Joanne Morreale (ed.), *Critiquing the Sitcom: A Reader* (Syracuse, NY: Syracuse University Press, 2003).

Hobbes, Thomas, *Leviathan* (London: Everyman, 1914).

Hole, Anne, 'Performing Identity: Dawn French and the Funny Fat Female Body', *Feminist Media Studies* vol. 3 no. 3, 2003, pp. 315–28.

Horowitz, Susan, *Queens of Comedy: Lucille Ball, Phyllis Diller, Carol Burnett, Joan Rivers, and the New Generation of Funny Women* (Amsterdam: Gordon and Breach, 1997).

Horrocks, Roger, 'Construction Site: Local Content on Television', in Roger Horrocks and Nick Perry (eds), *Television in New Zealand: Programming the Nation* (South Melbourne: Oxford University Press, 2001).

Horton, Andrew S. (ed.), *Comedy/Cinema/Theory* (Berkeley: University of California Press, 1991).

Hough, A., 'Trials and Tribulations – Thirty Years of Sitcom', in R. P. Adler (ed.) *Understanding Television: Essays on Television as a Social and Cultural Force* (New York: Praeger, 1981).

Housham, D., 'Primetime' in *Are We Having Fun Yet? The* Sight and Sound *Comedy Supplement* vol. 4 no. 3, 1994, pp.10–13.

Husband, Charles, 'Racist Humour and Racist Ideology in British Television, or, I Laughed Till You Cried', in Chris Powell and George E. C. Paton (eds), *Humour in Society: Resistance and Control* (Basingstoke: Macmillan, 1988).

Irwin, William, Mark T. Conrad and Aeon J. Skoble (eds), The Simpsons *and Philosophy: The D'oh! of Homer* (Chicago, IL: Open Court, 2001).

Jacobs, Jason, *The Intimate Screen: Early British Television Drama* (Oxford: Oxford University Press, 2000).

Jacobs, Jason, 'Hospital Drama', in Glen Creeber (ed.), *The Television Genre Book* (London: BFI, 2001).

Jacobson, Howard, *Seriously Funny: From the Ridiculous to the Sublime* (London: Viking, 1997).

Jenkins, Henry, *What Made Pistachio Nuts? Early Sound Comedy and the Vaudeville Aesthetic* (New York: Columbia University Press, 1992).

Jenkins, Ron, *Subversive Laughter: The Liberating Power of Comedy* (New York: The Free Press, 1994).

Jhally, Sut and Justin Lewis, *Enlightened Racism:* The Cosby Show, *Audiences, and the Myth of the American Dream* (Boulder, CO: Westview Press, 1992).

Jones, Gerard, *Honey, I'm Home! Sitcoms: Selling the American Dream* (New York: St Martin's Press, 1992).

Joyrich, Lynne, *Re-Viewing Reception: Television, Gender, and Postmodern Culture* (Bloomington and Indianapolis: Indiana University Press, 1996).

Kant, Immanuel, *The Critique of Judgement*, trans. J. C. Merideth (Oxford: Oxford University Press, 1952).

Karnick, Kristine Brunovska and Henry Jenkins (eds), *Classical Hollywood Comedy* (London and New York: Routledge, 1995).

Keane, J., 'Democracy and Media: Without Foundations', in Oliver Boyd-Barrett and Chris Newbold (eds) *Approaches to Media: A Reader* (London: Arnold, 1995).

Kehily, Mary Jane and Anoop Nayak, 'Lads and Laughter: Humour and the Production of Heterosexual Hierarchies', *Gender and Education* vol. 9 no. 1, 1987, pp. 69–87.

Keighron, Peter, 'The Politics of Ridicule: Satire and Television', in Mike Wayne (ed.), *Dissident Voices: The Politics of Television and Cultural Change* (London and Sterling: Pluto Press, 1998).

Kellner, Douglas, '*Beavis and Butt-head*: No Future for Postmodern Youth', in Horace Newcomb (ed.), *Television: The Critical View*, 6th edn (Oxford: Oxford University Press, 2000).

Keslowitz, Steven, The Simpsons *and Society: An Analysis of Our Favorite Family and Its Influence in Contemporary Society* (Tucson, AZ: Hats Off Books, 2004).

Kilborn, Richard, *Staging the Real: Factual TV Programming in the Age of* Big Brother (Manchester: Manchester University Press, 2003).

King, Geoff, *Film Comedy* (London: Wallflower Press, 2002).

Kirkham, Pat and Beverley Skeggs, '*Absolutely Fabulous*: Absolutely Feminist?', in Horace Newcomb (ed.), *Television: The Critical View*, 6th edn (Oxford: Oxford University Press, 2000).

Kisseloff, Jeff, *The Box: An Oral History of Television 1920–1961* (Harmondsworth: Penguin, 1995).

Klevan, Andrew, *Film Performance: From Achievement to Appreciation* (London and New York: Wallflower Press, 2005).

Kothari, Shuchi, Sarina Pearson and Nabeel Zuberi, 'Television and Multiculturalism in Aotearoa New Zealand', in Roger Horrocks and Nick Perry (eds), *Television in New Zealand: Programming the Nation* (South Melbourne: Oxford University Press, 2001).

Kozintsev, Alexander, 'Foma and Yerema; Max and Moritz; Beavis and Butt-head: Images of Twin Clowns in Three Cultures', *Humor: International Journal of Humor Studies* vol. 15 no. 4, 2002, pp. 419–39.

Krieger, Rosalin, 'Does He Actually Say the Word Jewish? Jewish Representations in *Seinfeld*', *Journal for Cultural Research* vol. 7 no. 4, 2003, pp. 387–404.

Krutnik, Frank, *Hollywood Comedians: The Film Reader* (London and New York: Routledge, 2003).

Lacey, Nick, *Narrative and Genre: Key Concepts in Media Studies* (Basingstoke: Macmillan, 2000).

Larsen, David, '*South Park*'s Solar Anus, or, Rabelais Returns: Cultures of Consumption and the Contemporary Aesthetic of Obscenity', *Theory, Culture, and Society* vol. 18 no. 4, 2001, pp. 65–82.

Leab, D., *From Sambo to Superspade: The Black Experience in Motion Pictures* (Boston, MA: Houghton Mifflin, 1975).

Levine, J. B., 'The Feminine Routine', *Journal of Communication* vol. 26 no. 3, 1976, pp. 173–5.

Limon, John, *Stand-Up Comedy in Theory, or, Abjection in America* (Durham, NC and London: Duke University Press, 2000).

Littlewood, Jane and Michael Pickering, 'Heard the One about the White Middle-Class Heterosexual Father-in-Law?', in Stephen Wagg (ed.), *Because I Tell a Joke or Two: Comedy, Politics and Social Difference* (London and New York: Routledge, 1998).

Lodge, David, *Therapy* (London: Secker & Warburg, 1995).

Lovell, Alan and Peter Krämer (eds), *Screen Acting* (London and New York: Routledge, 1999).

Lovell, Terry, 'A Genre of Social Disruption?', in Jim Cook (ed.), *B.F.I. Dossier 17: Television Sitcom* (London: BFI, 1982).

Ma, Sheng-mei, 'Yellow Kung Fu and Black Jokes', *Television and New Media* vol. 1 no. 2, 2000, pp. 239–44.

McArthur, Colin, 'The Exquisite Corpse of Rab(Elais) C(Opernicus) Nesbitt', in Mike Wayne (ed.), *Dissident Voices: The Politics of Television and Cultural Change* (London and Sterling: Pluto Press, 1998).

McCarthy, Anna, '*Ellen*: Making Queer Television History', *Gay and Lesbian Quarterly: A Journal of Lesbian and Gay Studies* vol. 7 no. 4, 2001, pp. 593–620.

McCarthy, Anna, '"Must See" Queer TV: History and Serial Form in *Ellen*', in Mark Jancovich and James Lyons (eds), *Quality Popular Television: Cult TV, the Industry and Fans* (London: BFI, 2003).

McCracken, Allison, 'Study of a Mad Housewife: Psychiatric Discourse, the Suburban Home and the Case of Gracie Allen', in Janet Thumim (ed.), *Small Screens, Big Ideas: Television in the 1950s* (London: I. B. Tauris, 2002).

MacDonald, Chrissie, *That's Anarchy! The Story of a Revolution in the World of TV Comedy* (Hartwell, Victoria: Temple House, 2002).

McEachern, Charmaine, 'Comic Interventions: Passion and the Men's Movement in the Situation Comedy, *Home Improvement*', *Journal of Gender Studies* vol. 8 no. 1, 1999, pp. 5–18.

McQueen, David, *Television: A Media Student's Guide* (London: Arnold, 2001).

Malik, Sarita, *Representing Black Britain: Black and Asian Images on Television* (London: Sage, 2002).

Marc, David, *Demographic Vistas: Television in American Culture,* rev. edn (Philadelphia: University of Pennsylvania Press, 1996).

Marc, David, *Comic Visions: Television Comedy and American Culture* (London: Unwin Hyman, 1989).

Margolis, J., 'Heard the One about the Racist Comedian?', *The Guardian,* 4 November 1996, G2 Section, pp. 2–3.

Marshall, Jill and Angela Werndly, *The Language of Television* (London and New York: Routledge, 2002).

Martin, Nancy San, 'Must See TV: Programming Identity on NBC Thursdays', in Mark Jancovich and James Lyons (eds), *Quality Popular Television: Cult TV, the Industry and Fans* (London: BFI, 2003).

Mast, Gerald, *The Comic Mind: Comedy in the Movies*, 2nd edn (Chicago, IL: University of Chicago Press, 1979).

Matthews, Nicole, *Comic Politics: Gender in Hollywood Comedy after the New Right* (Manchester: Manchester University Press, 2000).

Mayer, David, 'Acting in Silent Film: Which Legacy of the Theatre?', in Alan Lovell and Peter Krämer (eds), *Screen Acting* (London and New York: Routledge: 1999).

Medhurst, Andy and Lucy Tuck, 'The Gender Game', in Jim Cook (ed.), *B.F.I. Dossier 17: Television Sitcom* (London: BFI, 1982).

Meinhof, Ulrike H. and Jonathan Smith, 'The Media and Their Audience: Intertextuality as Paradigm', in Ulrike H. Meinhof and Jonathan Smith (eds), *Intertextuality and the Media: From Genre to Everyday Life* (Manchester: Manchester University Press, 2000).

Mellencamp, Patricia, *High Anxiety: Catastrophe, Scandal, Age, and Comedy* (Bloomington and Indianapolis: Indiana University Press, 1992).

Meyer-Dinkgräfe, Daniel, *Approaches to Acting: Past and Present* (London: Continuum, 2001).

Miller, Jeffrey S., *Something Completely Different: British Television and American Culture* (Minneapolis: University of Minnesota Press, 2000).

Milling, Jane and Graham Ley, *Modern Theories of Performance* (Basingstoke: Palgrave, 2001).

Mills, Brett, *No Laughing Matter: The Constraints upon Television Sitcom in Britain* (Unpublished PhD thesis: University of Kent at Canterbury, 1998).

Mills, Brett, 'Comedy Vérité: Contemporary Sitcom Form', *Screen* vol. 45 no. 1, 2004a, pp. 1061–76.

Mills, Brett, '*Till Death Us Do Part* and *All in the Family*', in Glen Creeber (ed.), *Fifty Key Television Programmes* (London: Arnold, 2004b).

Mills, Brett, 'New Jokes: *Kath and Kim* and Recent Global Sitcom', *Metro* no. 140, 2004c, pp. 100–3.

Milter, Shomut, *Systems of Rehearsal: Stanislavsky, Brecht, Grotowski and Brook* (London and New York: Routledge, 1992).

Mintz, Larry, 'Situation Comedy', in B. G. Rose (ed.), *TV Genres: A Handbook and Reference Guide* (Westport, CT: Greenwood Press, 1985).

Montgomery, Kathryn C., *Target Prime Time: Advocacy Groups and the Struggle over Entertainment Television* (New York and Oxford: Oxford University Press, 1989).

Moran, Albert, *Copycat TV: Globalisation, Program Formats and Cultural Identity* (Luton: University of Luton Press, 1998).

Morowitz, Laura, 'From Gauguin to *Gilligan's Island*', in Joanne Morreale (ed.), *Critiquing the Sitcom: A Reader* (Syracuse, NY: Syracuse University Press, 2003).

Morreale, Joanne (ed.), *Critiquing the Sitcom: A Reader* (Syracuse, NY: Syracuse University Press, 2003a).

Morreale, Joanne, 'Sitcoms Say Good-bye: The Cultural Spectacle of *Seinfeld's* Last Episode', in Joanne Morreale (ed.), *Critiquing the Sitcom: A Reader* (Syracuse, NY: Syracuse University Press, 2003b).

Morreall, John, *Taking Laughter Seriously* (Albany: State University of New York Press, 1983).

Morreall, John (ed.), *The Philosophy of Laughter and Humor* (Albany: State University of New York Press, 1987).

Mullan, Bob, *Consuming Television* (Oxford: Blackwell, 1997).

Mulvey, Laura, 'Visual Pleasure and Narrative Cinema', in Meenakshi Gigi Durham and Douglas M. Kellner (eds), *Media and Cultural Studies: Keyworks* (Malden and Oxford: Blackwell, 2001).

Musser, Charles, 'Ethnicity, Role-Playing, and American Film Comedy: From Chinese Laundry Scene to Whoopee (1894–1930)', in Lester D. Friedman (ed.), *Unspeakable Images: Ethnicity and the American Cinema* (Urbana and Chicago: University of Illinois Press, 1991).

Naremore, James, *Acting in the Cinema* (Berkeley: University of California Press, 1988).

Neale, Steve, 'Questions of Genre', *Screen,* vol. 31 no. 1, 1990, pp. 45–66.

Neale, Steve, *Genre* (London: BFI, 2001).

Neale, Steve, 'Studying Genre', in Glen Creeber (ed.), *The Television Genre Book* (London: BFI, 2001).

Neale, Steve and Frank Krutnik, *Popular Film and Television Comedy* (London and New York: Routledge, 1990).

Nerhardt, Goran, 'Incongruity and Funniness: Towards a New Descriptive Model', in Tony Chapman and Henry Foot (eds), *Humour and Laughter: Theory, Research, and Applications* (London: John Wiley, 1976).

Nicoll, Allardyce, *The Theatre and Dramatic Theory* (Westport, CT: Greenwood Press, 1962).

Nuttall, Jeff and Rodick Carmichael, *Common Factors/Vulgar Factions* (London: Routledge and Kegan Paul, 1977).

Oakley, Giles, '*Yes, Minister*', in Jim Cook (ed.), *B.F.I. Dossier 17: Television Sitcom* (London: BFI, 1982).

Olsen, Edgar, *The Theory of Comedy* (Bloomington: Indiana University Press, 1968).

Olson, Kirby, *Comedy after Postmodernism: Rereading Comedy from Edward Lear to Charles Willeford* (Lubbock: Texas Tech University Press, 2001).

Palmer, Jerry, *The Logic of the Absurd: On Film and Television Comedy* (London: BFI, 1987).

Paterson, Richard, 'Drama and Entertainment', in Anthony Smith (ed.), *Television: An International History*, 2nd edn (Oxford: Oxford University Press, 1998).

Paul, William, *Laughing, Screaming: Modern Hollywood Horror and Comedy* (New York: Columbia University Press, 1994).

Pearson, Roberta E., *Eloquent Gestures: The Transformation of Performance Style in the Griffith Biograph Films* (Berkeley: University of California Press, 1992).

Perren, Alison, '*Married . . . with Children*', in Michelle Hilmes (ed.), *The Television History Book* (London: BFI, 2003).

Pettitt, Lance, *Screening Ireland: Film and Television Representation* (Manchester: Manchester University Press, 2000).

Pierson, David P., 'A Show about Nothing: *Seinfeld* and the Modern Comedy of Manners', *Journal of Popular Culture* vol. 34 no. 1, 2000, pp. 49–64.

Pines, Jim (ed.), *Black and White in Colour: Black People in British Television Since 1936* (London: BFI, 1992).

Pollio, Howard R. and J. W. Edgerly, 'Comedians and Comic Style', in Tony Chapman and Henry Foot (eds), *Humour and Laughter: Theory, Research and Applications* (London: John Wiley, 1976).

Porter, Laraine, 'Tarts, Tampons and Tyrants: Women and Representation in British Comedy', in Stephen Wagg (ed.), *Because I Tell a Joke or Two: Comedy, Politics and Social Difference* (London: Routledge, 1998).

Press, Andrea L., *Women Watching Television: Gender, Class, and Generation in the American Television Experience* (Philadelphia: University of Pennsylvania Press, 1991).

Provine, Robert R., *Laughter: A Scientific Investigation* (London: Faber and Faber, 2000).

Putterman, Barry, *On Television and Comedy: Essays on Style, Theme, Performer, and Writer* (Jefferson, NC: McFarland, 1995).

Quinn, Michael L., 'Celebrity and the Semiotics of Acting', *New Theatre Quarterly* vol. 4 no. 1, 1990, pp. 154–61.

Rabinovitz, Lauren, 'Ms.-Representation: The Politics of Feminist Sitcoms', in Mary Beth Haralovich and Lauren Rabinovitz (eds), *Television, History, and American Culture: Feminist Critical Essays*, (Durham, NC and London: Duke University Press, 1999).

Radcliffe-Brown, Arnold, *Structure and Function in Primitive Society* (London: Cohen and West, 1952).

Real, Michelle, 'Structuralist Analysis 1: Bill Cosby and Recoding Ethnicity', in Joanne Morreale (ed.), *Critiquing the Sitcom: A Reader* (Syracuse, NY: Syracuse University Press, 2003).

Richards, Jeffrey, *Films and British National Identity: From Dickens to* Dad's Army (Manchester: Manchester University Press, 1997).

Rickman, Gregg (ed.), *The Film Comedy Reader* (New York: Limelight, 2001).

Riggs, Karen E., *Mature Audiences: Television in the Lives of Elders* (New Brunswick, NJ and London: Rutgers University Press, 1998).

Rivero, Yeidy M., 'Erasing Blackness: The Media Construction of "Race" in *Mi Familia*, the First Puerto Rican Situation Comedy with a Black Family', *Media, Culture and Society* vol. 24 no. 4, 2002, pp. 481–97.

Rixon, Paul, 'The Changing Face of American Television Programmes on British Screens', in Mark Jancovich and James Lyons (eds), *Quality Popular Television: Cult TV, the Industry and Fans* (London: BFI, 2003).

Roome, Dorothy M., 'Global Versus Local: "Audience-as-Public" in South African Situation Comedy', *International Journal of Cultural Studies* vol. 2 no. 3, 1999, pp. 307–28.

Ross, Karen, *Black and White Media: Black Images in Popular Film and Television* (Cambridge: Polity, 1996).

Rowbotham, Sheila and Huw Beynon (eds), *Looking at Class: Film, Television and the Working Class* (London: Rivers Oram Press, 2001).

Rowe, Kathleen, '*Roseanne*: Unruly Woman as Domestic Goddess', *Screen* vol. 31 no. 4, 1990, pp. 408–19.

Rowe, Kathleen, *The Unruly Woman: Gender and the Genres of Laughter* (Austin: University of Texas Press, 1995).

Rudlin, John, *Commedia dell'Arte: An Actor's Handbook* (London and New York: Routledge, 1994).

Russo, M., 'Female Grotesques: Carnival and Theory', in Teresa de Lauretis (ed.), *Feminist Studies/Critical Studies* (Bloomington: Indiana University Press, 1986).

Schechner, Richard, *Performance Studies: An Introduction* (London and New York: Routledge, 2002).

Schopenhauer, Arthur, *The World as Will and Representation*, trans. E. F. J. Payne (New York: Dover Publications, 1958).

Scodari, Christin, 'Possession, Attraction and the Thrill of the Chase: Gendered Myth-Making in Film and Television Comedy of the Sexes', *Critical Studies in Mass Communication* vol. 12 no. 1, 1995, pp. 23–39.

Seidman, Steve, *Comedian Comedy: A Tradition in Hollywood Film* (Ann Arbor: UMI Research Press, 1981).

Seidman, Steve, 'Performance, Enunciation and Self-Reference in Hollywood Comedian Comedy', in Frank Krutnik (ed.), *Hollywood Comedians: The Film Reader* (London: Routledge, 2003).

Shepherd, Simon and Mick Wallis, *Drama/Theatre/Performance* (London and New York: Routledge, 2004).

Shrum Jr, Wesley Monroe, *Fringe and Fortune: The Role of Critics in High and Popular Art* (Princeton, NJ: Princeton University Press, 1996).

Shugart, Helen A., 'Reinventing Privilege: The New (Gay) Man in Contemporary Popular Media', *Critical Studies in Media Communication* vol. 20 no. 1, 2003, pp. 67–91.

Sierz, Aleks, *In-Yer-Face Theatre: British Drama Today* (London: Faber, 2001).

Smith, Jacob, 'The Frenzy of the Audible: Pleasure, Authenticity and Recorded Laughter', *Television and New Media* vol. 6 no. 1, 2005, pp. 23–47.

Sontag, Susan, *Against Interpretation* (London: Vintage, 1994).

Stabile, Carol A. and Mark Harrison (eds), *Prime Time Animation: Television Animation and American Culture* (London and New York: Routledge, 2003).

Staiger, Janet, *Blockbuster TV: Must-See Sitcoms in the Network Era* (New York and London: New York University Press, 2000).

Stratton, Jon, 'Speaking as a Jew: On the Absence of a Jewish-Speaking Position in British Cultural Studies', *European Journal of Cultural Studies* vol. 1 no. 3, 1998. pp. 305–25.

Strinati, Dominic, 'The Taste of America: Americanization and Popular Culture', in Dominic Strinati and Stephen Wagg (eds), *Come on Down? Popular Media Culture in Post-War Britain* (London and New York: Routledge, 1992).

Swanson, Gillian, 'Law and Disorder', in Jim Cook (ed.), *B.F.I. Dossier 17: Television Sitcom* (London: BFI, 1982).

Tait, Alice A. and John T. Barber, 'Black Entertainment Television: Breaking New Ground and Accepting New Responsibilities?', in Venise T. Berry and Carmen L. Manning-Miller (eds), *Mediated Messages and African–American Culture* (Thousand Oaks, CA: Sage, 1996).

Taylor, Ella, *Prime-Time Families: Television Culture in Postwar America* (Berkeley: University of California Press, 1989).

Taylor, Rod, *The Guinness Book of Sitcoms* (Middlesex: Guinness, 1994).

Thompson, Ben, *Sunshine on Putty: The Golden Age of British Comedy from Vic Reeves to* The Office (London and New York: Fourth Estate, 2004).

Thompson, Kristin, *Storytelling in Film and Television* (Cambridge and London: Harvard University Press, 2003).

Thompson, Robert J., *Television's Second Golden Age: From* Hill Street Blues *to* ER (New York: Continuum, 1996).

Tinkcom, Matthew, 'Working Like a Homosexual: Camp Visual Codes and the Labour of Gay Subjects in the MGM Freed Unit', in Steven Cohan (ed.), *Hollywood Musicals: The Film Reader* (London: Routledge, 2002).

Tompsett, A. Ruth, 'Changing Perspectives', in Patrick Campbell (ed.), *Analysing Performance: A Reader* (Manchester and New York: Manchester University Press, 1996).

Tuan, Yi-Fu, 'Space and Context', in Colin Counsell and Laurie Wolf (eds), *Performance Analysis: An Introductory Coursebook* (London and New York: Routledge, 2001).

Tucker, Patrick, *Secrets of Screen Acting,* 2nd edn (New York and London: Routledge, 2003).

Tudor, Andrew, 'Genre: Theory and Mispractice in Film Criticism', *Screen* vol. 11 no. 6, 1970, pp. 33–42.

Tunstall, Jeremy, *Television Producers* (London and New York: Routledge, 1993).

Turner, Chris, *Planet Simpson* (London: Ebury Press, 2004).

Ubersfeld, Anne, *Reading Theatre* (Toronto: University of Toronto Press, 1999).

Vineberg, Steve, *High Comedy in American Movies: Class and Humor from the 1920s to the Present* (Lanham, MD: Rowman and Littlefield, 2005).

Waddell, Terrie, 'Revelling in Dis-Play: The Grotesque in *Absolutely Fabulous*', in Alice Mills (ed.), *Seriously Weird: Papers on the Grotesque* (New York: Peter Lang, 1999).

Wagg, Stephen (ed.), *Because I Tell a Joke or Two: Comedy, Politics and Social Difference* (London and New York: Routledge, 1998).

Wells, Paul, *Understanding Animation* (London and New York: Routledge, 1998).

Wells, Paul, *Animation and America* (Edinburgh: Edinburgh University Press, 2002).

Wexman, Virginia Wright, 'Returning from the Moon: Jackie Gleason and the Carnivalesque', in Joanne Morreale (ed.), *Critiquing the Sitcom: A Reader* (Syracuse, NY: Syracuse University Press, 2003).

Willemen, Paul, 'Presentation', in Steve Neale (ed.), *Genre* (London: BFI, 1992).

Williams, Raymond, *Communications*, 2nd edn (Harmondsworth: Penguin, 1968).

Williams, Raymond, *Drama in Performance* (Harmondsworth: Penguin, 1972).

Wilmut, Roger and Peter Rosengard, *Didn't You Kill My Mother-in-Law?* (London: Methuen, 1989).

Wilson, Pamela, 'Upscale Feminine Angst: Molly Dodd, the Lifetime Cable Network and Gender Marketing', *Camera Obscura* nos 33–4, 1994, pp. 103–32.

Winokur, Mark, 'Black Is White / White Is Black: "Passing" as a Strategy of Racial Compatibility in Contemporary Hollywood Comedy', in Lester D. Friedman (ed.), *Unspeakable Images: Ethnicity and the American Cinema* (Urbana and Chicago: University of Illinois Press, 1991).

Winston, Brian, *Lies, Damn Lies, and Documentaries* (London: BFI, 2000).

Zillmann, Dolf, 'Humor and Comedy', in Dolf Zillmann and Peter Vorderer (eds), *Media Entertainment: The Psychology of Its Appeal* (Mahwah, NJ: Lawrence Erlbaum, 2000).

Zillmann, Dolf and Jane R. Cantor, 'A Disposition Theory of Humour and Mirth', in Tony Chapman and Henry Foot (eds), *Humour and Laughter: Theory, Research and Applications* (London: John Wiley, 1976).

Zook, Kristal Brent, *Color by Fox: The Fox Network and the Revolution in Black Television* (New York and Oxford: Oxford University Press, 1999).

Zurawik, David, *The Jews of Primetime* (Hanover, NH: and London: University Press of New England, 2003).

List of Illustrations

The Simpsons, 20th Century Fox Television/Gracie Films; *Shameless*, Company Pictures; *M*A*S*H*, 20th Century Fox Television; *The League of Gentlemen*, BBC; *One Foot in the Grave*, BBC; *Hancock's Half-Hour*, BBC; *Father Ted*, Hat Trick Productions; *Open All Hours*, BBC; *The Office*, BBC; *Kath and Kim*, ABC; *Brass Eye*, TalkBack Productions; *Friends*, Warner Bros. Television/Bright/Kaufmann/Crane Productions; *South Park*, Comedy Central/Comedy Partners; *Absolutely Fabulous*, BBC/Comedy Central/French & Saunders Productions/Oxygen Media; *Fawlty Towers*, BBC; *Seinfeld*, Castle-Rock Entertainment/West-Shapiro; *Will and Grace*, KoMut Entertainment/Three Sisters Entertainment/NBC Studios/NBC Universal Television/ Everything Entertainment/New Dominion Pictures Inc.; *All in the Family*, Bud Yorkin Productions/CBS Television/Norman Lear/Tandem Productions; *Till Death Us Do Part*, BBC; *I Love Lucy*, CBS Television/Desilu Productions Inc.; *Roseanne*, Carsey-Werner Company/Wind Dancer Productions; *Butterflies*, BBC; *Coupling*, Hartswood Films; *Ellen*, Black-Marlens Company/Touchstone Television; *The Thin Blue Line*, BBC/Tiger Aspect Productions; *Gimme, Gimme, Gimme*, Tiger Aspect Productions; *The Cosby Show*, Carsey-Werner Company/NBC; *Yes, Minister*, BBC; *Rab C. Nesbitt*, BBC.

Index

Page numbers in **bold** indicate detailed analysis; those in *italics* refer to illustrations; *n* = endnote.